HORSES FOREVER

A Sequel to The Horses Know Trilogy

LYNN MANN

Coxstone Press

ISBN 978-1-9161721-5-9
Published by Coxstone Press 2021

In celebration of horses
and dogs everywhere

Prologue

WILL

The sight of the horses galloping ahead of me gives me as much of a thrill as the feel of Ember's power and strength beneath me. He's every bit as magnificent as I knew he would be. I glance down to where Maverick is racing along with us all, his eyes wild with delight. He isn't as big and strong as the horses, but we shift a little of our herd energy to him so that he has the strength and endurance to stay with us – for we move as one. We breathe as one. We feel as one. And we know what is coming. That which has been a flicker in the human collective consciousness has been steadily growing into a disturbance that my fellow humans will soon sense. Humanity is approaching another crossroads. The horses and I are ready.

ONE

Victor

I am afraid. Everyone else is too, I know they are, but they will never admit it. My parents taught me how to hide my fear when I was a small child, and then constantly reminded me to do it until they were taken prisoner more than five months ago. Without them to notice when I'm struggling, to prompt me to stand with my shoulders back, my chest sticking out and my feet apart, I worry that I'll forget to do it – I'll forget to look strong, balanced on my feet and ready to take on anyone thinking of challenging me; I'll look weak.

But standing like that doesn't feel natural to me. It never has; it makes my back hurt and my shoulders ache. It makes my heart thump in my chest as I wait for someone to notice the real me underneath. Not that they ever have. They're all too busy standing, walking and talking in the same way, so that they too appear invincible – because appearances are everything down here, even amongst we Disposables.

My parents were Disposables before I was even born; their lack of fight and ambition saw to that, for everyone is a competitor here in our underground city. Our survival as the consummate humans we are, the very survival of Supreme City, depends on it – or so we are all continually told, anyway.

Our ancestors saw the path the future was taking decades before the governments of our aboveground cities destroyed one another. They built what they told everyone was a new centre for research into further genetic advancement of both Enforcers and humans, extending it deep underground and reinforcing it throughout to withstand the blast they knew was coming. By the time everything above ground was obliterated, families and individuals selected for their intelligence, skills and physical prowess were safe underground. As the years passed, they burrowed towards the underground sections of other buildings, until the vast underground city was created that still supports and protects us all hundreds of years later.

So many generations have lived and died here, all encouraged to fight for their existence so that humanity could never become weak, so that we would survive and advance to the consummate beings we are now. The beings who, when it is deemed safe, will extend our dominion back above ground.

In the early years following the blast, a scouting party was sent above ground every twelve months to assess whether the conditions were suitable for us to return to the surface. The few that made it back below ground were always terrified and insane, muttering incessantly about ghosts and voices until they were put out of their misery. The interval between sending scouting parties above ground was increased to ten years, but when the results were always the same, it was gradually extended to one hundred years.

I've often wondered whether the ghosts exist at all, or whether we're just not mentally equipped to survive outside the safety of our underground cocoon. Saying that out loud would ensure my swift execution, so I keep quiet, even when my lips tremble so much that I have to bite them to stop myself screaming.

I don't think I have it in me to elevate myself above being a Disposable, even if advancing might mean that I could visit my parents; we have to fight our way up to Regular status, since only those with the necessary strength and aggression are deemed worthy of coming into contact with the majority of other Regulars, let alone the Elite. I have no more fight in me than my parents have in them, despite my weapons instructors telling me that they see potential for the battle rage that my grandfather possessed in abundance, to emerge in me.

My grandfather was born a Regular and fought his way up to Elite. It didn't get him far though; he was murdered before I was born. It's one thing fighting your way up to being Elite, but another having the wit and cunning to stay alive there, or so my father has always said. He has never seemed sad that he lost his father when he was eighteen, the age I am now. I think he has just focused on making sure the same doesn't happen to me, but what good is it him being alive when he isn't here to protect me, to help me?

He should never have said what he did; privacy, even in family apartments, is a luxury enjoyed only by the Elite, so he had to know he would be overheard when he told me, 'The best we can do, Victor, is to survive and take joy in seeing one another every day.'

Sure enough, The Force heard every word and within the hour, our front door was broken down and both of my parents were taken away for indefinite imprisonment for their "lack of fighting spirit". I was warned that I had six months in which to prove myself and if I didn't, I would be joining them.

I have two weeks left. My parents are still imprisoned and clearly have no intention of fighting their way back to me, so I either prove myself to be different from them and stay out of prison, or I join them there, where my only chance of leaving will be to fight my way back out.

I kick the grey, dimly-lit wall of the tunnel that leads to the many weapons halls where I, along with all others of teenage years, have to train for two hours every morning. My left eye is still swollen and my head still ringing from the beating I took yesterday, but as tradition dictates, I'll have the same partner again today, until I at least give an even fight. If I allow him to beat me again, I'll have to face him over and over until either he kills me or I "man up", as my instructor told me yesterday. The weak are not permitted to survive.

Fear courses through me as those who always win their fights jog past me, shoving me against the wall or kicking me without even breaking stride. My current training partner, Kudos, is thankfully not with them; he would have begun in the corridor that with which he meant to carry on in the training hall. I fear that today is the day I'm going to die.

I select a staff – the weapon I'm on rotation for today – and press the button on the handle so that it extends out from its current two feet in length. When it is as long as I am tall, I remove my finger from the button and slide it, locking the staff at the correct length. Remembering what I've been taught, I set my shoulders down and back before striding onward with an apparent confidence that I absolutely don't feel, to the square outlined on the hard, grey floor of the hall, in which Kudos is warming up. I grind my teeth together to stop them chattering.

'Here he comes, the weakling born of weaklings,' Kudos sniggers, dropping so that his buttocks touch his heels, then leaping high into the air before landing lightly on his feet. He throws his staff from one hand to the other and flicks the fingers of his free hand, beckoning me to him. I don't give him the satisfaction. I take up my fighting stance just inside the fighting square allocated to the two of us, and stare at him. Then I see it – a flicker of uncertainty in his eyes before they harden and stare right back. I remind myself of that which I've always known; I'm not the only one who is afraid. A cold focus steals over me. I'm still terrified, but my terror now fuels something deep within me, something I had no idea was there. I see Kudos's fear and I feel powerful, as if now I've seen his weakness, he can't possibly beat me.

Kudos advances. 'Come on then, weakling, let's finish this.'

I stay where I am, a grin spreading across my face. Kudos hesitates, swallows and then lunges at me, slamming his staff against mine. 'Your parents don't deserve their given names,' he sneers. 'Winner and Surpass? Weakling and Subservient, more like.'

Rage fills my stomach and then erupts into my throat. I growl as I let go of my staff for a split-second and punch him in the face, taking hold of my staff again before he even registers what has happened. He takes a step backward and I throw my weight behind my staff, pushing him further off balance. I lift my staff higher and ram the butt of it into the side of Kudos's head. When his knees buckle, I kick him onto his back and hold my staff across his throat.

'My father is Winner. My mother is Surpass. Say their names,' I snarl.

His eyes widen as I invoke the ritual that forces him to acknowledge my parents' superiority over him.

I take hold of his hair, lift his head and smash it back on the ground. Then I reposition my staff across his throat. 'Say. Their. Names.'

'Your father is Winner. Your mother is Surpass,' Kudos gasps.

'LOUDER,' I shout, sure that I can see a film of red in front of my eyeballs.

'I… can't,' Kudos whispers.

I throw my staff to one side and leap off him, grabbing him by the bloody collar of his training shirt and lifting him to his feet, then higher so that his toes dangle as he tries in vain to touch the ground. I'm strong and powerful. I have him at my mercy and it feels good – better than I ever thought it could. He frowns as he tries to focus.

'SAY MY PARENTS' NAMES SO THAT WE CAN ALL HEAR,' I yell.

'Your father is Winner…'

I nod. 'Yes, he is.'

'…and your mother is Surpass.'

'And who am I?'

His eyes widen again.

I shake him, glad that his throat gurgles as I turn my hands, tightening his collar around his neck. 'WHO AM I?' I roar.

'Victor. You're Victor,' he wheezes.

I drop him and he falls to the ground on his hands and knees, gasping. I kick him onto his back and put a foot on his chest.

'Don't you ever forget it,' I tell him.

Someone begins to clap. Others join in. Then the cheering starts. It's all false, I know that; they are making all of the right movements and sounds because we have all been told to applaud power and strength. While they're doing as they've been taught, they're watching me, assessing me, wondering how to beat me when their turn comes to face me. Deep down, they're terrified they'll lose. They hate me, but we all play this sick, twisted game because it's how we've been taught to live.

I grin and raise my hands above my head, acknowledging my victory, but as my terror-fuelled rage fades, I'm disgusted and revolted. Nevertheless, I force myself to punch the air with both fists and as ritual dictates, I nod to each and every spectator, challenging them to take me on. I wonder if their terror can possibly be as great as my own.

Thankfully, I don't have to find out. A strong hand clasps my shoulder and spins me around.

'As strong at eighteen as your grandfather was at twenty-five,' Vicious tells me, his eyes cold and hard as they bore into my own. 'And now your battle rage has shown itself. I knew you'd follow in his footsteps, eventually. I'm promoting you to Regular.' He leans forward and whispers, 'Don't forget who put you there. When I need you, you'd better have my back.'

A stunned silence fills the hall. Kudos sits up groggily and tries to focus on me.

This can't be happening. No one gets raised from Disposable to Regular after one fight, especially not an eighteen-year-old still in training. My brain races away with me, wondering what's behind this, what challenge for power Vicious is planning that he's recruiting so brazenly, but still, I remember to offer my hand in gratitude and acceptance, nodding my head the bare minimum so that I show my acceptance of his generosity without acceding power and status to him – he is, after all, only a Regular, as I now am myself.

I shower and put on the green trousers and vest of a Regular that I find in place of the brown shirt and trousers of a Disposable that I left outside the bathroom door. My heart sinks at the realisation that Disposables have been here. They will now clean my apartment, collect and wash my clothes, leaving fresh ones in their place, and prepare my food. I know how much they will hate doing it, just as I always have. But then my heart leaps at the thought that if I work hard and prove myself, I may be allowed to see my parents, and maybe even find a way to get them released.

A knock at the door causes me to frown in confusion, before I remember that I am no longer a Disposable and subject to people just opening the door and entering. Regulars are afforded the respect of a knock and a few minutes grace before whoever is outside comes in. The Elite alone can choose whether to allow entry to whoever is knocking.

I remember my status and stand to attention, chest out, shoulders down and back, feet apart. I must appear confident and strong, always, I remind myself. I've somehow made it this far and I won't stuff it up, not for myself and not for my parents.

A Regular in green vest and trousers that match my own, opens the door and steps into my apartment. She stands with her hands on her hips, looking me up and down as she decides whether she deems me worthy of having been raised to the same status as she. I don't speak; unless I challenge or taunt her, it is a show of weakness. I'm also not confident that my voice will come out as anything other than a squeak. I'm proud of myself that I manage to move my feet even further apart, put my hands on my own hips and stare levelly at her. She blinks. I smile. Victory.

She breathes in sharply and lifts her chin. 'Your presence is demanded at the Elite Forum in five minutes. Don't be late.' She marches out and slams the door behind her.

I want to run after her. I've never been to the Elite floors and have no idea where the Forum is, but to show weakness at this stage would see me back as a Disposable before I can blink. This is a test. I will pass it.

I march out of the door and make for the lifts. Mercifully, one is standing empty. My finger shakes as I select -50. The floors housing the Disposables and weapons halls are -1 to -20; they are closest to the surface and the most at risk in the event of an attack from above. The Regular floors – in which I assume I'll be assigned an apartment before the day is out – are -21 to -40. The Elite occupy the lowest, most protected, most luxurious floors of -41 to -50 and the Forum is on the bottom floor; I know that because I've been told, not because any Disposables are ever allowed down there.

Panic pierces my stomach and then my heart. Was I raised to Regular just so I could go to floor -50? My legs begin to shake and I steady myself against the juddering wall of the lift as it slowly sinks downward. Did my battle rage mark me as a suitable candidate for one of the Elites' games? They never fight one another openly; their power struggles are all covert. They scheme and plot and trap one another, sometimes ensuring a formal and public execution of their chosen rival, sometimes getting away with their murder to the horror and admiration of their peers. No, if they decide a hunt is in order, they choose Regulars for their entertainment. Disposables are too weak, too pathetic for the Elite to be able to take any pride in, or kudos for, their kill. Regulars who have distinguished themselves are a different matter.

It all makes sense; Vicious was ordered to select a fellow Regular for the Elites to hunt. Rather than expose whatever power play in which he is currently engaged to his fellow Regulars, he raised a Disposable – me – to fill the spot. I admire him and hate him all at once; he plays the game well.

All of my bravado and determination disappear, and I have to work hard to keep the contents of my bladder from streaming down my legs. What to do? I have nowhere to run and if I even try to go against a direct order from the Elite, both I and my parents will be executed. I sink to the floor and shift back into the corner of the lift, drawing my knees up to my chin.

For the first time since I donned them, I take in the scent of my new clothes. I decide that they must use different chemicals to produce the green clothes of Regulars. Come to think of it, the synthetic fabric does feel, as well as look, different. The first time I have ever had new clothes, and soon they will run with my blood. I wonder whether the Disposable who will be ordered to wash them will be able to get it out, and what will happen to them if they can't.

I snap back to myself. I can't let my mind wander. If I am to die, I need to ensure it is quick and that I show no fear. Only if I give a satisfactory account of myself will my parents' lives – such as they are – be safe. I get back to my feet as the panel above the lift door shows -45. By the time it shows -48, I have smoothed down my clothes and run my hand through my short, regulation length hair to make sure it is lying completely flat, its side parting dead straight and in exactly the required place. No deviation from the accepted appearance is ever tolerated and I want my death to be clean and rapid. If I give them any reason to make torture part of the game, they will take it.

When the panel shows -50, I take a deep breath and adopt the stance that has been drummed into me ever since I could first stand upright. The doors part and I step out into a corridor unlike any I have seen before. It is light! Not just barely, as ours are, with dim lights flickering continuously and giving the impression they will fail at any second, but brightly and with a different type of light. I look up at the ceiling and see that it is dotted with small, round spots from which the light appears to be coming.

Something snags at my memory. My father once mentioned that someone in the kitchens told him their son had been given the high-profile job of maintaining the Elite's light tubes. It was a brag, obviously, a way to try to gain superiority – however minimal – over the other kitchen workers, but my father seemed interested in the concept of light tubes itself, rather than any standing he might have lost during the conversation. I dismissed it at the time, but now I rack my brains, trying to remember. Light tubes carry natural light from the surface down to the Elite, I suddenly recall. It must provide some benefit over artificial light for them to bother. I immediately curse myself for an idiot. I've been summoned by the Elite, I'm about to die, and I'm pondering the benefits of natural light?

I cast about myself desperately. Which way to go? There are three options – left, right or straight ahead – and there is no one around to ask. That will be intentional. They'll be watching me though – I don't look for the cameras that I know will be there. My finger itches, wanting to go to my chin as it often does when I'm thinking. I clench my fist. Show no weakness.

I decide that the Forum will have pride of place down here. Those eligible to go within it will not want to deviate left or right when they exit the lifts from their apartments on the floors just above; marching straight ahead will be one of the many subtle ways that they put themselves above those who must deviate in other directions.

I march forward, my eyes flicking in all directions as I look for clues as to which door will be that of the Forum, while trying to appear as if I already have it figured out. None of the doors, all of which – in stark contrast to the brown ones of the Disposable floors – are brightly coloured and decorated, cause me to pause. Eventually, I find myself at the end of the corridor and facing red double doors that glitter, as if they have thousands of gems embedded in them.

My heart slows its frantic beating for a few seconds as relief courses through me. This has to be it. Then it thumps so fast and so hard, it feels as if it will jump right out of my chest. Hopefully, within an hour or two, this will all be over.

I knock on one of the doors and manage to merely blink when

it is flung open, instead of turning and running. I ensure that I am once more standing confidently, my palms flat to my thighs as is regulation when in the presence of those of a higher status, and staring straight ahead. If I am spoken to by an Elite, I must drop my gaze to the floor, but until then, I must appear ready and eager to be challenged; any sign of weakness at this stage, and they will add torture to the hunt.

'Enter,' a man says sharply. I don't need to look at him. I know he will be wearing the green of a Regular, but with red, horizontal stripes down his left arm to show he is permitted to serve the Elite.

I put my right arm across my chest so that the palm of my hand rests above my now painfully thumping heart, and march into the room. As soon as I am clear of the door, I stop and once more take up my stance.

My peripheral vision tells me that the room, like the corridor, is gloriously light, due to both the light tubes terminating at the ceiling, and the fact that the walls have been painted white and glitter in the same way as the doors. I make out a long, white table, around which fifteen people sit; one at the far end from me and seven down each side. All of them wear the red robes of the Elite, and all of their faces are turned towards me.

Even through my terror, it pleases me that their grey skin is identical in hue to my own and the mauve tinge to their silver hair matches mine. If I dared to look, I know I would find that their purple eyes also mirror those with which I was born. The Elite might not be required to keep their hair short, parted in the same place as the rest of us, and smoothed back at all times, but genetically, they are little different from the rest of us; the genetic engineers made sure of our uniformity in all aspects when they created us… except for the trait of battle rage, the predictability of whose inheritance they never managed to ensure. Yet it is a trait I have, and one that, it seems, will be my downfall.

'You may approach, Regular.' The woman's voice is warm and soft, like my mother's, as it reaches me from the head of the table.

I feel myself relax a little, and check myself. The Elite are anything but warm and soft. The woman sounds so because she has been schooled by her parents to use her voice as a means of disarming her opponents, just as she has been taught, since she uttered her first words, never to use the name of anyone of a lower status and to avoid using the names of those of equal or higher status. She knows my name is Victor. Acknowledging it, as I forced Kudos to, would be acknowledging me as just that to her, just as my parents intended. Just as all parents intend for their children when they name them.

I don't speak or acknowledge her instruction other than by dropping my gaze as soon as I hear her voice, and then doing as I am told. Once I am in position at the nearest short side of the table, I again take up my stance, my gaze still directed downward.

'It seems you have distinguished yourself in weapons training,' another woman says.

I remain silent; I would be an idiot to answer or react in any way, since I don't have any idea what game they are playing with me, and how long it will continue before I am released from the Forum so that the hunt can begin.

'I knew your grandfather,' a man says, sounding thoughtful. I bite down hard on my cheek and congratulate myself that I manage not to raise my eyes. 'He was impossible to beat when battle rage took him. It was disappointing to see he didn't pass it on to your father – you have my sympathies for having parents as pathetic as yours – but it's a pleasant surprise to see that it merely skipped a generation instead of disappearing from his line altogether.'

Blood pours into my mouth as I bite a chunk clean out of my cheek. I clench my teeth together and it takes every bit of self-control I have to keep my palm flat to my chest when it wants to clench and punch the man senseless. I slow my breathing as my mother taught me to do. Breathe in, slowly, quietly, then breathe out the same way. Control myself but don't ever let anyone see that's what I'm doing.

'He has control as well as aggression and half a brain. He'll do,' the first woman says, her voice still warm and now full of approval even though I know she's just identified me as a threat. The hunt will begin at any moment. My parents' faces flit through my mind, but I push them away. I have to be strong. For their sakes, I have to be.

'Regular, it has been one hundred years exactly since the last scouting party was sent above ground,' the thoughtful-sounding man says. 'Tomorrow, you will lead a party of five Disposables, chosen by yourself, above ground, where you will all remain for ten days. No more, no less. If any of you attempt to come back down here before you are due, you will all be executed. At zero seven hundred hours on the tenth day, if you are still alive and still sane, you will return to this room and report your findings.

I manage not to frown. What trick is this? I'm eighteen, I can't lead a scouting party; I don't know how to make decisions for myself, let alone for anyone else, I've never had to… but then I realise that I just did. I came straight here from my apartment on floor -4 with no deviations, in less than five minutes. I passed the test they set for me, a Disposable in all but name, elevated to a rank that will ensure control of those I take with me. I keep my breathing slow and even, not daring to believe I might be right.

'You will be shown to an appropriate apartment for one of your new status, where you will find everything you will need for your mission,' the man says. 'You will find the wallscreen in a Regular apartment dispenses far more information than that which has provided your education to date, including all of the information available regarding previous scouting missions and their findings. You will have two hours to look up the records of the Disposables you are considering taking with you. You will enter on your screen the names of the five you select before the two hours is up, or you will find yourself demoted back to Disposable. You needn't consider too carefully, since those you choose will probably all die or go insane, anyway. They are there to take whatever comes at you, so that you have a better chance of making it back here with your report. Remember that each is Disposable, just like your parents. Be at the lift to the surface at zero seven hundred hours in the morning. You may leave us.'

Breathe in, then out. Ignore his threat to my parents. Don't try to kill him, I'll never succeed. Swallow down the urge. Live to fight another day. If I distinguish myself, maybe they'll release my parents as a reward. Just breathe.

When the red door closes firmly behind me, I release a slower, longer breath. I can't lose control, they're still watching me. I march forward, my face blank, my breathing even. The light from the tubes above soothes me until I have to fight not to smile. Soon, I'll be bathing in natural light for real, something I never dreamt would ever be possible.

Terror takes me afresh. I'm going above ground where nothing is under control – that's why my ancestors created Supreme City in the first place. Those who made it back from previous scouting missions reported that it gets both too hot and too cold up there, and that it's wet and dry with no warning and no way of changing the conditions. They told of noisy, dirty, ferocious animals that do whatever they want, whenever they want, and they ranted about ghosts. But then they were all insane – they can't have been telling the truth. The ghosts they spoke of can't possibly exist and if there are any people up there, they won't be a match for us. Our strength is three times that of those who first lived down here and our weapons are deadly.

I will succeed where all of the others failed. I'll do whatever it takes to survive for ten days above ground, then when I get back down here, I'll find a way to get my parents back.

TWO

Will
___

My daughter giggles as Maverick licks her face. She's under a year old and not always steady on her feet, but whenever she wobbles, she, her mother and I have all learnt to count on one or both of our beloved dogs being there to steady her. Her hand rests on the black fur of Maverick's neck as she gurgles and squeals to him. When her fingers close around his fur, I'm Aware of her sensing how he feels, as if it's her ruff she's beginning to hold too tightly and not his. Immediately, she loosens her hold. There is no thought process involved, for she isn't capable of it, she just reacts to him in the same way he reacts to her.

When she's confident on her feet, Maverick darts in front of her and play-bows, daring her to chase him as he has from the moment she first stood upright. His acorn-brown eyes are bright and full of fun as she shrieks and toddles towards him. Delighted, he barks and runs away a few steps, his black brush of a tail held gaily aloft. When she catches up, he play-bows and runs again.

'Not near the mud, Tania, your mum will kill me.' Even as I

call out the words, I wonder what I'm thinking. As Lia is always reminding me, our daughter may have been born with the same abilities that I possess, but, exciting as it is when she begins to use them, for the most part they merely define whom she will become. For now, she is like any other ten-month-old who has ever lived, and has no idea what I just said.

Thankfully, Maverick comes to my rescue. Pleased as he was to lead Tania towards the mud that the ducks delighted in creating when the rain fell yesterday, he now runs around and around her until she turns in confusion, then he leads her back in my direction.

I relax back against the wall of the cottage that my mother and grandfather insisted on singing into existence for Lia and me when we married last year. Lia and I could have done it, but Mum insisted that whether everyone was capable of multiskilling or not, she and my grandfather had always planned to sing cottages for all of her children when they married, and she wouldn't be deprived of the joy of doing it for me, her firstborn, at least.

Lia chuckles as she sits down on the wooden bench beside me, her own dog, Breeze, jumping up to sit on her other side. 'You were actually more concerned about spilling your ale if you set your glass down to go and get your daughter, than you were about getting into trouble with me for allowing her to get muddy when I've just bathed her. I've said it before and I'll say it again, you spend too much time with Levitsson and Justin.'

I grin. 'It was you who created the potential for spillage by filling my glass to the brim.'

My wife raises her own glass of ale and chinks it gently against mine. 'I knew it would be your last for a while. I know he's coming for you.'

I nod slowly, smiling as Maverick now herds Tania, rushing at her and yapping excitedly when she heads in the wrong direction,

until she giggles and turns away, arms out either side to balance
herself. Then he dashes behind her and lies on the ground, ready
to spring to either side if she deviates again. Lia holds her arms
out, and Tania toddles as fast as she can to her mother, with
Maverick crawling along on his belly behind her. As soon as Tania
is on Lia's lap, Maverick licks my daughter's feet and then jumps
up beside me and puts his head on my shoulder.

I rub his chest. 'You feel it too, don't you, Mav? Ember's
coming for us. Makes a change from us having to go and find him,
doesn't it?'

'Don't pretend you don't love going off into the wilderness
looking for Ember and his herd when the mood takes you.' Lia
kisses Tania's head and settles her into the crook of her arm,
rocking her gently. 'So, it's nearly upon us then? Whatever it is
that's coming?'

'It is.'

'We've all respected the blocks you and Amarilla have in your
minds to stop any of us knowing about it, and we're grateful to
you both for saving us the hassle of having to block it from the
children, but now that it's imminent, I'm asking you to either tell
me, or allow me to search your mind.' She twists to face me, her
green eyes boring into mine. 'What's going on, Will?'

I draw her mind into my own and show her. It takes only
seconds for her mind to accept everything I have kept from her.

Her eyes widen. 'That's not possible,' she whispers. 'How...
how have they been down there all this time without us knowing?
How have they survived? It's been hundreds of years since The
Old regime imploded, since they all – well since we assumed that
they all – perished.'

I stay quiet, knowing she is now Aware of the answers to her
questions, and her brain just needs to catch up with what her mind
knows.

'You've known about this for months,' she says finally.

'I couldn't miss it when I felt the horses gathering above the underground city. I wondered to begin with why they've never picked up on the imbalance caused by those of The Old before, but it's not that they missed it, it's because it's never been ready to be corrected before. When the human collective consciousness shifted to include Awareness nearly thirty years ago, it called to the people of The Old every bit as it did to those of The New. Most of them were too set in their thought processes to feel its pull, but some of them felt it and still do, and a great many of those born since then feel it even more strongly; they care about people other than themselves and they're open to change. We and the horses can help them.'

Lia shudders. 'They're still violent, though. While you're doing what you need to do, the rest of us are going to have to work hard to shield those here who aren't yet strong in their centres, or they'll be driven mad as soon as they become Aware of the energy of The Old.'

I kiss her cheek and then that of my now sleeping daughter. 'You're here. Mum, Dad and my sisters are here, as are Am and Justin, not to mention the Kindred and a hundred others who are every bit as centred. You're all more than enough to protect the minds of those who need it.'

She nods but when she looks up at me, her eyes are full of concern. 'But what about you? We all know how strong you are, but you're planning to go and meet them alone.'

I chuckle. 'I'll have Maverick with me, and Ember, his herd and all of the other horses who have been drawn to where the energy of The Old is boiling over. I'll be far from alone, and don't forget, I already know how this will play out.'

She chuckles along with me. 'There is that. When are you going to let everyone else know?' She takes a sharp breath and then we both grin as we feel a familiar energy touch our minds. Amarilla is way too polite to monitor the thoughts and conversations of others, but Infinity has no such reservations and to all intents and purposes, they are one and the same.

I'll deal with it once you've left tomorrow, Will, my aunt tells me. *You're capable of much, but you're no match for your grandmother once she's built up steam, and she'll never let you go and do what you're planning, alone. I'll make sure my dad and both of my brothers are with her to keep her at home until she's calmed down, and then I'll let everyone know the situation. We'll all be ready when you need us.*

'Well I guess that's that sorted then,' Lia says as the sun finally sets on the warm, summer evening, and the last few birdcalls peter out to silence. 'It's so peaceful here, it's hard to imagine that it'll soon be anything but, isn't it?'

'It is. But it'll be peaceful again. Eventually.'

I'm up before dawn, wanting to go and meet Ember and his herd before they come clattering into Rockwood and ruin any chance I have of being able to leave the village quietly. I dress quickly, kiss Lia and stroke Breeze's head as it rests on my wife's stomach, then tiptoe quickly past Tania's nursery, tapping my leg to encourage Maverick to come with me. Lia won't thank me for allowing him to bowl his way into the nursery and wake Tania before time.

My dog follows me down the stairs and when I'm almost at the bottom, he leaps up behind me, landing on my shoulders. I put an arm over him to both steady him and discourage him from making a noise by leaping back onto the stairs. He licks my face excitedly, knowing that he and I are preparing to hunt. It doesn't

matter that we never actually go out to search for or kill animals –
whether we go for an early morning run by ourselves or with
Justin, or go off on one of our trips to find Ember and his herd so
that we can run with them for a few days before returning home,
it's all the same as far as Maverick is concerned; he and I are
going somewhere and it will be as brilliant as everything always
is. I love him for it. I always have and always will.

I put down a bowl of meat for him and make myself some
porridge and tea. I packed my back-sack before going to bed, so as
soon as I can feel that Maverick's stomach has settled after his
meal, we set off.

We've barely left the house when I sense that we aren't the
only ones up. I turn around, knowing exactly whom I will see in
the moonlight that bathes the cobbled side street of Rockwood.
Maverick lets out a high-pitched whine of excitement as he
catches my mother's scent, and launches himself at her, dirtying
her white dressing gown and almost knocking her off her feet.

I grin. 'Lia told you,' I say softly.

My mother nods and laughs as she holds Maverick away from
her. She tries to stroke his head but quickly goes back to using two
hands to restrain him as he bounces up and down on his hind legs.

'Mav, come here, boy,' I say, and my dog bounds back to me,
his eyes bright with excitement.

My mother follows him and hugs me. 'Don't be cross with
Lia, she was very careful to guard both her and my thoughts so
that no one else picked up on our conversation – she's better at
that than I am now, you know, and almost as good as you and Am.
She knew how much I'd want to see you before you go wherever
it is that you're going this time.'

'Am will fill you all in later. I need to get moving though, or
Ember will come here for me and if he wakes Gran up, I'll never
get going.'

My mother nods. 'Your dad will be sad not to have seen Ember when he's so close, but he'll understand.'

'You'll both see the two of us very soon and then you'll probably be wishing it was otherwise.'

Her eyes widen in horror as she wonders what I can be meaning. Then she laughs. 'Stop teasing me, you horrid child, and get gone.'

'I'm twenty-seven, Mum, and I was going before you held me up.'

She turns me away from her and gives me a little push like she used to when I didn't want to go to school. 'You'll always be my child, however old you are, which Lia appreciates even if you don't. Take care, Will.'

'Always.' I blow her a kiss and then set off at a jog, Maverick bounding along at my side.

It's getting light by the time we leave the forest that, along with the huge rock at the base of which the village nestles, gives Rockwood its name. I know the woods very well but even so, I was glad of Maverick's eyesight as he leapt forward ahead of me and then hurtled back, over and over, so that I could be confident I was still on the path that would lead me to the grassland where I know Ember and his herd are currently grazing.

We have many things to do together, Ember and I – we've known it ever since our eyes met when he was just hours old – but the days of horses bonding with humans, giving up their natural way of living in order to help their human Bond-Partners, are gone. Ember has a herd to look after and he won't ever leave them; if I want to spend time with him, I spend time with all of them. The fact that we both know where we are needed now makes no difference to that – Ember and I will travel with the rest of the herd, at the speed of the weakest member.

I see the horses in the distance and know the instant that Ember registers my presence. He lifts his head above the grazing horses and watches our approach. It is only when we are within a long stone's throw that he leaves the other horses grazing peacefully – they are so well used to my and my dog's presence that even Maverick's delighted barking and bouncing around at the sight of those alongside whom he has run so often, doesn't disturb them – and walks slowly, powerfully, majestically to Maverick and me.

Ember's fluted ears are pricked as he slows to a halt in front of us. Maverick runs around the back of him in celebration, as if he has brought Ember to me himself. The stallion's black coat gleams in the early morning sunshine, but as always, it is his amber-coloured eyes, blazing with strength and vitality, that take my breath away.

He steps closer, nips the arm of my shirt and tugs at it playfully as he used to when he was a foal. I chuckle and rub his nose. When he wanders back to his family, Maverick and I follow, also sensing that the brown lead mare has just made the decision to move on now that the awaited final members of the herd have arrived. She moves off at a walk, allowing the others to organise themselves behind her. Maverick and I walk just in front of Ember, at the back of the herd; we may not be horses but he still wants us in front of him where he can keep us up with the others. I sense when the lead mare is preparing to increase speed at the same time Ember does. I turn and vault onto his back while Maverick yaps excitedly.

Ember takes a step of walk and two of trot, then canters powerfully, effortlessly, after the other horses, my weight no more a burden to him than his own. The herd energy shifts a little towards both Maverick and the foals of the herd, ensuring they are able to keep pace. Then we gallop as we have so many times before; not because we need to, but because of the joy it gives us to feel our power, our balance, our strength.

The horses all return to canter at the same instant and maintain it for a while before, as one, we slow to a trot to give the weaker members a chance to regain their wind. Then we canter on again for a while before finally slowing to walk to a stream just ahead. Maverick scents the water and races on in front. I laugh when I see water droplets fly into the air, knowing he will have launched himself straight into the stream. I sense his relief as it cools him, and his joy as he then splashes towards the bank. He leaps out onto it and the lead mare snorts as he shakes in front of her, flinging water at her and the yearling standing at her side.

I slide down from Ember's back as he and the others go to the water to drink. They are all streaked with sweat, even though the early summer sun is only just beginning to gain any real strength. I look back the way we have come and realise that we've covered a huge distance.

I feel the pull that the imbalance in the underground city exerts on the horses whose energy can correct it. Most of those who are needed are already in position. Ember's herd members will push themselves hard to also get themselves into place. It would take two days for me to walk to my destination on foot. At the pace at which we have travelled this morning, and that I can feel the horses have every intention of maintaining in between rest stops, we'll be there by lunchtime.

THREE

Victor

$\mathcal{I}$ try not to frown as I consider who to include in my scouting party; those who report to the Elite will be watching me more closely than ever and I cannot appear to be indecisive. I stare at the screen set into the living room wall of my new apartment, and attempt to ignore the time counting down from two hours in the top right corner, which began the second I set foot in my new apartment. I still have more than fifty files open. Fifty Disposables from whom I need to choose five, and I only have five minutes left to enter my choices before I lose my status, apartment, parents and life, probably in that order.

I should choose tactically. Who is a good enough fighter to have my back, but not strong enough to challenge me if I show weakness? I curse silently. Who am I kidding? None of them will have my back, they'll try to stick something sharp in it as soon as they get a chance. Okay, so who is a lot weaker than I am? Who won't dare to try to fight me for my position as a Regular, for their chance to return here, victorious, in my place?

I let out a sharp but hopefully silent breath in frustration and fear as I realise that again, I'm kidding myself. It's unlikely that any of us will be returning victorious, if we even return at all. How many scouting parties have gone above ground during the hundreds of years my ancestors have been living down here, how many party leaders were determined to succeed where their predecessors failed, only to meet the same fate? Why will I be any different?

I feel as if something is pulling at my stomach. That's a new sensation. A new type of terror? No, it doesn't feel like it. It snags again, more strongly this time, and strangely, I feel a little more optimistic. I want to believe the feeling, but a glance at the time pushes it from my mind. Two minutes left. I don't have time to think, so I frantically begin typing in the names of those who were closest to me in weapons training a few hours ago.

Kudos. Ace. Prime. Hero. Adept. I hit enter with twenty-four seconds left on the clock.

Relief at having made the deadline is quickly replaced by panic. Was that another test? Should I have typed in the names with plenty of time to spare? Did I show weakness by taking so long to think? Will I hear the sound of marching feet in the next few minutes as The Force comes to take me away, or will the Elite be impressed by my choices? Will they think it was a good decision to take those whose strengths and weaknesses I know almost as well as my own, those who are a similar age to me and so more likely to take orders from me than older Disposables would be? Or will they think me a coward for choosing Kudos, who will still be sore after the beating I gave him, and for choosing those who saw me take him down?

I need to do something. I need to appear to be pleased and confident with my decision, and eager to get on with my mission. I decide to go through everything that is laid out on the living room floor, prioritise the items and pack them accordingly. That will be what they'll be looking for me to do.

As I kneel down on the floor, it dawns on me for the second time since arriving that I actually have a living room! My new apartment is more than double the size of the one I shared with my parents. The old one was grey-walled, dingy, and consisted of the bedroom shared by my parents, a bathroom and a hallway between the two where we ate and I slept and took my lessons from the wallscreen.

This one has walls painted a pale green, and there are even glitter stones at regular – if not frequent – intervals. There are two bedrooms leading off from the living room, as well as a bathroom and a room with long, floor-to-ceiling cupboards. One of the cupboards is for the Disposables to store the food they have prepared and delivered, another contains crockery and cutlery, and the last contains both an oven in which to heat my food if I want to, and a chute that takes my rubbish and dirty eating equipment back to the Disposables.

I feel a pang of guilt, remembering the smelly crockery, utensils and leftovers that used to land with a crash in a corner of the apartment I shared with my parents, at all times of the day and night, and the beatings that would follow if the rubbish wasn't immediately sorted and redirected, or the washing up wasn't done and returned to the apartments of the Regulars from which they came. When my parents were taken away, the duty fell solely to me, and I shudder at the memories of returning from weapons training barely able to walk, yet having to wash up and sort rubbish before being able to nurse my injuries.

I wonder how my parents are. Prison has to be way worse than living in a Disposable apartment. Does my father still believe that the best he can hope for is to survive and take joy in seeing my mother every day? Does he even see her every day, or are they separated? Maybe now, the best he hopes for is merely to survive. But I can't think of him now. I need to get above ground, then I need to fight to stay alive once I'm there. That means sorting through my kit and making wise decisions regarding organising and packing it. I get to work.

There are four sets of vests and trousers in the green of my new status, plus two long-sleeved shirts and a thicker garment that I've never seen Regulars down here wear, also with long sleeves. I nod to myself, remembering the reports of the changeable temperature above ground.

Thirty tubs of food are piled in three stacks of ten – three meals a day for ten days. Whoever decided on the food provision is more optimistic about my chances of survival than I am. I breathe sharply and grind my teeth. I can't afford to think that way, my parents' lives depend on it. With an air of determination, I pack half of the tubs into the bottom of my rucksack, followed by the clothes. Then I pack the rest of the food, telling myself that I will eat the contents of each and every last tub, and I will be back here in ten days' time, as ordered.

I put the long-barrelled gun and helmet with which I have been provided, to one side, and place the cloths and oils for maintaining my weapon in a side pocket of the rucksack. I pick up the metal torture headband and press the button that turns it on. Its fingerpad flashes red until I put my thumb to it, then flashes green as it registers the print that will activate it henceforth. While I have been instructed in the headband's use for cold-blooded punishment, as a Disposable, I was never allowed to use one. I place it on top of my food along with a water flask, and pull the drawstring of the rucksack closed.

I sit back on my heels. So. I haven't been allowed a staff or any of the knives with which we have all been trained to fight, and I have to assume that none of my party have been, either. The

Elite are limiting the damage we can do to one another to that which will either cost us in ammunition, or in strength if we fight using our bare hands. As a Regular, I will be alone in having been provided with a torture headband, which I now realise I may have to defend with my life. I put that thought to one side. Of all the things that could go wrong once we are above the city, that is the least of my worries.

The best way to win is to be prepared; that is what we are taught from the moment our wallscreens begin throwing information at us. If I am to win against everything that is above ground, I will need to know what I might face. I stand in front of my wallscreen and browse its menus. Soon, I have files open that contain all of the previous scouting reports. I'll start with those, then move on to those with more information on the conditions I'm likely to encounter, then I'll research all the different types of animals that live on the surface. I have a long day ahead of me.

My wallscreen wakes me at zero six hundred hours, as I instructed it to. It feels strange to be rising, for the first time ever, at a time of my choice. I shower, dress, eat and then check my gear. I slept with it by my bed, so it's unlikely anyone could have tampered with it, but I need to be sure. The strands of my hair tied around the rucksack's clasps are intact, as are those which I tied between one of its straps and the handle of my bedside table, and between its other strap and the chinstrap of my helmet which still rests atop it. Even so, I remove the helmet and open the rucksack, checking it thoroughly before carrying out an equally thorough check of my weapon and helmet. Everything is exactly as I left it.

I leave my apartment with the aim of arriving at the lift to the surface at one minute to seven. I have considered my timing carefully. When we have weapons training, the Regulars in charge never arrive before us; they want their inferiors awaiting their arrival so that they can march in and immediately start giving orders. I must do the same, however I am unsure whether any of the Elite will arrive to give last minute instructions, so I cannot risk not being there before them.

I try to appear sure of myself as I march to the lifts. Thankfully, I am the sole occupant of my chosen lift, so while it ascends to floor -1, I slow my breathing and check that my posture conveys confidence. When the door opens, I march to the lift that hasn't been used in a hundred years. I know it is serviced regularly in case of urgent need, and find myself hoping against hope that it doesn't fail – both for my sake and for those of the Disposables in charge of its maintenance.

As I stride through one identical, grey, dreary corridor after another, trying not to wince as all of the Disposables I pass – some of whom I have known all my life – stand to the side, their gazes averted, I wonder if I will ever see any of it, or them, again.

My stomach is queasy with fear and excitement, and I'm convinced that the breakfast I forced myself to eat will soon be making work for whichever unfortunate Disposable is closest when I throw it back up. I swallow firmly. No. I am in command, both of myself and of the five teenagers I can now see ahead of me, waiting by the lift to the surface. I glance down quickly at my wristwatch, which reads 06:58:36. Good. I will arrive exactly as planned. I force my shoulders even further down and back, and lift my chin.

When I reach my party, I say, in the same curt voice the Regulars always use, 'Helmets off.'

I'm unsure whether it is my voice or the fact that my clothes are the green of a Regular while theirs are the brown of Disposables, that has all of them immediately lifting their helmets off, placing them hastily between their feet and then smoothing their hair back down to regulation appearance. I don't care, I'm just relieved that they are obeying me.

Kudos stands nearest the lift. So, he was here first, determined to claim his place at the head of the party. He has a large swelling on the side of his head where I hit him with the end of my staff yesterday. That will cause him pain when both donning and removing his helmet, and probably all the while he's wearing it. Good. I'll remember that in case I need to use it against him.

Prime is next in line. His grey skin, mauve-tinged, silver hair, and muscular build are identical to all of ours, but he is a fraction taller than the rest of us and his purple eyes are a little smaller and meaner than average. I grin inwardly to myself. He'll be seething that Kudos beat him to the first spot, and will already be planning to take it from him; something else I can use to my advantage if need be. Prime's eyes flick between Kudos and Ace, who stands on his other side, her eyes as hard as ever. She is a competent fighter who wins as many bouts as she loses. I think she could win far more than she does, but she's calculating, winning enough that she isn't taken lightly, but not so many that she attracts attention. Prime is wise not to underestimate her.

Hero is anything but, we all know that, and I'm surprised he didn't arrive last. We've been taught to see him as a coward and a weakling, but I think he's stronger inside than any of us. I can't ever remember him winning a fight unless his opponent was already injured, and when he curls up and takes his beatings, the taunts and insults that we're encouraged to shout at him appear to bounce off. He gets up each time, limps back to his duties, and endures the pain.

Adept is the last in line and the closest to looking unsure of herself. I'm not surprised, since she's rarely without her cousin,

Stellar. The two of them are the closest any of us are to being friends – that is to say, if either has plans to bring the other down, they've managed to keep the fact concealed as yet. Their mothers are sisters and, similar in appearance as we all are, Stellar and Adept are identical. They rarely speak to anyone else and appear to gain strength from one another's presence. I've made Adept less of a threat to me by separating her from her cousin, but as with the others who stand before me, I would be stupid to underestimate her.

'I have no intention of checking you have correctly packed your rucksacks,' I say in as cold a voice as I can manage. 'If you've left anything behind, or packed essentials in such a way that they can't be accessed quickly when you need them, that's down to you. We could be under attack the second we appear on the surface, so I want your weapons primed and ready. If no threats are immediately obvious, we will spend today scouting in pairs, meeting back at the lift at twenty hundred hours this evening. The pairings are...' I pause in panic as I realise that I almost used my team's names, therefore acknowledging them as being superior over me in the way each name was intended. I recover quickly, relieved that sweat hasn't broken out on my brow, and point to Kudos and Adept. 'You two.' Prime and Ace nod curtly as I point at the two of them next. Hero's eyes widen as I stand in front of him and tell him, 'You will pair with me.'

I march back to the front of the line. 'Replace your helmets, then enter the lift behind me.'

Kudos manages to keep his eyes cast down as I touch the fingerpad by his shoulder, then press the button to open the lift door and enter ahead of him. I smile to myself, knowing how much he is hating having to show me respect and do as I say.

Unlike any other lifts in which I've been, this one has thick glass walls which I hope are bulletproof; just because none of the previous scouting parties reported having seen signs of humans, it doesn't mean there aren't any out there.

'Everyone, face outwards,' I order, and we all claim a spot around the perimeter of the lift as it begins to move.

The walls of the lift shaft are the same grey as those of all the upper floors. We are therefore all rendered speechless when, after a long ten minutes of rising at speed through a blur of grey, our eyes are suddenly assaulted not only by light brighter than any of us have ever experienced before, but, as our eyes slowly adjust, by a mind-blowing variety of colours.

I can't allow anyone else to speak before I do. 'The green stalks with green tops are all grasses,' I tell the others, grateful for the hours of study I did yesterday. 'Those with coloured tops, called flowers, are herbs. Lots of the animals we'll see eat both. Humans used to eat some of them too, before we were advanced enough to create everything we need synthetically. If you look up, the white masses are collections of water called clouds. Sometimes water falls from them. That bright light you can see is the sun. If you look directly at it, it will blind you. Its light is scattered through the atmosphere in all directions before it reaches us. Blue light is scattered more than other colours because it travels as shorter, smaller waves, so when we look up, we see a blue sky.' That should delay any early attacks on me; I have demonstrated that I have knowledge they need.

I blink frantically as my eyes continue to adjust. Eventually, I notice movement in the distance. 'Second visors down,' I order.

I press a button on the side of my helmet and a thicker visor drops down in front of the first, magnifying my surroundings. Hero, to my left, and Kudos to my right, both gasp and step backward.

'Disposables, back to your stations,' I bark, proud that my voice doesn't shake, for my visor is filled with huge, four-legged creatures of many different colours – every single one of which is standing, looking in our direction. 'Those of us looking to the west have spotted horses,' I tell the others. 'They're herbivores, so they won't be looking to kill us for food, but they are certain to want us dead before we can harm them. Can anyone else see any animal, of any kind?'

There is a chorus of voices answering to the negative.

'NO, WHO?' I roar, glad of the chance to shout my fear out.

Adept answers quickly. 'No, Victor.'

When Ace and Prime give the same answer, their monotones give away the control they are having to exercise over themselves in order to do it.

I glance to either side out of the corner of my eyes so that Hero's and Kudos's faces aren't magnified, and see that while Kudos is smirking at the others having acknowledged who I am to them, Hero has a look of wonder on his face as he stares at the horses. Why isn't he afraid?

My eyes snap back to the beasts who are still standing, apparently watching us – yet they can't be; they can't possibly be able to see us properly from that distance. Most of them appear to be chewing, some with long stalks of grass hanging out of their mouths. I grimace. So, it's true. They're eating food they've just pulled from the ground. How disgusting. They will be our first targets.

'Wait a minute, I see large animals too, and they're coming this way,' Adept says.

'Hold your positions, everyone,' I say, and step quickly beside Adept, looking to where my main visor now tells me is the south. 'More horses,' I confirm.

'I see some now to the east, also coming this way,' Prime says.

'And I see them to the north,' Ace reports. 'We're surrounded.'

'Everyone, outside before they get any closer,' I command, my heart racing. 'Take up your positions around the circumference of the lift and prepare to fire as soon as they are in range.'

I open the lift door and nod for everyone to step out before me. It is my fingerprint alone that both the internal and external fingerpads have been set to recognise, so I must exit last.

Hero lingers, still staring west with an awestruck expression on his face. I've never seen him like this. I glance outside to make sure that the others are following my orders, then say under my breath, 'What do you see?'

'They're beautiful,' he whispers. 'They see me. And you. I mean really see us; they see who we are inside. Can't you feel it?'

I glance at the others and see Prime watching Hero and me. 'Eyes outward, Disposable,' I order, and when he obeys, I hurry to Hero's side. 'Feel it? Feel what?'

'Just watch them. Look into their eyes. They're so... peaceful. They won't hurt us, they're here to help us.'

I can't help myself. Something about Hero's voice and demeanour makes me do as he says. I stare at a horse the colour of my skin. It has eyes so dark that they frighten me at first. Then it blinks and stares right back at me as if it knows I'm watching it, even though it can't possibly at this distance. It stops chewing, stalks dangling from both sides of its mouth. Its nostrils widen as if it can smell me. What I assume are its ears – two long, hairy things that swivel around on its head – stop moving and point towards me.

Then I feel it – the same relief I used to feel whenever I arrived back in our family apartment and shut the door, knowing I could have a break from pretending to be brave, confident and aggressive, and just be myself. The same acceptance I used to feel when my parents hugged me for nothing more than being who I am. I feel as if everything is alright, as if there's nothing to fear.

I frown. That can't be right, I have everything to fear. I shake my head, trying to free myself from whatever magic this is. Have the horses driven me insane? I can't be failing already.

'Out. Now,' I say to Hero.

'We can't shoot them. We can't k…kill them. They're peaceful, they're here to help us. You felt it too just then, I know you did. All any of us want is to feel safe, and they can show us how.'

'Get out now and take up your position, or I'll shoot you where you stand,' I tell him, glad that he doesn't dare raise his eyes to meet mine. I furiously blink away the tears filling my eyes, in case any of the others risk a glance in my direction.

Hero swallows a gulp and wipes his own eyes. I feel ashamed, but push him anyway as he steps out of the lift in front of me. I press the button to shut the door and stifle a gasp as what seems like a hundred different scents assault my nose at once. Several of the others have begun to sneeze, but a smile spreads across my face as I try to decide from where all the different scents can be originating. Then my attention is taken by a thumping sound in the distance and when I look back to the horses, I see that they are now running towards us from all directions.

'Stand ready,' I warn the others. 'Second visors away. Fire on my command.'

We all position our guns against our shoulders and wait. A quick glance to my left tells me that although Hero has obeyed my commands, he has no intention of firing; his shoulders are juddering with his silent sobs. I'll need to protect him if any of the others notice, but for now, I must keep us all alive.

By the time the horses are easily visible without our distance visors, they are almost in range. The horizon from left to right as far as any of us can see, is filled with them – hundreds of them, all running straight at us. I should be high on adrenalin, my heart hammering in my chest, my vision sharp, my hearing acute, my muscles twitching and ready for action. I should be giving the countdown to us all pulling our triggers... and yet something about them is giving me pause.

They all leave the ground at exactly the same time, then land back on it so lightly, it's as if they aren't touching it at all. Their long hair hangs in the air for what seems like forever before it lands to rest back on their necks and faces, as if time has slowed down. My breathing slows to the rhythm of their movement, as does my heart rate. All I want to do is drop my weapon and... smile.

Out of the corner of my eye, I see Kudos shake his head violently, as if trying to dislodge something that has landed on it – or in it. So, he's affected too. I don't dare look at any of the others, but wonder how they are faring. We're all going insane, we have to be. Our mission is over before it has begun. No. That cannot be.

'READY TO FIRE,' I shout. 'FIVE. FOUR. THREE. TWO...'

As one, all of the horses come to a stop in an enormous circle around us, just out of range of our weapons. Options flash through my mind. We could advance, or I could order everyone to change the settings on their guns so that their ranges are extended. The latter isn't advisable; we haven't trained at a range longer than that at which our weapons are now set, and the horses could come at us again while we're making the adjustments. But wait, I'm thinking about them as if they are intelligent, even though the information provided by my wallscreen led me to believe that all animals are mindless. They won't know they are no longer in danger if we lower our weapons to adjust them... yet they knew to stop their charge just beyond the point we would have slaughtered them. How did they know?

As I squint into the distance at the horses, a deep unease steals over me. What to do? I can't appear weak in front of the others.

'Prepare to advance and fire on my command,' I say. 'Advance.'

I take a step forward through the knee-high grasses and herbs and hear rustling as the others do the same. Immediately, the horses turn tail and run away from us – all except for one. Out of the dust kicked up by hundreds of hooves, strides a single black horse.

I flip my second visor down in disbelief, but I see my vision isn't deceiving me; the horse now fills my vision as if he were right in front of me, and he isn't alone. There's a man on his back! And what's that at his side? It can't be a dog? They're vicious predators and would never be in the company of a human and a horse. Yet according to those I saw on my wallscreen, that's exactly what this is. The dog's tongue is hanging out of the side of its mouth as it looks up at the brown-skinned man with almost white hair who is smiling down at it, his lips moving as if he is talking to it, and oblivious to the weapons trained on him.

There's something about the three of them that makes me feel... envious. I blink, several times, but each time I refocus on them, the feeling is still there. There is an ease about the three of them, a confidence that I wish I had, but it's more than that; they trust each other, I can see it. They... like each other. The only time I've seen that before is between my parents. I want what they have. Very much. But I have to maintain control over the others.

'Everyone, report,' I say.

All but Hero to my left, and Kudos to my right, report that the horizon is clear.

'All of you, form a line either side of me. No one is to fire unless I give the command,' I order.

'We should be firing now,' Prime snarls, 'not giving that abomination a chance to get closer.'

'Frightened of a horse, a man and a dog, are you?' I snap. 'Your insubordination has been noted. If it happens again, I will allow one of the others to shoot you. We are here to scout and report back. Hundreds of wild beasts charging us was one thing. What we have in front of us now is no threat to six of us with weapons. Stand firm, but do NOT fire.'

FOUR

Will

*T*heir fear comes off them in waves as they stand, feet apart, metal tubes held to their shoulders. Maverick feels their distress and is all for racing over to them to distribute his unique form of love and happiness, but I keep him with Ember and me by talking to him, which he always loves. As we get closer to the six young adults standing in a line, staring at us, I hold my arms out, inviting him to jump up in front of me. Ember tolerates Maverick's enthusiastic bark and subsequent leap onto his withers, knowing it is necessary.

The shock of our spectators at this latest development is almost as strong as the fear that has gripped them all since they were children. Prime, Ace and Kudos are on the verge of defying the orders they have been given, and attempting to kill Ember, Maverick and me. Hero and Adept want to throw their weapons on the ground, but don't dare. Victor is torn. His soul is urging him to acknowledge what he saw in the horses and what he sees between Ember, Maverick and me, but his parents are in danger and he thinks he can save them if he completes his mission. My heart goes out to them all even as I smile in the knowledge that everything will be okay.

'A very warm welcome to you all,' I call out as soon as I am close enough for them to hear me. The three who are most frightened brace themselves, even closer to firing their weapons.

'State your name, rank and purpose here,' Victor calls back.

I grin. 'Of course. My name is Will, this loon sitting in front of me is Maverick, and the horse doing me the enormous favour of carrying us both is Ember. I named him that on account of his eyes. Stunning isn't he? Our rank is equal, and our purpose here is to welcome you above ground after all this time, and to invite you and all of your people to come and live with us and around us as people of The New.'

Ember halts. Hero and Adept lower their weapons and there is a thud as Hero drops his in the grass.

'Equal?' spits Kudos. 'Your rank is equal? You can't possibly mean to us, so you must mean to a horse and, whatever that thing is in front of you? Have you no pride? No shame?'

I chuckle. 'None whatsoever, I'm afraid, Kudos. Maverick is a dog, by the way. He's desperate to meet you all, but I have a feeling you'll find his form of affection uncomfortable at the moment. Don't worry, I'll keep him with me for now.'

'Why would we worry?' Ace asks. 'Any one of us could drop all three of you in a heartbeat, and there are six of us.'

'It was merely a turn of phrase, Ace, of course you don't need to worry; none of us will harm you. You're quite safe, all of you, as are all of those still underground. I do hope you'll extend our invitation to everyone else?'

The teenagers look at one another in confusion, which is quickly replaced by rage in Prime, Kudos, and Ace.

Kudos's finger twitches on his weapon's trigger. Then it relaxes and he moves his eye away from the part down which he was squinting. 'You called me by my name,' he says. 'While it's acceptable that you acknowledge my superiority, you will tell me immediately how you know my name.'

'And mine,' Ace says. 'Tell me right now, or I'll blow your head off.'

'STAND DOWN. ALL OF YOU, WEAPONS DOWN,' Victor shouts while keeping his own weapon trained on me. 'Answer her, please,' he says to me. 'How did you know their names?'

I stroke Maverick's head to reassure him; he hates shouting. He turns and licks my face, and all of those before us grimace in disgust. 'In the same way that you could have known mine without needing to ask me. You're little different from me, you just don't know it yet,' I reply.

'How dare you,' Prime sneers, hoisting his weapon back against his shoulder. 'You come to meet six who are superior to you in every way, unarmed and spouting nonsense, and you have the nerve to suggest that we're little different from you?'

He is right in terms of his physicality being superior to mine – he is head and shoulders taller than I, and nearly twice as broad. His arms are the thickness of my thighs, as is his neck. He is the tallest of the group by a small margin, but they are all of similar size and stature.

Ember's skin ripples in front of my knee, and I flick away the insect biting him before turning my attention back to Prime. 'The biters really irritate him,' I explain. 'I agree, the differences between us do appear to be great. I can assure you, though, that as we spend more time together, you'll find that in essence, you all and I are very much the same.'

Prime's outrage explodes out of him only moments before three killing pellets blast from his gun at me, Ember and Maverick.

All time is now, so I have all the time I need to consider my course of action. I could drop my physical boundaries and allow the pellet coming in my direction to pass right through me, but then Maverick and Ember would feel significant pain for the few seconds it would take me to heal the injuries their pellets would cause them. In addition, the teenagers would assume I am one of the ghosts who used to haunt the city sites of The Old. I stick with the simpler option upon which I decided when I foresaw this event. I tune into the three metal pellets on their way to me and my companions, allow my energy to resonate with them, then cause them to disintegrate to their component atoms.

Prime looks at me, Maverick and Ember in turn, then at his weapon, and scowls. 'Hand me your gun,' he says to Kudos.

Kudos looks at me, then back at Prime. I sense his uncertainty at the strangeness he has just witnessed as he shakes his head. Prime freezes as the end of Victor's weapon is jammed into the side of his neck.

'Drop your weapon and remove your helmet right now, or I shoot you dead,' Victor says, his voice unwavering even though I know that his knees are shaking.

Prime does as he is ordered and I take in a sharp breath. I saw the humans of The Old in my mind when I saw what was coming, yet still I find myself unprepared for the vision before me. The lad's face is the same colour as his weapon and so many of the other machines he and his kind value so much. His eyes are purple and his hair makes him look like one of our elderly, even though he is barely nineteen.

'There's a headband in the top of my rucksack. Put it on him,' Victor orders Hero, who reaches into the sack on Victor's back, then rushes to Prime's side and lowers a metal band around his head. Victor puts his thumb to a pad on the headband, then presses a button. Prime drops to the ground immediately, unconscious.

Victor looks up at me. 'I'm sorry about that. He won't bother you when he wakes.'

I grin at him. 'He didn't bother me before. Please, remove the headband. Instruments of torture really aren't necessary.'

Victor removes his helmet and looks up at me with eyes that match Prime's in colour, but are a little larger. He shakes his head. 'You know nothing of our people. They are very necessary.' He glances at Ace. 'Take the insubordinate's weapon apart and report as to why it misfired. If the air up here is affecting our weapons, we're vulnerable.'

Ace pulls a cloth from a pocket of her back-sack and lays it on the ground beside Prime. Then she begins to dismantle his weapon, laying its constituent parts on the cloth.

'You have everything to hand in your back-sacks, don't you?' I remark.

Victor looks at me thoughtfully. 'In our rucksacks? Yes, we do. We have everything we need for the ten days we have to be up here before returning to the city.'

'You don't need to return, Victor. You and your people will be warmly welcomed by the villagers of The New, and taught everything you need to have a long and happy life. And by the way, there's nothing wrong with that weapon, it fired three perfectly aimed bullets.'

Victor shakes his head. 'That's impossible. If it had, the three of you would be dead.' The others all look at me as if I'm stupid.

There's no point arguing. They will arrive at the truth in their own time.

FIVE

Victor

*A*dept, Hero and Kudos are waiting for my orders, but I can't stop staring at the peculiar sight in front of me. Will is watching Ace taking Prime's gun apart as if there is nothing in the world more interesting, while his dog watches us all, his tongue dripping saliva onto the horse who stands with his ridiculous ears swivelling back and forth between us, sometimes pointing in different directions as he gazes in yet another.

Their calm, relaxed demeanour hasn't changed in the whole time they have been before us, yet I wouldn't choose to take any of them on; I have a strange feeling deep inside of me – with which I want to argue, yet find I can't – that I wouldn't win. And I realise that I don't want to. Much as Ember scares me with his size and bearing, I find myself wanting to get closer to him to see if the feeling of security that I had when I looked into the eyes of the grey horse, and which is steadily creeping over me in Ember's presence, will get even stronger if I touch him. I want to sit down with Will and ask him how it is that Ember carries him as if they were born joined together. And, despite having read that dogs are vicious and will bite to kill as soon as look at you, I want to experience the affection from Maverick that Will thinks I will find uncomfortable.

As soon as the thought has crossed my mind, Will lifts his leg over Ember's neck and slides to the ground. He sets Maverick down and the dog takes two leaps and lands in front of me. I take a step back in alarm and am aware of weapons being readied around me.

'Weapons down, we're not in any danger,' I say to Kudos and Ace, and hold a shaking hand out to Maverick, hoping upon hope that I'm right and he won't bite me.

'That's it, let him sniff you. Appreciate the moment, because he won't be this polite once he knows you,' Will says.

Maverick's nose is cold and wet, despite the heat beating down on us from above. I cringe as he presses it into my hand and takes lots of breaths in for every big breath out. When he's finished, he licks my hand as if it's covered in something tasty. I freeze, wondering if he will bite me. He doesn't. When I don't respond to him, he sits in front of me and makes a horrible noise, like a toddler whining.

'If I were you, I'd crouch down and stroke his head,' Will says, 'because if you don't... uh-oh, too late.'

Maverick leaps up in front of me and licks my face, leaving a stripe of slimy, disgusting saliva on my cheek. He lands back on the ground, then leaps up again only this time putting his front paws on my shoulders and hanging on. Instinctively, I grab hold of him and once I have him in my arms, he licks my face as if he'll die if he doesn't.

'He won't die,' Will tells me, 'he'll just be very, very disappointed.'

I start laughing, yet I have no idea why. I have a dog attached to me and behaving in the most revolting way, there is a horse standing in front of me who could crush me at any moment of his choosing, I've dropped my gun, and a man is answering the thoughts in my head as if I'm speaking out loud. I should be horrified, terrified and on the offensive, yet I don't want it to stop. I hear laughter joining mine, I think it's Hero's. Then I hear the bang of a bullet being fired.

'Stop! What do you think you're doing?' Adept cries.

'Stop your whining, or you'll be next. He's gone mad, letting a filthy animal maul him like that. What. Is. Wrong. With. This. Gun,' Kudos says through his teeth.

'Mav, come here,' Will calls, and I'm both relieved and disappointed when the dog obeys him. As soon as my contact with Maverick ends, however, I see Kudos taking aim at him.

'NOOOOOOO,' I shout and pick up my gun.

'Victor, it's okay, Kudos can't hurt anyone,' Will says, as if he's asking me to pass him something. 'Neither can you. Please, don't try. Remember how you feel when you look at the horses. That's who you are.'

Stunned, I drop my gun and turn to him. 'How do you know everything I think, everything I see, everything I feel? Are you even real, or are you a ghost? Have I gone mad? Have we all gone mad, and are just shooting at ghosts? Is that why the bullets don't hit?'

Ember lowers his head slightly and walks slowly towards me.

'Give me your gun,' Kudos says to Ace. 'I'll shoot the three of them down if it kills me.'

'Are you stupid? Our guns aren't working, and I can't even work out why,' Ace says. 'If the horse is going to kill him, let it, it's not like any of us will lose any sleep over it.'

Will chuckles as if he's genuinely never heard anything so funny. It's comforting, and I find myself smiling too, despite the fact that a part of me is annoyed that Will hasn't answered my question.

Ember stops an arm's length away and stretches his nose out to me. I'm ashamed that my hand is shaking as I reach out to him. He sniffs my hand and then touches it with his soft, black nose. Nothing else in the world matters in that moment. I feel safe, as if nothing can hurt me, and I feel strong, but not in the sense that I can win a fight or argument – in the sense that I don't need to. Like Hero. I glance at him and flick my head to the side, beckoning him over.

Hero doesn't need asking twice. He is by my side in an instant, holding a hand out to Ember, who sniffs it solemnly. Then, the big, muscular horse with his terrifying yet soft, pale orange eyes, takes a step closer to him and sniffs up his arm to his shoulder.

Hero smiles, not appearing in the least afraid of the enormous beast standing over him. Ember could strike out at any moment or bite him, or crush him, yet Hero reaches a hand up and gently strokes the horse's face as if they are old friends.

'Can I meet him too?' Adept says softly and comes to stand beside Hero. As Ember moves to sniff her, I note that Ace is watching the big black horse, her task of inspecting the inner workings of Prime's gun forgotten. She doesn't look scared, but more as if she's having an internal battle with herself. She frowns and glares, then her eyes soften and she leans forward a little as if about to stand up and go to stand with Adept... but then frowns again. I nod to myself. She's fighting herself, but she knows the horse is far more than he seems, every bit as much as Hero, Adept and I know it.

My eyes rest on Will, who is crouching down, stroking Maverick and watching me. He gives the faintest wink and flicks his eyes towards where Kudos is also now watching Ember, and behaving in exactly the same way as Ace. I study him more closely.

He's the same age as I, but has always acted older, more confident, more capable – more everything. Now, he looks more confused than I am. We've all been trained to spot worry and uncertainty in our opponents, so that we know when and where to press in order to win; whether a physical or a mental battle. And we've all been trained to hide it in ourselves so that we don't lose. Kudos isn't even trying, and doesn't seem to be aware of it.

When I turn back to where Will is now sitting in the grass, his dog lying across his lap and apparently asleep, the man grins at me. Then he looks at Prime and back to me.

Prime is the meanest of all of us. He isn't the best fighter because he doesn't have Kudos's reflexes or Ace's intelligence, but he gets by because he has an instinct for weakness and how he can use it to his advantage. So many times, I've seen him fight and wondered why he is suddenly going for what we're trained are "lesser targets" on the body instead of those areas that will cause maximum pain and the quickest win – only to see his opponent crumple in front of him. Not content with the win, he will always then go for a "greater target", inflicting damage and pain for the enjoyment of it. I'm fascinated to see what will happen when he wakes up and sees Ember towering over Adept, wiggling the end of his nose in her hair as she strokes his neck, giggling, her helmet and weapon abandoned. I've never heard anyone except my mother laugh like that, and that was in the relative privacy of our old apartment.

I put my thumb to the fingerpad on Prime's headband and then press the button that loosens it, allowing me to pull it off his head. His eyes open and flick around as he weighs up his choices. When they settle on me, I tell him, 'Sit up, then stand when you're ready.'

When you're ready? That isn't an order. Where the hell did that come from? I look at Will and find him smiling at me. He winks at me openly this time. The damned man knows what I'm thinking again, and he thinks it's funny. I start to feel annoyed, but then Hero's laugh joins Adept's as Ember includes him in his antics, and immediately, I calm down. I guess it is funny really; we all came above ground to this environment so full of foreign sights and sensations, in order to dominate it, and within less than half an hour, we've all been completely outmanoeuvred – and we don't even know how it's happening.

Prime shakes me out of my thoughts as he gets to his feet. When he sees that Ember is so close, he reaches for the weapon that would normally be slung over his shoulder or attached to his rucksack, but it isn't there.

'It's here, buttface. There's nothing wrong with it,' Ace tells him, looking past him to Ember.

Prime looks from her back to Ember, Adept and Hero. 'That repulsive beast is mauling and bewitching those imbeciles, and you're doing nothing?' he sneers. 'You're not fit to be part of this group.' Prime frowns as Ace not only doesn't answer, but the corners of her mouth soften and then twitch, as if she might smile.

Prime grabs her weapon from where she laid it in the grass in order to work on his, and aims it straight at her face. I rush to replace his headband, but see Will moving out of the corner of my eye. He's shaking his head at me. I stop in my tracks. Why am I obeying him? He isn't in charge here. But he's so relaxed, so confident, so… everything I wish I were.

I watch as Prime pulls the trigger at point blank range. Ace's gun fires just as Prime's did – yet her head is still intact on her shoulders. His blink at the bang of the weapon firing turns to a scowl. It is Prime who is in danger now.

Prime turns Ace's gun around and holds it like a baton as he crouches into his fighting stance. Ace adopts the same posture, but then sees Ember over Prime's head, and hesitates.

'So, you're going as crazy as the rest of them,' Prime sneers. 'This'll be easy then. When I've finished with you, I'll take the others, one by one, and then it'll be me who is the last standing, me who returns victorious with the results of our mission, me who gets promoted to Regular. I'll be Elite by the time I'm thirty and then they'd better watch out, because I'm cleverer than all of them. One by one, they'll fall at my hand and then everyone will have to acknowledge me as Prime. No one will dare tell me I'm slow again, or that I'm not as strong as I should be for my height, or that I should win every fight and not just some of them. No one will tell me I'm not good enough, or that they wish they'd never given birth to me. Everyone will... love me.' He blinks and then frowns.

'They totally will, Prime, as soon as they meet you. The people of Rockwood will love all of you,' Will says.

Prime looks at Will in disbelief, and snarls, 'Your people won't love us, and we don't want them to. They'll fear us. We'll conquer them and they will be our Disposables.'

'I'm as sure as I can be that they'll love you whatever you try to do,' Will replies cheerfully. 'They'll see the same in you that I do.'

'You see no weakness in me, you piece of filth, for I have none,' Prime growls.

'I couldn't agree more,' Will says cheerily. 'You're not weak, you're just desperate to feel loved. The great news is that the second you stop believing you have to achieve that by force, it will happen. Ace, please do feel free to go to Ember. Of all the horses who will be accompanying us over the next few days and weeks, he alone will tolerate being approached, so fill your boots while you can. You too, Kudos,' he adds and then looks back to where Prime is watching him with his mouth flopping open and closed as he tries to think what to say, Ace's weapon at his feet where he has dropped it, having apparently forgotten all about fighting her.

I'm fascinated and frightened all at once. Who is this man who can disarm both weapons – for now I'm sure that's what he's somehow managed to do – and people, with just his presence and his words? Is he real, or is he a ghost? Did we go mad the second our senses were assaulted by the sights and smells of this strange world?

Will grins at me as he approaches, his hand outstretched. I clasp it in my own, shocked that without thinking, I am greeting him as an equal. 'There you go,' he says, 'I'm as real as you are, which is to say, not very, but as much as we all need to be until we no longer need to be.'

Maverick stands on his hind legs and puts a front foot on each of our arms, as if wanting to be part of our formal greeting. His brown eyes gaze up into mine and I find myself accepting what Will has just said, even though I have no idea what he means. The man's handshake is solid and real enough, but that fact just leaves me with more confusion, a feeling I see I am not alone in feeling as Prime watches us as if seeing us both for the first time.

'Please,' I beg Will, now holding his hand in both of mine, 'tell me how you know us all, how you know what we're thinking, how you know what to say so we believe you even though we don't understand you, and how you disarmed our weapons without even blinking?'

Will puts his other hand on top of mine and holds it firmly. 'Please believe me, Victor, when I tell you that you will understand the answers to your questions far better if you feel your way to them for yourself. Even then, you won't always believe them, until you do. Then, you will have more answers than you currently believe possible.' His blue eyes pierce through me and his words follow, settling somewhere deep inside so that I feel them as well as hear them.

'I believe you,' I whisper.

He grins and releases my hands. 'I know you do. Now, would you like to extend the invitation of my people to your own? We don't have room for their thousands at Rockwood, but we can easily incorporate some of them, and our neighbouring villages will do the same. We can help the rest to build their own villages wherever they like.'

I sigh as I remember my mission. 'I'm not permitted to return below ground for ten days. My life, and those of my parents, will be forfeit if I do. The Elite are terrified of what's up here. They don't want to see it, to hear it, to know about it, unless I return, sane, with news that it's safe.'

Will nods as if he were expecting my answer. 'Then the six of you can be their advance party. You can come back to Rockwood with me and experience life how we live it. I'll have you back here in plenty of time for your deadline so that you can report your findings, then you and your people can begin your new lives. How does that sound?'

I nod and smile, and can't seem to stop doing either.

'I have a question,' Hero calls out.

'Yes, Hero,' he replies, 'my people are all nearly as strange as I am, and yes, Ember and Maverick will be coming with us. So will they.' Will points in a circle all around us, to the hundreds of horses now wandering back in our direction.

Prime reaches for the gun at his feet and shoulders it. Then his mouth, and mine, drop open as its barrel begins to shudder, then bends slowly upward and back on itself, rendering it useless. Prime hurls it to the ground and steps back in horror.

'Sorry,' Will says. 'I probably should have warned you. I just think it will save time and hassle in the long run if your weapons are out of action completely.' He waves his hand to where the rest of our guns lie abandoned in the grass. 'The rest are now in a similar condition, as is your instrument of torture, so you might want to leave them all here, rather than be burdened by their weight?'

I nod while watching the horses coming closer. 'How do the horses all know you've destroyed our weapons? How do they know they're safe now?'

Will puts his hand above his eyes so that he doesn't have to squint as he joins me in watching the horses' approach. I copy him and find that it is indeed easier to see. 'The horses know everything, without knowing anything in the way we know it,' he says. 'They respond immediately and honestly to everything around them, including us. There's no hiding anything from them, and no fooling them. Remember that, Victor. Notice their behaviour, because it's never random. Learn from everything they show you. Your people worship your wallscreens for all the information they can store and provide. When you realise what the horses can teach you, you'll never want to look at a screen again.'

There is a roar and Prime rushes at Will. Everything happens at once. Maverick leaps, snarling, between Prime and Will, and Adept shrieks as Ember spins around on his hind legs and thunders to the dog's side. The enormous horse spins around again, this time on his front legs, and kicks out with both hind legs. Prime flies through the air and lands on his back in the grass, gasping for breath. He doesn't get up.

Will strokes Ember's neck and Maverick's head as he passes them both. The dog trots behind him and peers down at Prime as Will does the same. 'Four broken ribs,' Will tells Prime. 'One of them has punctured your left lung. Give me a moment and you'll be fine.'

The rest of us look between Ember, Will, Maverick and Prime, dumbstruck.

'There. All done, up you get,' Will says. He holds his hand out to Prime who looks at it, but doesn't take it, or get up. There is terror in his eyes as he looks at Maverick and then at Ember. 'They won't hurt you now,' Will says. 'I think you've learnt the futility of trying to cause any of us physical harm, so we'll just draw a line under what's happened and move on, shall we?'

Prime gets to his feet without taking Will's hand, and puts his hands on his hips. 'I've broken two of those ribs before. They didn't heal right. Now they feel better than before that evil beast broke them. How did you do that? How did you make me able to breathe easily again? And why? Why didn't you just let me die?'

'Because it would have been the most awful waste. I healed your ribs and lung tissue by resonating my energy with theirs so that I could affect them with my intention. It's a useful trick to know, and one I'll be happy to teach you when you're ready.' Will turns to the rest of us. 'Ember, Maverick and I are leaving for Rockwood. If you'd like to come with us – and I sincerely hope you do – ditch anything you don't need for a three day walk and a few cold nights, and join us when you're ready. We'll be waiting just over there.'

'When you said they were coming with us,' Ace says, watching the mass of approaching horses nervously, 'did you mean all of them?'

'No, just those who are members of Ember's herd. The rest will stay here.'

'Why are they all here?' Hero says.

Will grins around at us all. 'Because they bring balance where it is needed. And it's very definitely needed here.'

SIX

Will
---

*H*alf an hour later, all in the group have repacked their rucksacks and joined Ember, Maverick and me, leaving a pile of discarded food, weapons and helmets behind them. The abandoned helmets belong to Victor, Ace, Hero and Adept, all of whom have chosen to believe me that they won't be needed. Prime wears his, however, and Kudos attaches his to his rucksack so that he can grab it at a moment's notice.

'Is everyone ready?' I say, and all except Prime nod. He glares at me, furious that since he has no weapon, and none of his food tubs will open without Victor's thumbprint, he has no choice but to come. I smile at them all and pass Victor a jar of ointment from my back-sack. 'You're all going to need to rub this on any skin that's exposed to the sun, or you'll burn. My aunt made it and she loves jasmine, so I'm afraid it's a scent you're all going to have to learn to like.'

Victor takes the jar, unscrews the lid and sniffs the ointment that Amarilla made especially for him and his friends. His eyebrows shoot up, almost meeting the hairline of his silver hair, and a smile spreads slowly across his face. He dips a finger tentatively into the jar and scoops some of the yellow ointment out with his finger. 'Just rub it in?' he says.

'Yep, start with your face and neck, and finish with your hands. I'd roll your sleeves up and coat your arms in it too, the sun's only just getting going and with the speed we'll be travelling, you'll be hot in no time. That's it, now you, Hero.'

Hero applies the ointment as liberally as did Victor, then passes it to Adept, who does the same. When she passes the jar to Kudos, he passes it straight on to Ace without speaking. When Ace has finished lathering herself in the ointment, she holds the jar out to Prime, who refuses to even touch it.

'I notice you don't stink of it like that lot do,' Prime says to me while nodding at the four who are sniffing their hands in delight. 'I'm not having any of it on me, for all I know, it's poisonous.'

I hold my hand out to Ace for the jar. 'I don't need it, my skin has darkened in the sun, so I won't burn. I advise you both,' I nod to Prime and Kudos, 'to cover your skin with your clothing as much as possible. I'll have the ointment easily to hand, so if you change your mind, just let me know.'

'If your people don't need this, how did your aunt know to make it for us?' Kudos says, narrowing his eyes at me. I sense the human collective consciousness drawing him towards Awareness. He wants to trust the very faint sense he has that I can help him, but his mind – suspicious of everyone and everything as he has been trained to be since he was a toddler – won't let him. Not yet. But Ember's energy calls to his soul while Maverick's lightens the atmosphere and brings comfort. He cannot resist us all.

'Amarilla is probably the only human you'll meet who will seem weirder to you than I do,' I tell him with a grin. 'She knows all sorts of things, and has a passion for herbs. She was delighted to create the ointment for you all. She made a remedy for hay fever too, but those of you who were sneezing seem to have stopped, so we'll leave that one for now. If you have itchy or runny noses, or runny eyes, and want something to provide relief, let me know. Come on then, let's get going.' I turn and begin to walk towards the hills in the distance. Maverick falls into place beside me on one side, Ember on the other. Ember's herd walk on ahead of us.

'Is that the fastest you can walk, filth?' Prime sneers from behind me.

'I'm no match for any of you in terms of speed and endurance,' I reply, 'but I think I could probably squeeze more speed out of my legs if I wanted to. Would you all like me to try?'

'I wouldn't, I want to walk slowly and take everything in,' Victor says. 'It's warmer up here than the constant temperature we're used to, and I like the way the sun feels on my skin.'

Hero says, 'Me too. And the feel of the earth beneath my feet. It's so much softer than we're used to…'

'And the smells are amazing,' Adept interrupts. 'Supreme City smells of sweat, machines and… fear.' I don't need to look around at her to know she has surprised herself, or to see that it is her side at which Maverick now trots. He'll be gazing up at her, his tongue lolling, his brown eyes reassuring her that she's just stepped further along the right path.

'It's the sounds that I can't get over,' Ace says in a quiet, thoughtful voice. 'All of them in the city are sharp and loud. All of them here are soft and light. Happy.'

I turn and face them all to find Kudos and Prime walking immediately behind me. Prime hates himself for stopping abruptly in order to avoid bumping into me. Victor, initially so careful not to allow any of the others to challenge him for his leadership, is bringing up the rear, the way Ember does with his herd. Hero is

just in front of him with Adept and Ace, a thrilled Maverick now
darting around in their midst.

'Shall we take a vote?' I say. 'All of those in favour of
wandering back to Rockwood at my leisurely pace, raise your
right hands into the air.' The back four immediately raise their
hands.

'We do not vote, we command,' snarls Prime.

I raise my hand. 'That makes five for wandering and two
against, although I suspect if Maverick could vote, he'd be on
your side, he loves to run,' I say and wink at Prime and Kudos.
Kudos frowns but says nothing.

Prime's face goes a darker shade of grey. 'Did you not hear
me, filth?' he spits.

'I heard, you command, you don't vote,' I reply. 'Do feel free
to command whoever would like to be commanded to walk faster,
and we'll see you when we reach Rockwood. You're going to
need to head for the hills, then when you reach the tallest of them,
head east a bit until you drop down out of them onto grassland
like we're walking through now. Then when you reach a forest,
you'll want to head east a bit more. You'll know the village when
you see it, it's a collection of grey stone cottages on the far side of
the forest, at the foot of an enormous rock.

Prime turns to Victor. 'You're not fit to lead this party, look at
you, taking up the rear and doing everything this moron says. I'm
assuming command.'

Victor's eyes flick to me and I grin. He feels the influence of
both Maverick and Ember very keenly and is relaxing into his
sense that he's safe with us – that for the next ten days at least, he
can enjoy himself. He grins at Prime. 'Go for your life,' he says.

Prime turns back to me. 'So, run.'

'I go with the vote, rather than the command,' I say.

Prime turns to the others. 'SO, RUN!' he roars.

Maverick whines and crouches low to the ground. Adept drops to the ground beside him and strokes his head and back.

Ace glares. 'Wind your neck in, Prime, you scared Maverick and you're making a prat of yourself. None of us will follow you and you can't go on ahead without us because you'll run out of food. You're terrified of this place anyway, you'll soil your pants on your own and you know it.'

'You called me by my name. You acknowledged my superiority over you. Do as I command,' Prime snarls.

'I called you by your name because it has no effect on me. Don't you get it? Our rules, our training, our weapons, none of them have any relevance up here. Will disabled our weapons without breaking a sweat, and healed you almost as quickly. Do you really think he can't kill you just as easily if he decides to? He or the horse?' Her eyes flick uneasily to me and Ember, who stands patiently beside me, then back to Prime.

Adept says, 'I see you, Ace.' She turns to the lads with her. 'I see you, Hero and Victor.' Then she looks to the two ahead of her. 'And you, Prime and Kudos. But I'm still Adept.' Maverick leaps up and licks her nose. Ember wanders to her side, his tail flicking left and right at the biters trying to land on him. He rests his chin lightly on her shoulder and breathes into her ear.

Victor's voice rings out across the grassland. 'I see you, Hero, Adept, Ace, Kudos and Prime.'

Prime staggers backward a few steps. Kudos looks around aghast as all but he and Prime acknowledge their peers' names. There are smiles and back-slapping between the four who are at last becoming friends, which fade at the sound of thundering hooves. Ember trots out of our midst and joins his herd as they canter slowly, beautifully, breathtakingly around us all.

Prime turns to me. 'What is this? Why are they doing that?'

'Because it's necessary and because they can,' I say, feeling the horses' energy swirling around above us all, drawing the teenagers further out of themselves, showing them what is possible.

Kudos is unable to take his eyes away from the horses. 'I see you, Adept,' he says uncertainly. His voice gets stronger as he speaks the names of the others as they all stand, staring at the horses. The lead mare peels away from the circle around us and canters slowly away, followed by the rest of herd, including Ember.

'Where are they going? Ember, don't go, please don't go,' Hero calls.

I feel the desperation that permeates the group as the horses' influence wanes and the teenagers are left to themselves. Maverick rushes to each of them in turn, pushing his head into their huge, grey hands, licking them and comforting them all as best he can – all except Prime, of whom he is wary.

'They travel with us, but not always alongside us,' I tell them. 'They have their own needs which must be met. Please don't ever doubt, though, that when you need them, they'll be everything you need them to be.'

'Will we be able to ride them, like you do with Ember?' Victor asks.

'That is for them to decide,' I reply.

'How do we ask them?' Hero says.

'They already know. Everything will become clear if you pay attention to everything you think and everything they do. Come on, let's get going.' Everyone except Prime nods.

'We haven't exactly made much progress, have we?' Ace says, nodding back to where the lift is still clearly visible.

I smile at them all. 'On the contrary, we've come a very long way.'

The Will, Maverick and Ember ensemble is as potent as ever,

Justin notes, his thought arriving in my mind just before Amarilla's.

Way to go, Will. Your grandmother's settling down now you've calmed the situation to her satisfaction, so we can all relax.

I grin as Maverick arrives back at my side. *Don't I know it. You said you'd block her from hammering at me, but she's been like a fly buzzing at a window.*

Don't pretend it bothered you in the slightest, son, my father chimes in. *You held all six of those youngsters in your Awareness at once; all the details of their current lives and all those they've lived before, and if I'm not mistaken – I'll tell you in a few weeks, when I finally finish sifting through everything you picked up in a matter of seconds – you also know everything about all those below ground as well. I wasn't happy about you going to meet them alone, but as always, you did well and I'm proud of you.*

Proud enough to shield me physically from Gran when I get back there?

I feel their humour, and my mother's as she replies, *I think, from past experience, we can count on her to be comatose the minute she sets eyes on your companions. She may be Aware but she's no less dramatic.*

AND SHE KNOWS WHEN YOU LOT ARE DISCUSSING HER! Gran is no more subtle in her thoughts than she is in person. *Will, how could you put yourself in so much danger? You may be who you are, but you're still human, and you have a wife and child to think of. And my poor Maverick, how could you put him in harm's way? I'm pleased to see you've made progress, but really, it could have gone either way...*

I love you, Gran, I tell her and put the suggestion of a block between her mind and mine. Amarilla, Justin, my parents and sisters could all blast past it without blinking, but Gran is... Gran. She's railing at my grandfather now, insisting that he tell me off in her place, and she'll do the same to my mother when she arrives to give Grandpa a break. I grin. I love my family.

We love you too, Will. Lia's thought comes to rest gently in my mind, intentionally soft where Gran's was anything but. I may have greater Awareness than anyone alive except for the person my daughter will be, but Lia uses the Awareness she has more wisely. She was trained to overcome any blocks she had to full Awareness by my mother, and in the process, picked up Mum's tendency to use it for sensing what others need above all else. I just sense what I sense and say what I think, often without considering whether it is the most helpful thing to do. Lia says it's because I spend so much time with Levitsson, my favourite of all the Kindred. I grin as he registers my mind brushing his and sends me a sense of the mischief in which he expects me to participate on my return.

You're ready for us then, thanks, mate, I tell him.

We are. The question is, will they be ready for us?

I look behind me at where the youngsters are stumbling their way through the grass, tripping on even the smallest of tussocks with their over-sized feet, and jarring themselves when they step into the slightest of dips. They may be the superhumans that their ancestors envisaged in terms of power, strength and intelligence, but in the world that we of The New have created for ourselves, they are unbalanced in every way.

Yet still, it is easier for them than it will be for the older generations. The collective consciousness has called to them to feel their connection to everything – to be Aware – since they were born, and as such has kept their minds open to change. Hero, Victor and Adept grasped the inklings of Awareness they felt the instant the horses' energy highlighted it for them, and have been running after it with their arms wide open ever since. Ace and

Kudos aren't too far behind them, though Kudos still resists what he feels.

Prime will fight it with everything he has as a result of his parents having spent all of his nineteen years beating out of him any tendency to question the regime, and forcing him into every situation that might advance him, and therefore them, within it.

They'll be as ready as Maverick, the horses and I can get them, is the best I can offer my friend.

SEVEN

Victor

$\mathcal{I}$ don't know what I thought was going to happen up here, but it definitely wasn't this. In the space of a few hours, I've given up my command, my weapon, my helmet and very possibly my sanity, and yet I couldn't be happier. Every now and then, I think of my parents and feel guilty that I can't stop grinning up at the sky, down at all of the colourful herbs, and all around me at the sights, sounds and scents that bombard my senses.

I'm relieved to see that the horses have stopped to eat the grass ahead of us; hopefully we'll catch them up soon. While I trust Will – how weird is that, when I've only just met him and have never trusted anyone except for my parents – and feel happy whenever Maverick is near me, I've felt a sense of loss since Ember went off with his herd. I should be terrified of the horses, yet I'm not. I want to be near them and for them to look at me, so I can feel again that sense that it's okay to just be me. I want to ride one as Will rides Ember, because I want to experience the ease the two of them have in one another's company, the trust, the… whatever it is that makes Will who he is.

None of us have ever met anyone like him. He's heavily outnumbered and he's smaller, slower and weaker than any of us, yet he's supremely confident in himself and, as he's already proven, more powerful than all of us put together. We've been taught to recognise weaknesses since we were toddling, and we all see that despite his appearance, he has none. I'm in awe of what he can do and I want to be like him. Prime is terrified of him, and I don't think he's given up on the idea of defeating him, which I'm pretty sure Will knows, just like he knows everything else.

In complete contrast to the ease and confidence Will has in this strange world, we're all staggering around like we've only just learnt to walk. It's exhausting. Our bodies have only ever walked on flat, level floors, and here we have no way of knowing exactly where the ground is under all the grass and herbs that stretch as far as our eyes can see – which is much further than they've ever been able to before, and in a quality of light to which we've never been exposed before now. My nasal passages feel like they're burning as I draw in air much warmer than I've ever breathed before, and it feels strange to have sweat break out on my skin just from walking. I'll need to keep drinking to keep my body hydrated, but I don't have enough water to replace the amount I'm losing.

'Drink as much as you need to, when you need to,' Will calls over his shoulder. 'You'll have plenty of opportunity to refill your water flasks from the streams and watering holes we'll come across. There's water just ahead of the horses, so we'll make that our first stop. We'll need to veer to the right a bit so that we reach it upstream from the horses, otherwise it'll be silty from them swirling it up as they cross.'

'Upstream? What does that mean?' Adept says.

'The water is free-flowing from that direction,' Will points ahead and to the right, 'to that one.' He points ahead and left. 'Upstream means closer to the source of the water, downstream means closer to whichever body of water it will flow into. I guess that seems strange to you, with all your water being recycled and coming out of a tap.'

'Don't try and impress us with everything you think you know about us,' Prime snaps.

'Oh, give it a rest, will you?' Kudos says to him. 'He clearly knows everything about us. The only one still trying to impress anyone around here is you.'

'So, you drink from water that's just lying around, like the horses do? And we'll have to do that too?' Ace asks Will, who nods. 'Isn't that unhygienic?'

'Yes, blissfully so,' Will replies. 'Don't worry though, my very thoughtful aunt has supplied me with herbal preparations for you all that will soothe your stomachs when they become irritated by everything to which they haven't yet been exposed, and will expel any parasites you ingest.' Maverick makes the noise that Will calls a bark, as if reinforcing Will's assurance.

'There are parasites in the water? That's disgusting, I'm not drinking it,' Prime says.

'Then you'll die of thirst,' Will tells him cheerfully. 'Especially if you intend to carry on wearing your helmet as the heat builds. By the way, I also have a jar of ointment that will soothe the skin of your hands and neck when it starts stinging from the sunburn you're inflicting on it. Best to put it on last thing, before you go to sleep, so I'll give it to you later if I can find it amongst all the other jars and packets Amarilla gave me. I only just managed to fit in my food and one pullover to wear at nighttime.'

My head begins to spin. Will talks about changes in

temperature, skin problems, finding water to drink, parasites and trying to keep warm as if they're all a normal part of life and nothing to worry about, but how can that be? There's so much to consider. My stomach begins to churn with panic. What else do we have to learn to survive up here? Will we just continually lurch from one challenge to the next until we're so turned around, we don't know our own names? Was it that which drove the previous scouting parties mad, and not ghosts at all?

'No, Victor, that was definitely the ghosts,' Will says from right next to me, making me jump. 'Prime, Kudos, just keep heading to the right of where the horses are grazing,' he calls to them.

Maverick licks one of my hands, then darts around to my other side and licks the other. I take a breath and feel my panic subside a little. He's so happy being with us all, as if it's all that matters. I wish it were.

'It's easier if I walk at the back, so you can all hear what I'm saying without me having to walk with my head on the wrong way around,' Will explains. Hero, Adept and Ace all turn and nod, their faces strained and pinched. So, I'm not the only one panicking.

'When your ancestors blasted one another to oblivion,' Will continues, 'many of them refused to believe their bodies had been killed, and instead of releasing their hold on their lives here, they hung around, fuelled by hate, rage and fear. Whenever any of your people came above ground to see if the conditions were safe for the rest of you, the ghosts spoke to them in their minds, terrifying them with threats of what they would do to them and encouraging them to turn on one another. None of them made it more than twenty paces from the lift and the few that survived long enough to return below ground were, as you know, even less balanced than when they came above ground.'

'So where are the ghosts now? Did you get rid of them?' I ask him.

Will smiles. 'No. Adam and Peace did that more than seventy years ago.'

'Peace. What a lovely name,' Adept says.

'They were dear to you?' Ace asks.

'They certainly are that.'

Hero turns to look at Will. 'Are? How old are they?'

Will shakes his head. 'Sadly for all of us, neither Adam nor his horse are still here in the flesh. I never met them when they were, but I've come to know them very well. They're with us now, and they couldn't be happier that you're all here with me and are adapting so well, despite the fact that you're beginning to feel a little overwhelmed.'

Prime and Kudos spin around, both dropping into their fighting crouches, their eyes darting all around. The rest of us look around nervously.

'They're dead?' I manage to say. 'But they're here? How? Where?'

Will chuckles. 'This is one of the many situations where my wife would do a much better job than I'm doing. There's no need to be afraid. Yes, Adam and Peace left their bodies some time ago to return to All That Is. I'm Aware of All That Is, so I can be Aware of them whenever I want to, and whenever they want me to be. They're not ghosts; they don't hang on here, annoying people like those that they helped to move on, you don't need to worry about that.'

'You're Aware of All That Is,' I repeat. There is something about the words that makes me think there is more to them than their simple meaning, but I can't put my finger on what it is. Yet all of my panic melts away.

'You can all be Aware too,' Will says. 'I understand it's hard when everything is so new and so strange, but don't ask any more questions, either of me or of yourselves, for now. Take in everything you see, hear and smell. Taste the air, feel the grasses and flowers as they touch your hands and brush your legs, relish the sun's rays touching your skin. Let your five senses catch up with your new situation, then when you're ready, we'll help you to discover the sixth.'

'We? You and Maverick?' Ace asks him.

'I think he means the horses,' Hero whispers. We all look up to where the horses were grazing – but aren't anymore. Just like when we first saw them, they have all turned to face us, their heads held high, their ears pointing towards us. 'I told you, they're here to help us.'

'We don't need their help, or yours,' Prime says to Will.

Kudos looks at Prime and shakes his head, then walks onward, forcing Prime to hurry to walk just ahead of him. The rest of us follow in silence.

When we finally reach a narrow strip of water flowing from right to left, just as Will said it would, most of the horses have already drunk from it and moved on. The last few horses are standing with their front feet in the edge of the water, drinking. Ember is one of them. I feel better for being near him again, and am disappointed when he lifts his mouth, dripping, jumps to the far side of the water, and wanders off behind two other horses, one brown, one white.

Will instructs us to drink as much as we can from our flasks and then refill them. We all do as he says, even Prime. When he takes off his helmet, he has sweat pouring down his face and his hair is soaking wet. He drinks most of the water he is carrying, then pours the rest over his head, slightly disrupting his regulation parting. Ace glances at him and grins at me before kneeling down and holding her flask in the stream.

I kneel down next to her. I can't resist running my fingers through the soft, damp earth beside the water. My fingers come away dirty and there is soil under my fingernails, but for some reason, it feels good; good to feel something I have never felt before, good to be dirty – good to be breaking the rules. I hold my flask in the water and delight as the soil is carried away from my fingers by the deliciously cool water. I can see to the bottom of the stream, and reach down to pick up one of the stones that lie there. It is white with orange lines running through it and is smooth to the touch. It is beautiful. I throw it into the air and catch it. I put it in my pocket, a reminder of my first day in this amazing place.

I cup my hands in the stream and throw water at my face. I don't care if it hasn't been filtered and treated to make it hygienic. I don't care that it might carry parasites. It looks and smells different from any water with which I've come into contact before, and I count that a good thing. I throw water over my head and rub my hair until I can feel it sticking up in all directions. Ace's eyes go wide, then she grins and does the same. Her hair is longer than mine and looks shockingly untidy by the time she has tousled it out of its regulation style. I start laughing and she joins in, followed by Will.

Hero jumps into the water and splashes it all over himself while Maverick leaps up and down beside him, barking and trying to catch splashes of water in his mouth. One by one, the rest of us copy him until Prime alone stands on dry ground.

Kudos climbs out of the stream and shakes his head so that water droplets land on Prime. He ignores Prime's glare and says to Will, 'Can I have some of the ointment that will stop my skin burning in the sun?'

Will grins and, still standing knee deep in the water, reaches for his rucksack. 'Here you go,' he says, handing the jar to Kudos. 'You've already started to burn, unfortunately, but this will stop it getting any worse, and you can rub some of the soothing ointment on it later. If you'd like, I also have a preparation that will take that swelling down on the side of your head, and another that will relieve the pain.'

Kudos looks uncertain and glances at me. I grin at him and nod, and he blinks, frowns and looks back to Will. 'Er, okay, yes. Thanks. I mean please.' Furious as I can see he is that he looked to me for my opinion, I realise that where once I would have revelled in his slip, now I'm just pleased his head will feel better soon.

It is my turn to frown in confusion. Only this morning, I was glad that the injury I caused Kudos would give me a weak spot to exploit, and now I'm happy that it will no longer be so?

I remember Will's advice. Don't question anything for now, just let myself catch up with everything with which my senses are bombarding me. If it's all this good, I can't wait.

'I think now would be a good time to eat, then we can cool off in the stream again and drink more before we carry on into the afternoon,' Will says.

Everyone else looks at me; I may have given up command of them, but they still need my thumbprint to activate their food tubs.

'Sounds good to me,' I say. 'Everyone? Shall we vote? Those for eating now?'

Hero, Ace and Adept all grin and raise their hands. Kudos puts his hand to his forehead, then rubs his eyes before finally raising his hand.

Prime barges past all of them and holds his food tub out to me. 'Just open the damned tub.'

I look at Will and grin while holding my thumb to the pad on the lid of Prime's meal. 'All seven of us are for eating now, no objections.'

'I object to everything,' Prime grunts and stomps off.

'Totally objectionable. Noted,' Will says cheerfully.

Everyone except Prime laughs. He sits apart from the rest of us and glares at Will as he eats, his face dark grey with anger, his eyes even narrower than normal.

As we walk through what Will calls "the heat of the afternoon", following the horses, the mounds on the horizon for which we have been heading get gradually larger.

'When we reach the hills, we'll stop for the night,' Will says. 'There's more water there, and bushes and rocks that will shield us if a breeze gets up. The movement of air can soon take the heat out of you if it has a chill to it, which it will this early in the summer.'

The horses stop to eat the grass and herbs again, and I'm delighted that they remain stationary when we catch them up. I want to wander amongst them, stroking them as I did Ember, so I'm shocked, disappointed and angry when all of them except Ember move away to either side of us, well out of reach.

Ember lifts his head and when he spots Will among us, makes a soft, deep sound in his throat. Maverick rushes up to the horse, barking, and Ember tosses his head and snorts at the dog. Maverick races back to us, his tongue hanging out of the side of his mouth and looking ecstatic, as if he has achieved the exact outcome he wanted. My anger subsides a little. Ember ignores everyone in front of us as they move out of his way while he makes for Will, who has been walking with me and Hero.

'Hey, mate, how are you doing?' Will doesn't touch Ember

until the big black horse nuzzles Will's shoulder, then he strokes Ember's neck.

'Why did the others all move away?' I ask him.

'They're just responding to their instincts. Ember's more used to overcoming his when necessary, so it isn't such a big deal for him having you guys around.'

Hero takes a step towards Ember and the horse snorts and steps away. 'You know me,' Hero says softly. 'You let me stroke you before, you'll let me stroke you now.' He takes another step towards Ember, whose ears turn to point backward. The long hair sprouting out of his rear end flicks from side to side as he steps back again. Adept squeals and hops out of his way.

'He's swishing his tail and putting his ears back because you're irritating him. He's giving you the opportunity to realise your advance is unwelcome,' Will says.

I grab hold of Hero's arm. 'You have to let him come to you if he wants,' I say.

'But he likes me, he blew in my ear this morning. He was so gentle, he wants to help us all, I felt it,' Hero protests.

'What do you feel from him now, Hero?' Will says.

Hero stops pulling against me and stands still. I let go of his arm as he stares at Ember. 'Something has changed.'

'Because you've changed,' Will says gently. 'You were right, the horses are here to help you and they're doing it in every single moment they're near you, whether you're conscious of it or not.'

Hero suddenly seems much younger than his seventeen years as he says, 'So why don't I feel like I did before? I was happy then, when the horses were looking at me and when Ember was sniffing me and letting me stroke him.'

Ember moves back to Will's side and hangs his big head over Will's shoulder, his pale orange eyes watching Hero.

'Because he's giving you the help you need, regardless of

whether it's the help you want,' Will says and reaches a hand up to stroke Ember's cheek.

'How is he helping me now?' Hero said.

'That's for you to work out for yourself. As I advised Victor earlier, consider how you're thinking and feeling, and watch how the horses behave, because one always affects the other. You'll learn more than you thought possible, and more than any human can teach you.'

'What if we don't care to learn from dumb animals who can't think, can't talk, and aren't capable of doing anything other than eating, drinking, defecating, running around and procreating?' Prime scoffs.

'What if you've already learnt from them, without realising you have?' Will says, still stroking Ember's face.

Prime glares at him and Ember in equal measure. Ember watches him, blinking slowly, and Prime's eyes widen slightly.

'You're remembering how it felt to be taken down by Ember, how powerless you felt, how much pain he caused you and how frightened you were when you coughed up blood and thought you were going to die,' Will tells him. 'But remember the rest. Let yourself remember what else you felt.'

Prime opens his mouth but then clamps it shut again.

'I think you probably felt what I did,' Adept says softly. 'I felt envious of Will that Ember didn't hesitate to protect him. No one has ever protected me. I can trust my parents and my cousin not to hurt me – and I know that's more than you've ever had, Prime – but they won't protect me. When it comes down to it, it's just me against the world.'

Maverick snuggles against her leg and whines until she crouches down and strokes him. He pushes into her arms and tentatively, she folds them around him. He licks her neck and face until she giggles.

'In case you're in any doubt, that's Maverick's way of letting you know that while that may have been the case, it isn't any more. Not for any of you,' Will says, looking around at us all. 'The challenge we all face is that you don't believe it yet. You might feel reassured by my words, but whenever you feel uncomfortable or challenged, you'll believe you're on your own, until you know for certain that you aren't. That's what the horses can teach you.'

Prime looks as if he's choking. His breathing is rapid and he keeps swallowing as he pulls the round neck of his shirt away from him, even though it is loose-fitting.

'Breathe in and out slowly, Prime,' I tell him. 'My mum taught me to do it whenever I was scared. It helps you to calm down even when you think you're going to pass out. I used to do it before fighting any of you, so you wouldn't know how terrified I was.'

Kudos chuckles. 'We knew.'

'Only because we were all as scared,' Ace says, looking down at the ground.

'None of you can have been scared fighting me,' Hero says.

'I was,' Kudos says, 'but only because if I didn't beat you in less than a minute, I'd know I was slipping.' He grins at us all uncertainly. I grin back and so do all of the others except Prime, who stares at the horses, still swallowing, his breaths still coming too fast. Maverick creeps up to him, staying low to the ground and glancing frequently back at Will. When he reaches Prime, he lifts his head very slowly and rubs it against the outside of Prime's hand.

Prime flinches and pulls his hand away. Maverick flinches too and leans away, ready to run. He is trembling but he doesn't move. He whines and very slowly leans back towards Prime. The rest of us are silent. I glance at Will, who is watching Maverick with the same look on his face that my mother wears when she looks at me.

Maverick moves each foot so slowly that I can barely see him moving at all, until he is just touching Prime's leg with his side. He very slowly lowers his bottom to the ground and sits down, then shifts his weight so that he's slightly leaning against Prime. I feel like I don't want to breathe. Maverick slowly lifts his nose, looks up at Prime, and whines again, so softly I can barely hear him.

Prime flexes his fist and I shift my weight forward, ready to fly at him. Will puts his arm out in front of me and shakes his head.

Prime's fingers relax and he lowers his hand back down so that it rests on Maverick's head. Maverick shuffles closer to Prime's leg and pushes his head upward, so that Prime's fingers spread around the dog's skull. The big, mean nineteen-year-old, who I've hated forever, could crush the dog's head in an instant if he wanted to... but he doesn't.

He stops swallowing and his breathing slows. He moves his hand so that it rubs Maverick's head. He glances down at him and then quickly back to the horses, as if he's afraid to see what is happening between himself and dog. No one moves. The only sounds are the high-pitched squeaks made by the small animals flying through the air above us, and those of the horses chewing on the grass they've torn from the ground.

Eventually, Prime turns and walks towards the hills, Maverick trotting at his side. Adept and Ace both let their breaths out.

Will grins round at us all. 'Shall we?' he says, nodding his head after Prime.

EIGHT

Will

_____

*W*hen we reach the hills, I announce that it's time to stop to eat and rest. The teenagers are exhausted; they may be fitter and stronger than I am, but their minds are on overload and they aren't used to the heat. No one argues, not even Prime.

The horses take it in turns to drink from water that sprouts out of the hillside into a small pool before disappearing underground, then they spread out over the grassland behind us to graze.

The teenagers all lower their rucksacks to the ground and extract their food tubs, which they take to Victor to be activated. When the tubs open, I see that the contents are the same as at lunch – white, lumpy and with no smell – but they eat it without complaint.

When I begin to eat my cheese sandwich, some of them watch it all the way to my mouth, as if they are intending to pounce on any pieces I drop.

'I'm happy to swap with anyone?' I say as we sit cross-legged in a circle, and they all hurriedly shake their heads. I don't blame them. Enough is enough for one day.

Prime sits further back than the rest of us, so that he is slightly removed from our circle. My beautiful, loving dog sits at his side, just about touching him but careful to look away so that he gives Prime no reason to feel threatened. The others steal glances at the two of them every now and then, and I sense their interest, curiosity and envy.

Once we've eaten, I present each of the teenagers with a white packet of herbal preparations marked with their name and containing a variety of smaller packets. Each of the smaller packets is labelled with the ailment the preparation will ease, and the dosage. I instruct the teenagers to open any they think they need.

'This aunt of yours not only knew my name but she knew I would refuse the sun ointment,' Prime says, his voice harsh against the gentle sound of water flowing into the pool nearby. 'She thought I would want whatever foul-smelling rubbish this is, to "soothe your system from the inside while the aftersun ointment Will has, works from the outside".' His voice is sarcastic as he reads the words Amarilla has written on one of his packets. 'So, your people have not only found a way to know everything about us, but you have some kind of computer that can predict the future. That, our Elite will want to know about. Maybe this trip to your village won't be such a waste of time after all.' Maverick pushes his head against Prime's knee, and without thinking, Prime strokes him.

'I'm glad you think so, there's so much we're looking forward to showing you all,' I reply.

'Will the horses come with us to your village? I mean they seem to need grass and lots of space,' Hero says.

'They'll stay with us until we reach Rockwood, then they'll

graze the surrounding pasture. Everyone will be so excited to have the horses nearby.'

'You talk about the horses as if they're admired. Important,' Kudos says.

'They are our teachers. Without them, our ancestors would never have survived after leaving the cities. We wouldn't have learnt who we really are, and I wouldn't be sitting here with you now.'

All except Prime turn to watch the horses, confusion and wonder on their faces.

Prime licks the remainder of Amarilla's anti-parasite paste off his finger. 'Who you really are? Well I can tell you that, you're a human of an old, inferior race that doesn't deserve to exist now that we of Supreme City are here.'

The others all turn back to look uneasily at me.

I grin at Prime and feel the tension ease. 'That's one way of looking at it. Here's the aftersun ointment.' I hold it out to him and Maverick thumps his tail on the ground. 'Anyone apart from Kudos want it after Prime? You might have missed some places with the sunscreen. If you did, they'll be stinging and feeling hot. No? In that case, I think you have everything you need. Amarilla packed enough herbs to support your bodies for a couple of days, which is perfect...

'Of course it is,' sneers Prime.

'...because at the speed we travelled today, we'll be at Rockwood the day after tomorrow.'

'Thanks, Will,' Victor says, echoed by most of the others.

I nod. 'No problem. The sun is nearly down now, and the temperature is dropping. You'll want to put your extra clothes on top of those you're wearing, so you don't get cold. Maverick and the horses will alert us if there's anything around that we need to know about, so you can all rest easy.'

'How can we rest easy when we have no weapons? It's all very well the dog and the horses letting us know if we need to worry, but what are we supposed to do if that happens?' Kudos says.

'I didn't say you would need to worry; you never need to do that. And we don't need weapons, Maverick and I are more than capable of persuading any predators roaming in the area to hunt elsewhere.'

Everyone looks at Maverick and then at me, with a mixture of horror and disbelief.

Kudos gets to his feet. 'Just what sort of predators are we talking about?'

'There may be the odd pack of dogs or family of wild cats roaming around that will pick up our and the horses' scents. Cats are bigger and stronger than dogs, by the way, but hunt in smaller groups. Neither will cause us a problem.'

'Because you have the means to kill them how, exactly?' Prime says.

'I won't be killing anyone, it isn't necessary,' I say, pulling on a jumper.

'So how would you and Maverick persuade them to go away?' Victor says. Unlike most of the others, he believes me.

'I know it's hard to imagine, but when he and I combine our energy, we can be very frightening. I'm going to sleep now, it's been a long day. Rest easy, everyone.'

There is a stunned silence as I make my back-sack into a pillow, lie back against it and close my eyes. I hold my arm away from my side when I sense Maverick is on his way, and he snuggles up alongside me and rests his head on my shoulder. I hear Ember and his herd tearing at the grasses, swishing their tails at the last few biters of the day, and snorting their nostrils clear of pollen and dirt, and I feel the warmth of my beloved dog. By the time I drift off to sleep, I'm smiling.

Maverick and I wake at the same time. A low growl escapes his throat, and in an instant, I have him wrapped in a net of calming energy that reassures him I am on top of the situation and he need not intervene; much as his instinct drives him to comfort the lad currently creeping in our direction, his instinct to protect his pack is greater.

Prime has forgotten his earlier observation that I already know what will happen. His fear is the greatest of the group and his ability to trust and relax, the least. He's exhausted, but won't allow himself to sleep. The sounds of the horses moving around and eating grate on him, as do the gentle snores coming from Hero and Kudos, and the deep, regular breaths emanating from the rest. The noises of the night animals both close and distant have caused his muscles to tighten further and further, and he now has a desperate need to remove what he thinks is the source of all of his fear, rage and frustration – me.

He has spent some time observing the horses in the moonlight, and has decided that since they are either asleep or occupied with grazing, they are no danger to him. He has also watched Maverick and me for a while. He thinks if he moves slowly and quietly, he will be able to take each of our necks in one of his huge hands and crush them before we can react. His lack of compassion for the dog who has comforted him is easily explained by the fear that drives him and blocks out everything else.

Neither Maverick nor I move as I send a gentle flow of light to Prime. It surrounds him in a white haze that highlights him like a beacon as he crouches in the grass. He freezes in panic and looks all around himself. All is still. As far as he can see, all of us are asleep. Then he notices the glint of Maverick's eyes as my dog watches him. I feel the fresh wave of fear that roils through him, and I increase my flow of light. I sense his confusion as it penetrates the crack Maverick managed to make in his beliefs, his training and the fear that has gripped him for so much of his life, and soothes him.

He stays where he is as I increase the flow of light further and further, until exhaustion begins to overtake his fear. He sinks to his knees and kneels in the grass for some time before slowly rising to his feet and creeping back to his gear. I lessen the flow of light towards him until it is no more than a very faint glow. Once he has drifted off to sleep, I withdraw the flow and relax the net I'm holding around Maverick. My dog licks my face, sighs deeply and goes back to sleep.

I wake as the first rays of sun brush my face. I sit up to find all of the others still sound asleep, which pleases me; I know that none of them have ever slept this deeply or for this long before. Maverick and I get to our feet and my dog shakes the dirt and dust loose from his coat before trotting down to the pool with me.

Maverick laps up the cool, clear water while I quickly wash, taking care not to allow any water to splash back into the pool and contaminate it. Once I've also had a drink, the two of us wander amongst the horses, stopping to greet those who stretch towards us for a nose touch with Maverick or a scratch from me. Ember wants more attention than the rest of his herd combined, and by the time I've scratched him from his withers to the top of his tail, then at two spots he can't reach on his belly, the teenagers are all awake.

Hero and Adept stand watching us and talking quietly to one another, while the others rub their eyes, stretch, and strip off their extra clothes.

Just as Maverick and I are beginning our wander back to them, Hero and Adept suddenly drop down into their fighting stances. Adept launches herself at Hero with a yell, and the two begin wrestling and punching one another. The others crowd around to watch, Victor and Ace in shock, Kudos with interest, and Prime with eagerness and satisfaction.

I sigh. Hero and Adept are hoping that if they attack one another the way Prime attacked me yesterday, one or more of the horses will intervene in the way Ember did. They're so desperate to be near the horses, they're risking injury from one another and from any horses who might barge into the fray. I grin to myself as I remember being so desperate to be near a herd of horses that I too behaved in ways that now seem ridiculous.

I understand how the two of them feel – the horses have given them a glimpse of what is possible, and they are bereft without the feeling of connection to those who can so effortlessly show them the truth. But I know that the horses have no intention of acting as a conduit to truth indefinitely; the teenagers must find their way to it themselves.

Maverick rushes ahead of me and circles Adept and Hero, both of whom are now panting and sweating as they crouch, ready to rush one another again. Adept has a swollen lip and blood runs from Hero's nose as they both glance at the horses, then at me.

'Anyone want to swap one of your food tubs for the fruit I'm just about to eat?' I call out to them all. 'I have a mixture of ripe, sweet and very delicious berries.'

Victor raises his hand. 'I will.'

Hero rushes at Adept with a roar.

'It won't work, you know,' I say as I pass the two of them.

'Come and eat with the rest of us, and take the herbs Amarilla prepared for this eventuality. They'll take the swelling down and bring the bruising out more quickly.'

Hero and Adept both stand and look at me in shock.

'What won't work?' Ace says. 'These two trying to convince us all that they've gone mad?' She turns to the two who are still staring at me and says, 'You both hate fighting. What the hell are you doing?'

'We just wanted the horses to come and protect us,' Adept says.

Prime and Kudos laugh. 'Why would they protect you?' Kudos asks, holding his stomach as if he's never seen or heard anything so funny.

'Ember nearly killed Prime in order to protect Will yesterday,' Hero says sulkily.

'That isn't why he did it, actually,' I say, bending over Hero's and Adept's packets of herbs and rummaging around for the preparations I know are there somewhere. I feel the love and intention for rapid healing with which Amarilla has infused the herbs, and smile as I sense both her and Adam – from whom she learnt the trick – observing the current situation with interest.

'Then why did he kick my ribs in and leave me for dead?' Prime says, his interest sparked by the idea that maybe I'm not as protected as he thought.

'He did what he needed to do to bring you closer to balance,' I tell him. 'Ah, here they are. Come and get them when you're ready, you two,' I say to Hero and Adept, putting the relevant preparations on top of the rest. I hand a food parcel to Victor. 'Here you go. If you enjoy the berries, I'll show you where to look for more as we travel today, there should be plenty around.'

Victor looks bemused, but takes the food parcel and hands me an open food tub. 'Err, I hope you enjoy that too, although enjoy isn't a word I usually associate with food. It'll fill you up and make you strong, though.'

I grin. 'Good enough, thanks.'

I open a parcel of meat and put it on the ground for Maverick, then sit beside him as he eats.

I put a spoonful of white, lumpy gloop in my mouth, and frown as I try to decide whether I like it or not.

'Wow, these are amazing,' Victor says, a trickle of raspberry juice running down his chin. He picks up a blueberry, inspects it thoroughly and then puts it in his mouth. His eyes light up. 'Oh no, wait these blue ones are better. What are they?'

'Blueberries. The red ones are raspberries.'

'Seriously? The blue ones are called blueberries? It's not very imaginative, is it?' He grins at me, his purple eyes shining.

Ace shuffles next to him on her bottom. 'Can I try one?' she asks.

'In exchange for a mouthful of yours? No chance,' Victor says, then grins and passes her a blueberry. 'Just one, though, I'm hungry. Will's going to show us where to look for more, then you can eat as many as you can find.'

Two figures block Victor and Ace from my view. Hero and Adept glare down at me whilst rubbing Amarilla's starflower paste into the injuries they have inflicted on one another.

'AF?' Hero says, holding the other herbal preparation I looked out for him in front of my eyes. 'It says AF on it. What does that stand for?'

'After fighting,' I say with a grin. 'That's it, rub the paste into your bruises, then take that one by mouth like it says to.'

Prime laughs nastily. 'It seems your stupidity was predicted.'

'Just like yours yesterday, when you wouldn't use the sunscreen,' Ace retorts.

Victor and Kudos chuckle and Hero and Adept look sheepish.

'So anyway,' Adept says to me, 'how do we get the horses to bring us closer to balance, as you say Ember was doing for Prime?'

I grin up at her, glad to hear the passion in her voice. 'They already are.'

'But they're not, they won't come near us,' she protests.

Hero whispers, 'They give us the help we need, even if it isn't the help we want.' His huge, purple eyes bore into mine. 'So, they're helping us by avoiding us? It feels... horrible though, the fact that they helped us to feel as if there was nothing to be afraid of yesterday, and now they won't help us to feel that way again. Taking that away from us is worse than if we'd never felt it at all.'

'They haven't taken anything away, they just showed you what is possible. You can feel that way any time you like, you just need to find how to do it for yourself.' I hold a hand up. 'And before you ask, I have no intention of telling you how to do it, since I'm also inclined to give you the help you need rather than the help you want. Eventually, the two will become the same but in the short term, you'll find me very irritating. I had teachers just like me, so I know how it feels. I found that punching the ground relieves the frustration, but does nothing for the skin on your knuckles. Regardless, if you need to do it, the lovely Amarilla has also prepared herbs with those activities in mind.'

I sense Amarilla's amusement as she remembers nursing my hands. *You know, an aunt can take offence at being described as irritating,* she informs me.

Yet an aunt who is also Infinity both deserves it and is completely unaffected, I retort.

Fair point, eloquently made. The entwined essences of my aunt and the horse who was her Bond-Partner purposely withdraw from my thoughts. They know they don't need to – I can easily hold them in my Awareness at the same time as the six in front of me and all of the thousands currently living underground – but it's their way of expressing their confidence that I can be who I need to be for those currently watching me eat my white gloop with a mixture of confusion, fear, anger, and in Victor's case, interest.

Prime's stare is calculating. 'So, if I were to attack you again in the future, I wouldn't necessarily need to be concerned that Ember might intervene?'

'No, not necessarily,' I reply. 'Why, are you considering attacking me again?'

He narrows his eyes as he remembers the night's events and tries to figure out whether I know what he was up to. 'Did anyone see a strange light during the night at all?' he asks.

The others look between each other, shaking their heads, and then back at him.

'Why, did you, Prime?' I ask him.

He glares at me, expecting me to look away. I hold his stare.

'No,' he says finally. He sits down with his tub of food and Maverick leaves my side and goes to sit beside him, this time leaving a little space between himself and the big, grey, silver-haired lad. My heart swells with love for my boy, as it so often does. He feels it and squints his acorn-brown eyes at me while thumping his tail. If I call him, he'll come, but we both know where he is most needed.

We spend the morning climbing and descending hills covered in rocks, bushes and grass. The teenagers are no more agile or graceful than they were yesterday, but also not a whole lot less, despite the more challenging conditions underfoot.

The horses trail us, sometimes grazing for long enough that we lose sight of them in the hills, then catching us up in a graceful, rhythmic pounding of hooves and following us once again, but always at the same distance they have insisted keeping between them and the teenagers since we all began travelling together.

Hero, Adept, Ace and Victor walk in a line at the back of the group, looking repeatedly and longingly over their shoulders. Kudos walks just behind me and Prime walks beside me at the front, and just ahead whenever he can manage it, with Maverick trotting along between the two of us.

Whenever I spot bushes with ripe berries, I point them out and Victor and Ace rush to pick them and share them with Hero and Adept. Kudos accepts any fruit offered to him but otherwise remains distant. Prime stands waiting with a look of thunder on his face every time we stop, but says nothing. Maverick remains at his side, hopeful for any opportunity to get closer to him.

When we stop for lunch, Victor again accepts my offer to trade my food for his, and then shares my large slice of vegetable pie with Ace while I once again tuck into the white gloop. I explore it with both my senses and my Awareness as I eat it. It is nutritionally balanced and in one sense it is filling and satisfying – yet at the same time, it is devoid of everything I am used to sensing in my food, and leaves me feeling that I am eating something insubstantial.

The pie that Victor and Ace are enjoying isn't just filling their stomachs and providing them with nutrients; it carries the love and joy my grandmother felt as she made it for Lia, Tania and me, as well as the vitality of its ingredients that were grown outdoors and nourished not only by the sun and rain, but by the energy and intention of the Tree-Singers. It nourishes the mind and the soul as well as the body, causing Victor and Ace to smile as they eat it. When they begin to share Ace's white gloop, their faces fall.

'I don't want to go back to the city,' Ace announces suddenly.

'Then don't,' I say. 'Any of you who want to stay with us at Rockwood are more than welcome to do so.'

Victor looks at me desperately. 'I don't want to go back, either, but my parents…'

'Will lose their lives if you don't. I know. You, at least, will need to go back, Victor, but it will be temporary. Once you've reported what you've seen up here and secured your parents' release, you can all come to live in Rockwood.'

'What about the rest of our families if we don't return?' Adept asks.

Victor says, 'As long as there's no evidence you've done anything other than go the same way as previous scouting parties, your families will be safe, at least until they all come above ground, and then no one will be, you know what our people are like. So, we'll just enjoy the peace up here while we can, shall we?'

Adept shuffles around in her spot on the ground. I feel her conflict. She wants to tell the others that the peace will be even more short-lived than they suppose; that in a desperate attempt to be free of Supreme City, she and her cousin, both members of the engineering department and as Disposables, given all of the dirtiest, most dangerous – and therefore least supervised – jobs, have for some time been slowly and systematically damaging the life support systems that keep everyone alive below ground. She wants to warn them that it isn't a hundred years since the previous scouting party was sent above ground, but nearer eighty, and that the Elite, believing their underground city to be failing at last, are growing desperate and will flood above ground as soon as they know it is safe. But she doesn't trust Prime or Kudos.

Finally, she says, 'Supreme City is failing. The Elite are keeping it a secret from everyone because they don't want there to be panic and rebellion, but I know. I saw the deterioration of the systems every day. I was ordered to fix them, but all I could do was patch things over, when they really needed replacing from scratch with materials that have finally run out.'

No one speaks. I sense their large, genetically enhanced brains working at triple speed as they process what Adept has told them. A sneer spreads across Prime's face as he calculates how to use his newly gained knowledge of the situation below ground to his advantage; if he can get a measure of control over those of us above ground, or even a handle on how to do it, he will be promoted to Regular and maybe even Elite.

The others consider the futility of allowing themselves to enjoy the way of life that Maverick, I and the horses have begun to show them, when as soon as Victor reports back to the Forum, then the Elite, the Regulars and everyone else will swarm above ground and the teenagers will be forced straight back into the regime to which they are fast becoming desperate not to return.

Victor is horror-stricken. 'If for any reason I can't convince the Elite it's safe for them up here, they'll start killing Disposables to prolong however much life support remains, for themselves. They'll start with the prisoners, including my parents, whether I've made it back to report or not.'

Maverick races to his side and snuggles into him, nudging him with his nose for a fuss until Victor raises a hand and strokes him. I feel some of the tension leave the lad, and even greater determination settle in its place.

'You're not on your own in this, Victor,' I say as Maverick makes his way back to sit with Prime.

A rustling of grass behind Victor, Ace, Adept and Hero announces the arrival of Ember and four of his mares – one brown, one grey, one chestnut, and one as black as Ember himself.

Prime and Kudos instantly reach for weapons that aren't there.

'Relax and carry on eating, there's no need for concern,' I

advise them. Ember stares at Prime for a few seconds before lowering his head to tear at the coarse grass. 'All of you, just enjoy their company.'

All four mares move closer to the four teenagers who have been so desperate for their company all morning. One sniffs the back of Hero's head, but when he reaches a hand back to touch her, she flinches and moves away.

'Keep still,' Victor whispers.

The black mare reaches out and blows softly down the back of Ace's neck. A smile of delight spreads across the girl's face, making her look younger than she is. She was never allowed to be a child, and I'm glad she's finally being given a glimpse of how it feels to be carefree.

As the four of them sit unmoving and in various stages of rapture, the other two, watched studiously by Ember as he continues to graze, also remain still. It's all I can do not to chuckle; they are scared of him where they have no reason to be. He merely holds them in place so that his mares can help the other four. While they sit there with images running through their minds of what Ember did to Prime yesterday, his energy combines with that of the mares and weaves its way through each and every one of us, searching for where there is imbalance, drawing it to recognise itself as such, and nudging it to announce itself to the body so that it can no longer be ignored.

My dislike of Prime comes to the forefront of my mind. It is a normal reaction for a human to dislike one who treats any member of his family with contempt, but it is an energy that has no place in me. Maverick bears no ill will towards Prime's treatment of him, and knowing what I know, sensing what I sense, I should know better. I release the negative energy and send love to Ember for highlighting it to me.

I look at Prime and see a frightened lad who is just doing what he thinks he must in order to survive. The horses' energy latches on to the fear held most deeply within him, and draws it to the surface. His face contorts as he feels afresh the terror of disappointing his parents. He thinks he deserved all the beatings they gave him, just as they deserved all the beatings their parents gave them in order to make them stronger, cleverer, and able to survive long enough to constantly challenge for promotion to the status of Regular. I feel the horses tease from within him the desperation to succeed, to excel, to prove they were worth something, that he absorbed from his parents before he was even born. It isn't his and he doesn't need it. It oozes out of him and is reabsorbed by All That Is, once again recognisable as the love it has always been, now that it is no longer disguised as fear.

When the horses wander off, all seven of us are both less and more than we were before.

NINE

Victor

*T*he horses leave us – yet they don't. I can hear them ambling away through the grass, and their scent fades, but it feels as if they are still with us.

When I heard them approach and felt the warm breath of a horse behind me, I turned my head so slowly that my neck hurt. I was determined to have an image in my mind of what was happening so I could savour it later, as I was terrified that the horse would go as quickly as she arrived. It was an orange-red mare who helped me – that was definitely what she was doing, I could feel it in a way I can't describe and don't understand how I can even recognise.

It was like nothing I've learnt about or felt before. All of my life, it's just been me on my own in my body, in my head. When I first saw the horses yesterday, it was like all my worries and fears fell away and there was just me left – the real me, underneath it all. I've wanted to know that person, to be that person, ever since. Then, just now, I was that person and more; it was like the mare reached inside and pulled out everything I didn't want to feel so that there was just me left on my own... yet not on my own, because she was in here with me. How did she do that? How was she inside my body with me like she was part of me?

My face is frozen, just like everyone else's, except for Will's; he is grinning at me like he always does. His blue eyes stand out against his brown face and pale hair, and seem to pierce straight through me... and I feel him with me in my mind. I know it's him. He isn't doing anything, he's just there at the edge of my thoughts in the same way that because Ace is sitting so close to me, it feels as if her arm is touching mine when it isn't. He winks at me and I almost feel something from him... then it's gone.

Will looks around at all of us as he says, 'Trust what you all just felt, because it was as real as the ground you're sitting on. Let it sink in, that's always the best way to learn, then if any of you have any questions, just ask.'

No one answers. I feel my eyelids drooping and snap them back open. I can't be tired; last night I slept more deeply and for longer than I've ever slept before, and we've only been walking for a matter of hours. I look around at the others and see that they all look in a similar state, although Prime is blinking like mad, trying to shake it.

'Let yourselves sleep,' Will says. 'Maverick, the horses and I will watch over you. Shade your faces and any other exposed skin, lie back, and rest.'

When I open my eyes, for a moment, I think I'm still dreaming. Something is covering my face, I'm hot down one side, and there's a weight on my chest. I sit up with a start and the spare shirt that was shading my face slides off me, as does Ace, whose head was on my chest.

My heart hammers. I should never have been able to sleep while she snuggled up to me like that, let alone when she fell asleep not only so close to me, but on top of me. How did I not wake? My parents trained me from when I was small to sense someone approaching me while I slept, and to wake at the slightest thing. By the time I was ten, I would have a weapon in my hand and be on my feet by the time I opened my eyes.

I look down at Ace, who appears unaware of either her actions or mine when I so suddenly stopped being her pillow. She's every bit as well trained as I am, yet she sleeps on like a baby. I realise that was how I was sleeping too; as I haven't since I was a baby, too small to protect myself and nestled in between my parents.

I look around at the bushes behind which I can hear the monotonous, yet somehow comforting, sound of horses chewing grass. As always, I am learning, it is a constant background noise to the louder sounds of them moving around, snorting, grunting and farting. As I listen to them, I begin to feel the way I did when the mare was right behind me earlier… and suddenly realise that she's with me! And not just her, but all of the horses – they are in my head, my body even, yet they're nowhere near me.

A rustling causes me to turn back to the others. I jump at the sight of Will squatting down in the grass at my feet, restraining a wriggling Maverick. When he sees that I have noted their arrival, Will releases the dog, who leaps onto my lap and licks my face all over. Maverick loves me, I can feel it. He barely knows me but he loves me. How can that be? No one has ever loved me except for my parents, and even then, I never felt it from them like I do from this dog. What's happening to me?

Will puts a hand on my leg. His eyes are kind as they bore into mine. *You're becoming Aware of your connection to All That Is.*

I start to wriggle away from him, panic burning at my stomach, lungs and heart. How am I hearing him in my head? Maverick licks me even more frantically, and I hesitate.

Will lifts Maverick off me and strokes the dog's head, and Maverick turns his affection on Will instead.

The horses, Maverick, you and I are all part of All That Is, it's impossible not to be. We're all aspects of the same oneness and you've opened up to that connection, that oneness. You're doing extremely well, Victor, Will tells me.

I don't understand what's he's telling me, what's happening, and yet I do. *How did I open up to it?* I think the words back to him without even understanding what I'm doing.

Will sinks into the grass and crosses his legs. His thoughts are accompanied by a sense of patience and kindness as he tells me, *Before you were born, the horses helped those of us living above ground to be Aware of our connection to everything, and because we're all connected, that Awareness became part of the human collective consciousness. You're human. Ever since you were born, the collective consciousness has called to you to know of your connection to everything else, despite all of your training and conditioning to the contrary. Your soul felt an opportunity approaching that would allow you to get closer to the horses so that your personality would remember what your soul has always known, and it nudged you to not only get yourself in this position, but to bring with you those most likely to recognise the horses' teaching.*

Inadvertently, I glance at some of the others. *Prime and Kudos? Are you sure?*

Will nods. *They will need more time than the rest of you, but they'll get there. You're the first to open to your Awareness, so don't expect the others to feel what you now can. Let them find their way in their own time. Okay?*

Okay, I think. I nod down at where Ace is still asleep beside me. *If I live that long. If she wakes up to find herself that close to me, I'll be dead before either she or I know it.*

Will grins. *Don't be so sure. She's not far behind you.*

So, I don't mention I can hear you in my head?

It's up to you, but I find that people have a better understanding of something when they come to it by themselves.

I nod. *This is kind of cool.*

Will chuckles. *It totally is, and there's the difficulty. It's so cool that you'll be tempted to put all of your attention into what you can now be Aware of – the horses, that bee buzzing around by Kudos, the mouse giving birth just below ground over there, how constantly delighted Maverick is, the thoughts and feelings of all your friends – and you'll withdraw from your personality. Your physicality. In order to make the best use of your Awareness, you need to be able to balance it with your other five senses; with the person you are.* He snaps his fingers in front of my face and I jerk back to the world around me.

'See what I mean?' Will whispers. 'You were so absorbed in everything I pointed out to you in your Awareness, we could all have moved on and left you sitting here and you wouldn't have noticed.'

I look over at where Prime is still asleep. 'Okay, I understand the danger.'

Will shakes his head. 'In reality, danger doesn't exist but if it did, the biggest one you would need to be concerned with is that of a missed opportunity. For you – for all of you – to play a part in helping your people to know themselves and be happy instead of terrified and violent, you're going to need to be present in the physical world as well as Aware of everyone and everything around you.'

'My parents,' I whisper back. 'I can use this to help my parents?'

Will nods. 'You can use it to help them all.'

My stomach suddenly feels firmer, somehow. 'What do I have to do?'

Wander down to the horses. Act according to what you sense from them, how you feel. While you're doing that, I want you to count up to five hundred while also counting how many of each colour horse there are. I want you back here, standing in front of me when you reach exactly five hundred – not four hundred and ninety-nine, not five hundred and three, but five hundred. Got it?

But they'll run away from me... I stop in mid-thought as I discover that I know they won't.

Will grins, his teeth bright white against his skin, his eyes as penetrating, as knowing as ever. *Got it?* he repeats.

I find myself grinning back. *Got it. I'll be back on the count of five hundred.*

I can't get to my feet quickly enough. I turn to the horses and search for the feeling of them in my mind that I had before – but I don't need to search. I feel them all right here with me, as if they have always been here and I've just had to notice.

'You haven't started counting.' Will's voice jolts me back to the physical world.

Right. Sorry. One. Two. Three...

'Out loud, Victor.' His voice now sounds coarse against the softness of the horses in my mind, the beauty of who they are... I flinch as he continues, 'It will help you to remember yourself as a physical being, as a person, when your fascination with your Awareness will cause you to forget. Victor?'

I look over my shoulder as I tiptoe away from the others. 'I'm trying,' I whisper much too loudly for my own comfort – but then even the quietest whisper would have been too loud.

Will appears at my side. 'If you're trying, then you're not doing,' he says in a low voice. 'You're stronger than this, Victor, and you need to be. Come on, count with me. One. Two. Three. Four...'

'Five. Six. Seven. Eight. Nine...' The chestnut mare raises her head to watch our approach. I feel her total lack of concern at two who are part of her herd. Two? Where's Maverick? I turn to look for him but then sense him sitting back with Prime, watching him as he sleeps, his head tilting from side to side at Prime's snores. I grin.

'Victor?' Will says.

'Sorry. Ten. Eleven. Twelve...' Will stops walking and I sense both his wish for me to complete my task alone, and his reluctance to be too far from Maverick's vigil over Prime. He knows how much his dog is helping Prime, but he also knows how scared and volatile Prime is... wow! The events of last night blast into my head, both from Will's point of view and from Maverick's.

The next thing I know, I'm flat on my face in the grass and I have a sharp pain in my back. Warm breath blows on my cheek, and I look up to see Ember staring down at me. I curse myself for being so caught up in Prime's attempt to kill Will and Maverick that I didn't notice that which I'm now Aware happened; Ember disciplined two of his sons and where the other horses moved out of the way, I stood in the middle of it all until a stray hoof caught me in the back and knocked me flat.

I sense Will's amusement. *Remember your task.*

Can you heal me like you healed Prime?

Yes. But I'm not going to. The pain will help.

The horses involved me in their dispute on purpose.

They don't do things on purpose as such, they just respond to everything around them. Their energy will always encourage yours towards balance. It's who they are.

I get a sense of what he means, but I can't seem to fit it in with what I know of life, of how people relate to one another.

It's all a bit overwhelming, isn't it, which is why you need to be counting, Will reminds me.

I clench my fists and begin to sweat. *I can't do it, it's too hard.*

Only because you still haven't made the decision to do it. Count, and then carry on counting until your task is complete, then you'll feel a whole lot better. Trust me, Victor.

The sense I have of him is so like the sense I have of the horses, and I realise that I trust him completely, even though he has refused to heal my back. I count with each stab of pain, and begin to wander between the horses, leaving Ember to graze in peace. Counting how many horses there are of each colour means that I really see each of them, as well as feel them. The little white mare has brown flecks in her coat, and her eyelashes are so long and thick, the flies don't bother her as much as they do the others. As I add her to my tally of white horses in the herd, I sense that she's two years old and will be leaving this herd before long, to find a male who will father her offspring.

The big, solid horse whose coat is the same grey as my skin, is male and one of those who has begun to challenge the other males in the herd. He reminds me of Prime and Kudos.

When I come across a brown male, large in stature but gentler in nature than most of Ember's other sons, I feel as if I'm looking at who I would be if I were a horse. He alone wanders over to me as I stand, still counting every stab of pain in my back – now up to three hundred and forty-seven – as well as adding him to my tally of brown horses.

I feel the need to look away from him and to turn sideways on to his approach. Even so, I feel him walk an arc behind me so that he approaches me from behind my right shoulder. He is curious about my interest in him; my recognition of him as a similar character to me has made him more conscious of himself as an individual than his kind – who are so much one with each other – normally are.

He sniffs my shoulder and then takes the collar of my shirt in his teeth and pulls at it. I grin at the ripping sound as he tears it off, and turn slowly to see him tossing his head up and down, the strip of fabric flapping up and down in his mouth. He drops it and paws it with his hoof. I feel his Awareness that two of the young foals in the herd are interested in his discovery, and as a consequence, so are their mothers.

He knows exactly where each member of his herd is in relation to him both physically and in terms of their position within the herd hierarchy. He knows that there are no predators in the area and that he is safe to indulge in play. He knows exactly who I am and why I am here. And whilst knowing all of that in a fraction of an instant, he is totally focused on the shred of clothing. It's so easy for him. He's Aware of everything, all the time, and yet that's as far as it goes; he's Aware of it without being distracted by it, just like Will wants me to be.

I smile at the horse as I've never smiled at anyone or anything before. He's magnificent, and not just because his brown fur shines in the afternoon sun, or because his dark eyes are bright with the intelligence I can feel within him, or even because he's so big and powerful. He's magnificent because he's a horse and everything I'm beginning to realise that entails.

A particularly painful stab in my back reminds me I'm up to four hundred and thirty-one. I look up the hill towards the bushes behind which I know Will is playing with Maverick – and in front of which, Hero and Ace are now standing, rubbing their eyes in disbelief.

With a last glance at the brown horse, I turn to make my way back to Will. Then I smile as I realise that I haven't left the horse behind me; he is part of me in the same way he is part of his herd… and everything else. I sense the moment he picks the fabric scrap back up with his teeth and then as I feel him gather himself together and launch into a flat out run between and then around the rest of his herd, I punch the air with both fists. Between counting, I shout, 'YAHOO,' up to the blue sky, whilst being very careful to not look at the sun.

'How did you do it? How did you get them to let you near them?' Hero asks as I reach him and Ace.

'I didn't do anything,' I say, realising it for the first time. I stop in my tracks, frowning to myself, but then at another stab of pain, I say, 'Four hundred and ninety. Sorry, I've got to get to Will.' I hurry past them and around the bushes. When I reach Will, I say, 'Five hundred. Now will you heal my back?'

Will lets go of the stick that Maverick is trying to pull away from him, and grins. *You can heal it yourself, but that might be a bit much for your first hour of being Aware so yes, Victor, I'll heal your back.*

I feel a strange sensation, as if the rib that feels as if it's broken is moving. Then the pain disappears. I rub my back, and can't even feel a bruise.

I healed the tissues too, Will tells me. *Sometimes it's good to have the remnants of an injury as a reminder of what caused it, but in your case, I think it has well and truly served its purpose. Well done.*

I almost go to speak out loud in my excitement, but catch myself. The others can't know what I felt from the brown horse, not yet; having experienced what I just did, I well and truly know that they have to find it out for themselves. *That horse, the brown male…*

The colt, Will interrupts.

The colt, Ember's son, he's... he's...

Everything you need him to be. I know, Victor, and I'm pleased for you, but you need to start talking out loud. Your lips move when you use mindspeak and its unsettling the others.

I sense them all watching me. Hero and Adept are envious of me for having been accepted by the horses, and are desperate for me to help them achieve the same. Ace is envious too, but there's something else there – pride? She's proud of me. And she's confident I'll share my secret with her of how I did it. That will cause a problem. Prime and Kudos are more focused on the fact that I'm behaving strangely towards Will. I flinch and realise I'm staring at him as I interpret what I'm sensing.

'Um, sorry, that felt very weird. Better though, thanks, Will, I'll try not to be so careless as to get kicked again,' I say, and hurry back to my rucksack. I pull off my ripped shirt and try not to blush as I sense Ace's approval of my bare chest. I pull on the spare shirt I used as a shield against the sun, and stuff the ripped one into my rucksack. 'Sorry if I've held you all up, are we moving on again now?'

'Yes, I think we should,' Will replies. 'We want to be near the woods of Rockwood by this evening, then we'll arrive at the village tomorrow with plenty of time left in the day for you to get your bearings and settle in.' *Victor, as we travel, I want you to focus on your physical surroundings with every bit as much focus as the colt did on his new toy. If I nudge you with either my mind or my elbow, find your sense of him and remind yourself how it feels to be him – how it feels to be centred between your personality and your Awareness. Okay?*

I don't trust my ability to prevent my lips from moving if I answer him, so I just nod, and immediately realise how unnecessary it was to do anything. Will is Aware of everything I think and feel. I sense his amusement and his approval. *You're doing great,* he tells me in my mind at the exact same time he uses his voice to suggest that we all reapply the sunscreen ointment.

Stunned at how he can hold two conversations at once, it dawns on me just how much I have to learn.

TEN

Will

*V*ictor is doing better than he thinks. When he has the time to sift through everything he can pick up in his Awareness, he'll learn how long it took me to get to where he is. My personality may have ensured that once I was Aware, being centred was easier for me than it is for Victor, but his advanced brain ensures that he learns incredibly quickly – which is fortunate considering the small amount of time he has between now and everything he will soon be facing.

I have held my attention away from all of the atrocities I know his ancestors committed in order to create the superhumans they thought would give them their place in history. I choose not to dwell on all of the experimentation, the torture, fear and indignity they inflicted on their test subjects when deciding which of them expressed the synthetically created traits they inflicted on the human genome to an acceptable degree, and which of them would be bred with which others in order to give them the greatest chance of producing progeny with more of the same.

Grey skin and violet eyes were easily produced and replicated, as were greater size and strength. The brain chemistry that results in the battle rage that the Elite find so desirable, however, was tricky to perfect; for many generations, the geneticists struggled to produce anything other than aggressive fighting machines with no ability to think when their rage took them. When they finally created humans with the ability to use their intelligence in conjunction with maximum aggression, they congratulated themselves on having achieved their goal – only to find that the trait wasn't inherited predictably. For all of their brilliance, they only ever considered the mind and body in their experiments. It never occurred to them that there could be a third element involved in the expression of inherited traits – and the soul is unswerving in nature and purpose.

It can be dampened down and shouted over by the minds of those with strong personalities, but it never misses a chance to make itself heard. So many of those currently considered Disposable by the people of Supreme City, are those whose souls are responding to the call of the collective consciousness, ever encouraged by the love sent downward into the city by Adam and Peace during their cleansing of the area of its ghosts. Their souls urge them to question why constantly training to inflict damage on one another is an enjoyable way to live, and encourage their intelligence to over-ride the aggression that has been bred into them.

It gives me great pleasure to see the six teenagers in front of me experiencing that regardless of what has been done to their bodies and minds, they can still hear their souls when they are shown how.

As they shoulder their rucksacks and fall in behind Maverick and me, I sense the lead mare following us more closely, shadowed by the rest of her herd. Victor senses it too and looks behind him just before the horses round the bushes.

I grin to myself. The human collective consciousness may have drawn his mind to the door upon which his soul, and those of his parents, have been banging for so long, but it is the horses who pulled him through – it is the horses who will pull them all through.

I sense Victor picking up on my thought. *They bring us closer to balance, that's what you said. They're amazing and incredible and more powerful than any of my people living underground will believe is possible, but most of the Disposables are hostile and violent, the Regulars are vicious and calculating, and the Elite are terrifying. I hated my life and wanted to be someone other than who I was, but they don't, not the Regulars and Elite, anyway. How will the horses bring balance to them when they don't think they need it?*

I grin. *One step at a time. For now, we'll concentrate on the five we have with us. Fair warning – you'll be having your first experience of riding soon.*

'WHAT?' Victor shouts from behind me. Then he says, 'Really, Hero?'

'Well you stopped suddenly,' Hero says sullenly. 'If you don't want people bumping into you, don't make yourself into an obstacle.'

'You could have avoided me. You bumped into me on purpose because you're angry the horses let me near them when they still won't let you,' Victor says with wonder in his voice. He is firmer as he says, 'I suppose I would feel the same way. I'm sorry I can't tell you what I did, but honestly, I didn't do anything, I just felt differently.'

I carry on walking. Prime, momentarily distracted by the conversation at the back of the group, hurries until he is a fraction of a step ahead of me, and Maverick barks excitedly at Prime's increased pace.

I reach down and stroke my dog's head. 'It's a bit warm to run now, mate.'

'How did you feel?' Ace asks.

'Like I was one of them,' Victor replies. 'And the horses let me know it was true.'

Prime spins around. 'The horses came back when the rest of us were asleep?' He tries to disguise the fear in his voice as anger, but Victor can't be fooled as the others still can. I feel his shock as he senses the depth of Prime's terror – far greater than anything Victor has ever experienced.

I turn around too, but stay quiet. Victor has this covered, though he doesn't know it yet; he's standing still with his mouth opening and closing as he tries to think what to say. There would have been a time when he would have used Prime's fear against him, but he won't do that now. He wonders whether to lie, but then he remembers how he felt when he connected with the bay colt. Everything was simple, uncomplicated.

'No. They didn't come back while you were asleep,' Victor says. 'I just woke up and remembered how it felt when the orange-red mare was standing behind me, how it felt as if she was in my head. And when I remembered that, it was like all of the horses were in my head, and I knew how to be around them as if I was one of them. Then I walked down to them, and it was true.'

'What are you, stupid? Insane? Both?' Prime sneers. 'You didn't feel them in your head, you imagined it because you're all obsessed with mindless beasts who we should have shot when we had the chance.'

'He didn't imagine it, I felt it too, kind of,' Ace says, glaring at Prime, then at Kudos, daring them both to contradict her.

'And me,' Hero says and is echoed by Adept.

Prime shifts on his feet and Kudos looks everywhere except at the rest of us. Maverick trots to Kudos, his tail held gaily aloft, and sits in front of him, gazing up at him.

Kudos shakes his head. 'I don't know what's happening here, but I don't like it.' He looks at me. 'Will, are you going to just let Victor spout this rubbish and not say anything?'

Maverick shuffles closer to Kudos and licks his hand. Kudos's shoulders sag and he drops to his heels. He strokes a delighted Maverick, who leaps all over him, licking him wherever he can.

'You felt it too, didn't you, Kudos?' Victor says. 'Even though the horses didn't interact with you directly like they did with me and the others, you felt something from them. Well anyway, that's what happened, so shall we just keep going?'

I carry on towards Rockwood and Prime snorts and storms after me. Kudos hesitates and then hangs back to walk with the others. I sense that he, like all of them except Victor, glances over his shoulder at where the horses stopped to graze amongst the bushes and boulders when the teenagers stopped, but are now beginning to trail us again.

We call the red-orange coloured horses chestnuts, I tell Victor. *The young males are colts, older males are stallions. Young females are fillies, older females are mares. The brown colt you were so drawn to has a black mane and tail, so we call him a bay. White horses are only white if they have pink skin, otherwise they are known as grey.*

That's it? I just helped Kudos a bit closer to Awareness and that's all you have to tell me?

I grin to myself. *What is it you would like me to tell you?*

That I did a good job? You told me to let them find their own way to the horses, but then Prime asked me straight out and you just left me to it.

Did you need my help?

Well, no, I suppose not.

But what you do need my help with is learning about horses so that when I tell you something, you understand what I mean.

I feel his confusion; he is used to envy and grudging respect from all except his parents when he gets things right, and gloating and threats when he gets things wrong. He felt approval from me earlier and now he is desperate for more, but it is a desire that will hinder him.

Remember your connection with the horses, the bay colt in particular, I tell him as he wanders along behind me, ignoring the attempts of his friends to get him to advise them on what to do next. *And tell me how you feel then.*

It's so easy for him to find the horses in his Awareness now he knows they can't be anywhere else. Instantly, he calms down. *I feel like it doesn't matter what you think,* he tells me. *Like nothing matters, really.*

Stay in that place while you chat with your friends, Kudos included.

He doesn't have kudos over me, does he? Any more than I'm a victor over him, or Prime and Ace are number one to our lesser numbers, or Adept can beat any of us. It's not about any of that. We've been made into fighting machines when there's no reason to fight. There's absolutely nothing to fight about, ever. Our whole existence is pointless. I sense his shock at his realisation. His next thought is faint. *We're not supreme humans, we're weak and pathetic. We're ugly outside and inside, we're... we're monsters.* He flickers in and out of Awareness as anger and fear flood through him.

I turn and jog back to him, Maverick at my side. I take hold of his arms and hold his stare as Maverick jumps up between us, rests his paws against Victor's stomach, and whines. 'Victor, breathe slowly, in and out, just like your mother taught you. The bay colt is coming for you.'

Victor blinks and turns around. 'He is?'

The bay colt gallops out of the herd, his thick, black mane and tail held aloft by his speed, his brown eyes flecked with the orange of his father's. Ember is just behind him.

The other teenagers gasp and move out of the way, fearing they will be crushed as the colt and stallion head straight for us. I wrap Maverick in a net of calming energy so that he remains quiet at my side.

Victor smiles and I feel his Awareness flicker back... but as soon as he is Aware of the horses, of me, he compares himself, his life, his existence, with ours, and all of his fear and anger rise back up within him.

Victor, you feel me with you just as the colt is with you. Do you trust us?

Victor's fists open and clench and he begins to drop into his fighting crouch. The bay skids to a stop in front of him and reaches down to touch his muzzle to Victor's cheek. I feel Victor flicker back to us.

Victor, he and I can help you. You're going to need to ride him, but you don't know how. I can show you if you allow my mind to control your body. Can you do that? Can you trust me and allow your body to move the way I can guide it to?

Victor looks at me, his eyes full of pain. *What do you mean?*

We can help you through this. Do you trust us?

I sense the colt, Ember and the rest of the herd shifting some of their energy to Victor. Maverick and I join in; Victor is part of our herd now and what is ours is his.

His eyes widen as he feels us surrounding him, wending our way through him, supporting him where he feels weak. He puts a shaking hand on my shoulder. *I trust you. Help me?*

I nod. *Let me move your body. Focus on feeling everything you need to feel. The colt and I will do the rest.*

I feel his fear rise again, and the herd energy shifts towards him even more. He nods.

I turn to the others. 'Wait here, we won't be long.'

'Ready?' I ask Victor and he nods again.

The bay moves alongside him and he yells as I vault him onto the colt's back at the same time that I vault onto Ember's.

Ace gasps and Prime laughs nastily, but Victor doesn't hear either of them. All of his attention is taken by what he feels in his body and mind as the colt begins to move beneath him.

Victor's body is dense and heavy, but pleasingly supple. It responds easily to my instructions as I rearrange it so that its muscles are relaxed where they need to be and contracting where they need to be – apart from when I suggest that they allow him to relax his lower back so that he can sit into his pelvis, rather than on the front of it, and when I want his chest to relax and lower slightly, and his shoulders to relax down his back instead of being wrenched into position there. The fear and lack of confidence that have, so many times, forced him to stick his chest out and his shoulders down, causing his back to hollow and ache, so that he could give the appearance of strength and self-assurance when he felt anything but, still hold him in that position now. It is time he released them.

Feel your connection with the horse who carries you. That's all you have to do, Victor. Feel your way with him while I ride him through you.

The rest of the herd watch us lazily as Ember and the colt walk past them. Once we're clear of the horses, Ember heads for a flat, grassy expanse between two hills. The herd energy stays shifted towards Victor, with a little also now extended to Maverick as he trots alongside us, barking excitedly. Ember rears and as always, I delight in his balance and strength. As soon as his front feet touch the ground, we fly.

My body responds to Ember's with no conscious effort from me, so well used are we to being in perfect balance with one another. We rejoice in the added appreciation of our physicality that this interaction between our bodies gives us, even as we support Victor and the colt, who are already falling behind us as we gallop at full speed. Some of the herd energy shifts towards the colt, supporting his body that, while strong, is unused to carrying any rider, let alone one who isn't completely balanced.

The collective consciousness of the horses holds the pattern for perfect balance so strongly within it that the colt maintains both the perfect arrangement of his limbs, and his ability to make the hundreds of instant adjustments necessary to keep them arranged that way, as he runs. But Victor's less than perfect balance jars on him, tiring him and preventing him from moving at the speed Ember is achieving... and Victor feels it. His revulsion at his body, his training, his life, his existence, returns. Sharing his experience of his body as I am with him, I feel his chest, shoulders and pelvis stiffen even more as waves of anger and fear begin to course through him again.

I relinquish my control over his body a fraction – just enough for him to slip slightly to one side. Shock overrides his fear and anger, followed by a sense of loss for the feeling of connection he has lost with the colt. Immediately, I right his body.

I feel him sink back into his connection with the colt. Again, he feels how his body is affecting the horse beneath him and again, he hates himself.

So, be who you want to be, I suggest. *He's showing you how.*
I can't.
So long as you feel your way with him, you can do anything.

ELEVEN

Victor

*T*hey're both pulling at me; Will pulls at my body and the colt pulls at my soul. But I can't follow them. I want to, but I can't. I can't let go of the protection that, time and time again, has kept me alive. If I let it go and then find I'm no good at surviving without it, what will I do? How will I manage? Who will I be? Who will help my parents if I turn into someone who isn't strong enough to fight, or who just doesn't care to? It's all very well knowing who I really am and feeling blissful about it, but life isn't that simple… and yet it is. I feel it from the colt, and when I stay with him in my mind, I believe it. But then when I feel Will relaxing my shoulders, my chest and my lower back, I resist him. My ability to pretend to be someone I'm not is who I am.

The thought jars on me every bit as much as my body jars the colt's beneath me, and I feel, more than hear, my soul whispering, *It's who I have been.*

The rhythmic movement beneath me, the warm air belting past my face, the feeling of closeness, of partnership, of being at one with a horse who is so strong, so powerful yet so patient, moves me further and further away from the person I was. I want to hold on to that person because I know him, I know everything of which he's capable, I know he won't stop until he has either saved his parents or died trying. And yet he feels as weak as the horse who carries him is strong. Sticking out his chest and pretending he is a force to be reckoned with has never fooled anyone, because they all do exactly the same thing for exactly the same reason. Fear.

Supreme City exists because of fear. It is run by fear. It will never be conquered by fear. As long as I'm fearful, my parents are vulnerable. I would be strong, like the colt is and like he knows I can be. Like he's showing me how to be.

Will pulls gently at my lower back again, and this time I don't resist. I smile. I feel better and so does the colt, who speeds up beneath me. I feel my shoulders relaxing along with Will's suggestion, but when my chest begins to soften, I panic and stiffen. The colt hesitates beneath me and I feel some of the power drop out of his strides. He is the way forward; I know that better than I've ever known anything. He is putting all of his focus, all of his strength into showing me the way, and I have to follow him. I relax.

Suddenly, everything feels easy. Where I thought I would feel vulnerable, I feel strong, as if nothing can bother me, because nothing really matters… but my parents do, a little voice says in my head. Instantly, I'm Aware of them both. They are hungry and tired, since prisoners are forced to work even harder than normal Disposables. Their living conditions are squalid, yet apart from their constant concern for me, they are more content than when they lived more freely.

Understanding floods me as I remember the words my father spoke that got him and my mother arrested for lack of commitment to the city's regime; "The best we can do, Victor, is to survive and take joy in seeing one another every day." At the time, I hated him for being so defeatist and saying the words that he had to have known would be heard and would result in him being taken away from me. Now, I feel his determination to try to teach me what he and my mother knew, regardless of the risk to them both.

He wasn't speaking out of hopelessness, but from a position of enlightenment. He was trying to tell me that the best things in life are the little things. My heart goes out to him. He knew he would be arrested, but he was willing to risk it. He was devastated when they took my mother too, and struggled with himself for a long time, wondering whether it was worth it when I likely wouldn't have understood what he was trying to tell me anyway.

I understand now, Dad, I do, I think to him, knowing he can't hear me, for he isn't Aware... yet I feel him hesitate in his scrubbing of the prison floor. He can't hear me, but he felt something. I sense his soul urging him to reach back to the sensation he felt, to find me, but he can't. Not yet. I sense an energy supporting him in his feelings, his beliefs... then find that it swirls around him and everyone else in Supreme City. I follow it in my Awareness and eventually, it leads me back to Will. Adam and Peace. He told us they got rid of the ghosts, and immediately, I'm Aware of how they did it. The force of their positive energy lifted the residues of fear and hatred to a point that they could peacefully move on, and permeated the air, ground – and everything below ground – for miles. Their love sustains my parents and everyone else, softening hard edges and corners of personalities and minds wherever it can. There's an inevitability about it that makes me smile. Everything is going to be okay, because how can it not be?

The colt veers to the left behind Ember as we approach the end of the valley, jolting me back to our physicality.

I'm going to pull my mind back from you a little at a time, Victor, Will tells me. *The pattern for perfect balance is strong within the human collective consciousness thanks to the Horse-Bonded, so now you've released everything that was holding you from it, you can ride on your own. Your body knows what to do. Stay with the colt in every way and be everything you can be.*

I nod, my smile so wide that my ears feel as if they're in the wrong place. I know exactly what he has just said. I understand it, because I feel it.

The colt catches up with Ember and overtakes him, then tears up a shallow hillside. We race through the tall grasses bending in the breeze, around rocks, then downhill and along the floor of the next valley, all the time bolstered and supported by the herd energy that flows our way. Will, Ember and Maverick are nowhere to be seen. When the colt finally begins to slow down, I wipe the tears from my eyes and see his herd grazing where he left them, Ember among them as if he had nothing to do with our mad dash around the countryside.

Maverick races to meet us, barking, and as the colt slows further, the dog circles behind us and runs just below my foot. The others are standing, watching us with their mouths open. The colt slows to a stop in front of them and I lean forward and throw my arms around his neck. It is for me, rather than for him, because I find that I know he doesn't need my gratitude. He has helped me to find my balance – it's who he is and what he does, just like Will said. I slide to the ground and the colt makes a soft, low sound in his throat and then wanders off.

Will smiles and nods after him. 'He whickered to you. You'll come to appreciate what a compliment that is. There's a water hole over there. Follow him and once he's had a drink, wash the sweat off him. Then, pick some grass stalks, the toughest ones, and scrape the water off him.'

'I'll help you,' Ace says. 'I've just watched Will do it for Ember.'

'So did we all, I can help him,' Hero says, sticking his chest out. He's never tried to make himself look more confident than he is before, but I feel how much this means to him. I want to put my hand out and push his chest back in, to tell him how unnecessary it is, but I know it won't help him any more than it would have helped me. And besides, I'm finding it difficult to walk.

'I think the colt will let you know if he wants any of you to help him,' I say, knowing he won't. Sure enough, when Ace, Hero and Adept follow me as I hobble to where the colt is now drinking, he steps aside and snorts. Where his brown, orange-flecked eyes were soft, now they're wide and hard, and white shows around the outside of the brown. His ears flicker between my friends, his herd and me.

'Just move back, please,' I say. 'Please? He's thirsty and hot, and needs to be washed down, but if you don't move away, he'll go straight back to his herd.'

'But it's not fair,' Hero says, walking backwards. 'You wouldn't have seen who the horses really are if it wasn't for me, you would have shot them without even looking at them properly. And now it's you who they let near them, you who gets to ride one of them.' He sounds like a child whining because he doesn't want to go to bed.

'Thank you for making sure I saw them,' I say, looking at Ace and Adept with my eyebrows raised until they follow Hero's example and move away. 'Honestly, Hero, I'll always be grateful. But instead of focusing on what's happened to me, concentrate on what you feel from the horses. Find your own way to them, I know you can.'

'How do you know?' Adept calls out.

'I can feel it. Where the horses are concerned, how you feel is more important than what you do,' I say.

The three of them stand stock still, thinking, and are still there after I've washed the colt down, scratched the spots where I could sense he would appreciate it – as if I've always known that kind of thing – and watched him meander back to his herd.

Will is fielding questions from the other two while Maverick sits at Prime's side. As I shuffle back to my friends, I sense the dog's concern for Prime, his desire to comfort him and persuade him that life is fantastic, and it pulls me up short. Prime has ignored him and frightened him and, I remember, only just stopped short of trying to kill him, yet Maverick is unwavering in his desire to make Prime feel better. How is it possible for a creature to be so forgiving?

Because he doesn't recognise the concept of having been wronged. Refreshing, isn't it? Will grins as he chats to Kudos, reminding me that I need to try to keep a hold on what is going on around me, as well as working through what I pick up through my Awareness.

'Are you coming back to the others?' I ask Hero, Ace and Adept.

All three nod and follow me without speaking. I smile inside as I sense them going over and over everything they have felt from the horses, from their first glimpse of them up until earlier today, when Ember and the other four stood behind those of us closest to Awareness. They'll get there soon.

'So, we're just going to carry on to Rockwood as if all that never happened, and you're not going to tell us how to get near the horses and ride, even though they could get us there in half the time and by the look of what we just saw, in a far more enjoyable way?' Kudos is saying to Will.

'The horses could get us there in less than a quarter of the time, but that is beside the point. Ember and the bay colt didn't carry Victor and me for our convenience or entertainment, and Victor has already told you what you need to do for the horses to let you near them,' Will replies at the same time as telling me, *You're fit and strong, but we just pushed your body way past anything its ever done before. You'll find a packet of herbs labelled AR in the supplies I gave you – AR stands for after riding. Don't worry, Amarilla knew exactly which herbs would be needed, you'll be walking normally again before you know it.*

I grin and nod to him as I hobble towards where I left my rucksack.

Kudos looks between Will and me as if he knows something passed between us, but he says nothing. I sense his desire to be part of whatever it is. The survivor in him recognises that Will is strong in a way Kudos can't pin down, and he wants that for himself, but he's too scared to let down his guard and go after it in the way I have. He watches and waits for further proof that it's safe to follow the path I've taken.

Within minutes of swallowing a dose of the herbs that Will's aunt prepared for me, I feel a whole lot better. While the others are shouldering their rucksacks, I do a few of the stretches I would normally do before weapons training, and then heave my own rucksack onto my back.

I look over to where the bay colt is grazing. He has rolled on the ground and has dirt stuck to his damp coat, and dried grass stuck in his tail – but I've never seen anything or anyone so beautiful. I'm Aware that he has found for himself, and eaten, some of the same herbs I have, and the slight soreness caused by my seat bones before I learnt to sit on them properly, has gone. He's Aware of my attention and interest, and of everything else around him, all at once, just like Will seems able to be, but when his tail twitches at a biter and he walks on a bit to get out of

Ember's way as the stallion rounds up his herd ready to move on, I feel the effortless balance he has between his Awareness and his five senses. I blink, remembering Will's advice that I should concentrate on achieving the same, and follow the others.

Ace looks over her shoulder, hesitates and waits for me. She smiles and I feel her uncertainty as we walk together. 'I'm jealous of you,' she says, 'but weirdly, I'm pleased for you too. When you rode away on that horse, you looked awkward, as if you didn't belong there. I was worried you'd fall off and break your neck, especially when he started running so fast. Then you disappeared and I worried we'd all got everything wrong and he'd taken you off to kill you. When Will and Ember came back without you, I was ready to fight, to make Will tell me where you were, but you know what he's like, he said you were enjoying yourself and for some reason, like with everything else he says, I believed him. Then the horse came racing around the hill and for a second, I couldn't see you. It was like you were part of him, and he was part of you.' She drops her voice to a whisper. 'I actually thought I was going to cry, and I haven't done that since I was five.' She swallows and continues, 'And now I hate you for leaving me out of whatever you have with the horse, for not telling me how to have a horse of my own, and, and... for walking like Will does, as if you're stronger than the rest of us without even trying to be.'

'A horse of my own,' I say, her words reminding me of a glimpse I caught from Will of people who used words like that. I frown as I strain to remember. He told me he would withdraw from my body and leave me to ride on my own, which I would be able to do because the pattern for perfect balance was strong in the human collective consciousness as a result of... the Horse-Bonded.

'Yes, I want a horse of my own, like you have,' Ace insists.

My brain feels as if it will explode as my mind is flooded with images of people riding horses, as well as everything about who the Horse-Bonded were – why they came into existence, the role they played in establishing the communities of The New, how they helped the horses to move beyond their history of servitude to humans and how in the process, they became as perfectly balanced as the horses themselves... and became Aware.

Count all of the bushes you can see, Victor, or you'll get lost in it all, Will tells me. *VICTOR!*

I wince and then nod. I put my hands up to my head to try to hold in all of the information, in case it spills out. *One.* 'We aren't the Horse-Bonded, with Bond-Partners of our own,' I murmur to Ace. *Two, three.* 'They had their roles and their time has passed.' *Four.* 'You won't have a horse of your own any more than I do.' *Five.* I have a sense of everything the colt is, and compare it with the sense that swirls around in my mind of the bonded horses and all the aspects of being horses that they gave up in order to fulfil the roles their souls chose. They were content in those roles, but the colt could never be. He will never follow my lead when I ride him – where would the sense be in that, when he knows so much more than I do, when he feels so much more than I do? He brings balance wherever and whenever he can, that is why he and I are drawn to one another; for now, our purpose is the same, that is all. 'The colt isn't mine,' I say. 'How could he be?

'Who are the Horse-Bonded? I've never heard of them,' Ace says. 'Oh, wait, did you learn about them on your Regular wallscreen, when you were learning about life up here?'

I grimace. 'Our people know nothing about the Horse-Bonded or what they achieved. They think they know everything of importance, but they know nothing at all. Absolutely nothing.'

TWELVE

Will
_____

I am glad of Prime's silence as the two of us walk on through the scrub-covered hills, Maverick trotting between us as always. The sight of Victor and the colt returning to us looking like the single entity they are, has affected Prime deeply, but he doesn't understand how he feels. Usually when that happens, he responds by increasing his aggression, so the fact that he hasn't yet said a word is encouraging.

Shall I take over with Victor, so you can concentrate on the others? my mother asks.

I grin. *You know very well I can monitor all six of them at once.*

Yes of course I know that, Will, every bit as well as you know that helping people to centre themselves between their Awareness and personality is something I do all the time. As such, I have learnt that subtlety is usually more effective than allowing a newly Aware person to access a whole load of information at once, then yelling at them to count out loud so they don't get lost in it all.

You have your way of doing it, I have mine. The lad can take it, I tell her.

I feel her fondness as she tells me, *You're every bit as impossible as you always were. You may be Aware to an extent that none of us are, but that doesn't mean you have to do everything yourself, you know.*

I'm not doing it all myself – in case you've forgotten, Maverick's here and so are the horses.

I hear her sigh as surely as if she were standing in front of me. *I know. I've just been worried about you. I understand you wanted to go to meet them alone because giving them just one of us to deal with is the least threatening we could be, and I know you can be Aware of everything at once, but…*

You're my mum, you love me, and despite knowing what I'm capable of, you still want to protect me. I know and I love you too. We'll be there tomorrow, then you can take some of them under your wing and leave me in peace.

She senses the humour I attach to my thought and gives me a sense back of her pulling at her own hair.

See you, Mum.

She withdraws from my mind, leaving a sense of anticipation behind her. She's right, she's a lot more practised than I am at easing people into their centres by giving them exactly the right mental exercises to do to help them to stay grounded in the physical world, whilst exploring what they can sense in their Awareness. I know I can help Victor, though. His parents did well by him, teaching him what he needed to survive while tempering what they taught him with hints as to what they sensed to be real. His mind was primed and ready for the horses' energy to reach inside and draw him out from behind the fear and conditioning essential for survival of the Supreme City regime, and as such, he is ready for all the information to which he now has access.

We wander on through the afternoon, largely in silence. Occasionally, Kudos catches up with me to ask a question about the horses and what he thinks he might have felt from them, and when he does, I sense Prime's interest. I answer as honestly as I can without revealing anything that has happened to Victor, and Kudos falls back to think as he walks.

Those walking with Victor have given up asking him questions, since he is making little sense when he answers at all in between counting now how many rocks he can see, how many birds of each different size are flying above, how many clouds waft slowly through the sky above us, and describing his friends' appearances in minute detail – all of the exercises I give him, one after the other, to prevent him disappearing into his Awareness. His mind is flat out sifting through everything he can sense, and everything that Awareness then leads on to.

We drop down out of the hills, onto gently undulating grassland. 'See that dark line on the horizon?' I ask.

Prime nods before he can stop himself, and after a short pause, five voices behind me confirm that they see it too.

'That's the woodland separating us from the village of Rockwood. Not too far now until we stop for the night, and the going will be much easier now we're out of the hills.'

I sense the horses spreading out to graze the lusher grass and the herbs that were unavailable on the scrubby hillsides we have been traversing.

'Can we wait with the horses?' Hero calls out. He's nearly there; he feels the horses, but thinks it's because they've been following more closely for the last few hours.

'How you feel is more important than what you do,' I remind him with a wink. I sense Adept and Ace watching him, wondering whether he will wait, and if so, whether they should do the same.

'You're almost there, Hero,' Victor says, then adds, 'fifty-four pink flowers, although one might be red, it's too far away to be sure.'

'What?' Ace says.

You said that out loud. Good counting, but concentrate, I tell him, sensing his frustration and exhaustion. *You're doing very well. Keeping from the others that you're Aware while also exploring your Awareness, doing the exercises I've set you, and communicating silently with me, is a balancing act that far more experienced people would struggle with. I know you can do it, Victor. Just keep going.*

Victor doesn't answer and Ace doesn't push him. She's not far behind Hero; she feels something that she knows she only feels when the horses are near. Whenever she feels it, she has a sense that Victor is working through something as a result of his experience with the colt, and is far from the crazy lad he appears to be as he stumbles through the tall grass and meadow flowers, muttering to himself.

I sense Hero, Ace and Adept make the decision to walk after Victor. All three search their feelings, trying to keep the sense they all have of the horses' presence, and trying to figure out if anything is changing as the distance between them and the horses slowly increases. Any moment now...

Hero's eyes light up as he realises he can still sense the horses. His soul nudges his mind to reach out past his concern that he isn't good enough, and embrace what he feels. He flinches when he senses the irritation of the grey mare who stood behind him earlier, then smiles as he is Aware of her knocking a biter from her belly with her hind foot.

Hero stops and turns around in amazement just as Ace opens to her own Awareness. She turns to the horses, then back to Victor, and doesn't even try to stop herself staggering backward. She lands on her bottom in the grass and stares up at him.

He grins and crouches down in front of her, using mindspeak to explain what is happening to her, just as I did when it happened to him.

Ace and Hero open the path for Adept to follow, and her mind does, willingly. She turns to look back at the horses in wonder.

I don't look back as I narrow my thoughts so that only Victor picks them up. *I've got them, Victor. I need you to help me keep the other two walking while you carry on with your exercises. The sooner you can stay centred, the more help you'll be to them and the rest, and the better able you'll all be to help your people.*

Victor is immediately Aware that I need Prime and Kudos to keep moving away from the others. He squeezes Ace's hand and leaves her sitting in the grass, without argument.

'Come on, Kudos, they need space to work things out,' I hear him say. 'If you want, I'll tell you what happened when I rode the colt.'

Kudos falls in beside him as he outlines his experience, leaving out anything Kudos won't yet understand. I sense Prime listening avidly.

There is a whinny and hooves pound against the ground. We all stop and turn around to see Hero, Ace and Adept disappearing among the horses now circling them. I sense their delight and total lack of fear as the horses canter slowly, rhythmically around them, drawing them further out of themselves, past their belief that they have to fight for survival; past their fear that they are alone; past any tendency to hold themselves apart from one another. The horses won't give them the time they gave Victor. He has opened their minds to the possibilities the horses represent, and they are ready to ride, to find balance.

Adept. Hero. Ace. You can feel what the horses want you to do – what you need to do. I'll help you, just as I did with Victor earlier. I show them how I helped Victor to ride and sense their amazement and relief as they understand. *Ready?*

Are you kidding me? Of course we're ready, Hero tells me, and I sense the girls' agreement.

Hero already knows it will be the grey mare whom he sensed first, who will come for him. He watches her slow her canter until she is moving at the speed of a walk, then adjust the sequence in which she moves her legs, so that she walks gracefully to stand by his side. A chestnut filly comes for Adept, and a dark brown colt for Ace. I'm with all three teenagers at once, both in their Awareness and in their bodies. None of them resist as I vault them onto the horses who are prepared to help them, and rearrange their bodies as far as I can.

Like Victor, they have all been trained since they were little, to adopt a posture that gives them the appearance of strength, confidence and readiness for a fight. Each and every threat they have ever received has lodged itself into the parts of their body upon which they were trained to focus. The pain of each physical blow, the anger that accompanied every insult, the fear of death and loss, all keep them from sitting into their pelvises, where real confidence lies; from relaxing their shoulders so that their self-assurance is real; from opening their chests in self-expression instead of false bravado.

I'm with them every step of the way as the three horses leave the herd and trot off. I grin at Kudos as he gasps, and send a wave of love to Maverick as he shuffles closer to Prime's leg.

Keep counting, Victor, I tell him.

Oh, for the love of all that's powerful, how are you doing that? he replies. *You're riding three horses at once through three different people while showing each of them where they need to let go, and you still have time to be on my case?*

Never forget it. Keep counting. You've done all the pink and red flowers you can see, move on to yellow now. Victor? I nudge his mind firmly with my own as Adept achieves perfect balance. *Count.*

Fine. Wow, she was quick. I get it, her parents were a lot softer with her than Hero's and Ace's were, so she had less to release. I'm up to twenty, by the way.

I know. Keep going.

The three horses are galloping now, and, keen as they are to avoid both the hills and the woodland behind us, they remain on the grassland where we can see them. Adept's chestnut filly is pulling away from the other two. Hero has allowed me to reposition both his chest and shoulders – he rarely pretended to be confident and ready for a fight – but he's having trouble relaxing into his pelvis. He doesn't believe the confidence he's starting to sense there; he doesn't think it can be part of him.

The grey mare beneath him knows differently. She veers left and then right, then left and right again. I keep him in place but he bounces slightly, his forward-tilted pelvis and rigid lower back unable to absorb the extra movement. The grey mare isn't galloping as fast as Adept's filly, but her pace never waivers. Hero feels her confidence that whatever she does, he will stay with her, and begins to trust that over his worry that he's letting her down like he's always let his parents down. He allows me to sit him into his pelvis a little more. The mare veers left and right again, and he bounces less. He grins as he relaxes his lower back and sits into the confidence he finds there. His mare speeds up and races along just behind Adept's.

Ace is struggling, as she always does when she isn't in control. Her parents taught her that physical prowess and fighting ability are matched equally in importance by the ability to outthink everyone else, and she has always used their advice and training to full effect. She has never expended more energy in a fight than necessary to either win, draw or sometimes even lose according to her calculation – usually several fights before – of which outcome will suit her overall strategy the best.

When she was chosen as a member of Victor's scouting party, she calculated that getting close to him would give her the most and best options as the situation played out, but this wasn't one of the options she foresaw. She has no plan. She's found herself following her feelings, which she's never even considered as an option before. They've brought her physically, mentally and emotionally close to the brown colt in a way that is incredible and moving and… overwhelming. She doesn't know how to manage everything she feels, let alone everything she can feel waiting for her, everything that will be released if she allows me to help her body to move in better balance with the colt's. She needs to stop trying to manage every situation in her path, and the colt senses it.

He slows to a canter, then to a trot. Ace frowns in confusion as the other two horses and riders tear away from her and the colt. He distracts her by turning away from them and trotting a large circle, then he slows to walk for a few strides before moving back up to trot, then canter, then back to trot. Throughout, he balances both his weight and hers on his hindquarters, easily adjusting for the fact that her weight is too far forward. His body calls to hers to mirror his balance while his mind draws hers to notice how he occupies his body with all of himself – how he cannot be balanced physically if there are any parts of his body he avoids knowing about, any parts filled with anything that would keep out his mind and soul. She is fascinated. As he moves back up to canter, he takes her with him in every way.

I withdraw from Ace as I have from the other two, both of whom yell with delight as the brown colt takes Ace at a gallop across the middle of circle they have galloped, to meet them. All three horses race alongside one another towards us. They glide to a halt before us in one continuous, beautiful movement and stand just long enough for their riders to slide to the ground. Then they are off again. The colt bucks and the grey mare squeals and kicks the air to his side, both without breaking the rhythm in which all three are cantering. When they reach the other horses, they slow and then head off in different directions to take up their places alongside favoured companions. They blow for a few minutes, then drop their heads and graze. Where they singled themselves out as the personalities – the energies – most likely to help each of the three teenagers, now they release their individuality. Like snowflakes melting to water, their energy blends back into that of the herd, along with that which the others shifted to them to support their efforts.

Ace flings her arms around Victor, who at first has no idea what to do. Hero grins at him and slowly, Victor lifts his arms around Ace and hugs her back. *Well done, you were amazing,* he tells her and she laughs delightedly.

Then she stands back from him, wincing at the aching in all of the muscles her body has just used so differently from ever before. 'How long have you been able to do that?' she asks Victor. 'Oh, I see, I should have known. You've been talking to Will all this time, haven't you, without the rest of us knowing?'

It was supposed to be a secret so you could all come to your Awareness in your own time, but you've well and truly scuppered that plan for Prime and Kudos, Victor informs her. *Not that it was a plan, because plans aren't always helpful, you know that now, right?*

You know everything I went through? You spied on me when I was struggling? How could you?

We're both Aware, Ace. Nothing is private, in fact the others are listening in right now.

Ace glares at Hero and Adept, both of whose grey skin

darkens. Then they look at one another, shocked to be Aware of embarrassment other than their own.

Here, Victor announces. *This is what happened to me when I rode the colt.* He shows the three of them his experience and their eyes widen. *Now we're all even. You're just going to have to get used to the fact that we're all in each other's heads, oh, and that Will is a tyrant.*

Ace, Hero and Adept all turn as one to look at me. Prime and Kudos look from the three of them to me in confusion.

'Does anyone feel like explaining what's going on and why you're all acting weird?' Kudos says. 'Victor and Ace, if you're going to move your mouths as if you're talking to one another, breathe properly so that your words actually come out, or you just look like idiots.' He looks at me. 'What did Ace mean, you and Victor have been talking without the rest of us knowing?'

'Victor has been Aware of his connection to everything that exists since the nap you all took earlier. That means he's been Aware of me in the same way that I've always been Aware of him and the rest of you, and we have been able to communicate by thought. He's not used to it yet, so he moves his mouth as if he's talking.'

'And clearly, Ace can now do it too,' Kudos says. He nods to the other two who have just ridden. 'And both of you?'

Hero grins. 'Yep. We can all hear each other, and everything else, in our heads. Well, it's not like hearing, really, being Aware, it's just like, whatever I think of, I suddenly know about, like I knew the grey mare would come for me. Oh, and take that blue flower by your shin. It opened earlier today for the first time. Before that, it was closed tight, but when it felt the sun on it this morning, it was the right time for it to open. It's already had some tiny animals visit it and then fly away again...'

'Hero, count how many blue flowers there are,' Victor

interrupts. 'HERO! Stop babbling. You have to count, just like Will has had me doing, or you'll lose yourself in your Awareness. And all three of you, take a dose of the herbs Will gave you, labelled AR for after riding. If you don't, you won't be able to walk. Take more whenever you start hurting as much as you are now.'

'I thought you said it's Will who is the tyrant,' Adept chuckles. Ace joins in, followed by Hero, but they all do as Victor told them and rummage in their rucksacks for their herbs.

'I am,' I confirm. 'Hero needs to count blue flowers. Victor, you're still on yellow, Ace, you take pink, Adept, go for the red ones. I want to know how many you see between here and the trees as we walk. You can all sift through everything that comes into your Awareness, but don't stop looking for more flowers and counting those you see. Got it?'

Victor rolls his eyes and continues his count. The others nod without speaking.

I turn and walk on towards the trees.

Kudos hurries to walk between Prime and me. 'That's it?' he says. 'That's all you're going to say?'

'Yes. I'm hungry, aren't you? I plan to focus my energy on reaching the trees as soon as possible, so I can eat the gloop of whoever wants to swap food with me this time.'

'I do,' Kudos says. 'If they all get to ride horses and talk without speaking, I get to try the new food.'

I turn and grin at him. He'll be next.

THIRTEEN

Victor
___

I am so preoccupied with sharing thoughts with the others, exploring everything that bombards my Awareness and counting all of the cursed yellow flowers I can see, that when Kudos stops in front of me to stare up at the huge structures I recognise from my wallscreen as trees, I bump into him.

'I thought you were supposed to be Aware of everything,' he grumbles.

'Sorry. Wow!' His focus on the trees takes mine with it, but where he sees a long, brown trunk with smaller branches growing out of it, all sprouting green leaves, I feel it. All of it. I feel the water that is drawn up through the massive plant, distributing nutrients absorbed from the ground as it hydrates each and every cell. I feel the miniscule, perfectly designed openings on the underside of each leaf that allow the excess water to pass out and evaporate into the atmosphere, drawing more water up the tree to take its place. I feel the fluid that passes downward, taking nutrients manufactured in the leaves to everywhere else. I feel the animals who crawl all over the tree; lots of different sizes, colours and types, all intent on their own business. I feel the birds who have made nests in the branches, and the embryos developing in their eggs. I feel...

Victor. Count the branches, and while you're doing that, eat, or you'll forget to, Will interrupts.

Can't I just rest for a bit?

You can rest when you're asleep.

Your mum would let me rest.

I feel Will's smile as well as see it. I sense his closeness to his mother and feel a pang of guilt and shame that I've barely thought about my own.

Yes, she would let you rest, Will tells me. *I, however, know your full potential and have every intention of pushing you as hard as my teachers pushed me. Now, count.*

I can feel that he's telling me the truth. Even when I wasn't Aware of it, I kind of was; I trust Will as if he's always been my best friend, and somehow, I've only just remembered it. But that can't be right; his best friend is called Jonus.

I frown as I concentrate on counting branches as Will told me to, at the same time as activating all of the food tubs held under my nose by the others, and then beginning my own meal. I grimace. After having had two meals of Will's food, the white gloop – as he calls that which we are used to eating – tastes and feels as superficial as the rest of my existence has been. How did I manage to get through each day as I used to? Compared with my life now, it was such a one-dimensional existence, living purely to clean up after others and fight those who would crush me.

I shake my head. Jonus. I want to focus on him, and I need to count so that Will doesn't shake me out of my Awareness again.

I feel Jonus's closeness to Will, the bond they share, their similarities... and their differences. Jonus isn't in charge of himself in the way Will is. He isn't centred like Will, or even as much as I am – he isn't even Aware! Yet he and Will communicate just like Will and I do. How is that possible? I probe further. He has a horse; Jonus is Horse-Bonded. But the Horse-Bonded no longer have horses, theirs have all passed on and no more have taken their place. I put my food tub in my lap, hold my head in my hands and try to slow down the flow of information as it pours into my mind, so that I can sort through it and hopefully make sense of that which currently makes no sense at all.

I start with Will. I follow the link from him to Jonus – except that it isn't a link; Will's energy resides within Jonus! He's in Jonus's body just like he was with me in mine when he helped me to ride... oh. That's how it started. But why did he need to do that? The Horse-Bonded taught one another to ride, I've already seen that... but Jonus had no one to teach him. I suddenly remember why his name seems familiar; I learnt about him when the Horse-Bonded first entered my Awareness. He was the first of them. He had no one to teach him to ride, so Will did... my hands fall away from my head in shock. Will taught the first Horse-Bonded to ride. He found the first Horse-Bonded in his Awareness, managed to reach him across time while Jonus was alive in the past – and still does – and helped him to come to terms with the fact that a horse had chosen him as a Bond-Partner. He taught him what he needed to know as the first Horse-Bonded, including how to ride!

I sense another presence with Will and Jonus as their friendship developed, but I can't seem to grasp who it was. Each time I try, I come up against something that turns me away, that makes me want to think about other things... but I want to think about this. Who else was involved in the impossible? WHO ELSE? I batter against the obstruction in my mind, but it holds firm.

Finally, I let go of my head, exhausted and look across at where Will is sitting, chuckling at the expression on Kudos's face as he eats Will's food. He glances at me and winks as he often does when he's giving answers to our questions that aren't really answers at all and only lead to more questions – which he answers in the same way. Everything is circular where Will is concerned; there's never anything to take hold of whether it be physical or mental, he just slides around, letting us bounce off him until we get to where we understand for ourselves. It was he who was in my mind, blocking me from knowing who helped him to reach Jonus. I know it.

'Who were your teachers, Will?' I ask him loudly. 'You said you only push me as hard as your teachers pushed you, but I can't find them. Every time I go near them in my Awareness, you block me.'

He smiles and I sense both his approval and his delight. The other three who are Aware feel it too, and look between Will and me, frantically trying to raid my Awareness for what I know. Kudos and Prime also look between the two of us. Kudos is uncomfortable, just wanting the day to end without anything else happening that he doesn't understand. Prime narrows his eyes, pleased by the challenge in my voice and keen to see a rift develop between Will and me. Maverick shifts a little further away from him.

'I've had many teachers,' Will says, his blue eyes piercing through me, almost making me wish I hadn't asked. Almost.

'Your parents. Their friends, most of whom were Horse-Bonded – Rowena, Marvel, Vickery, Holly, Justin.' I sense more of them just beyond Justin in my mind, but it's like trying to see through a barrier that while made of a clear material, is so thick, it is opaque; I can see blurring on the far side of it, but I can't see who is there. It absorbs all of the punches I throw at it with my mind as I try to break through, then slides to the side when I try to dart around it. 'Why are you hiding them from me? What aren't I allowed to know?' I demand of Will.

'There's only so much your mind can cope with. When you're afraid, or tired as you are now, it can cope with even less. What you perceive to be a block keeping you from knowing who else awaits you in Rockwood, is a suggestion to your mind and nothing more. When you're ready to know who is beyond it, you will.' He looks around at the four of us who are all now pummelling at the barrier to the knowledge we want.

I stop my efforts. He's holding all four of us off as if we are specks of dust hitting glass. He's too strong. Too clever. Too... everything.

I am daunted by how long it will take me to work through everything of which I am now Aware, because I can only think of one thing at a time. Will can hold multiple mindspeak conversations at once, as well as holding verbal conversations. He is constantly Aware of where Maverick is and how Prime feels towards the dog, in case Maverick needs his help. He responds to all of us who are Aware whenever we stray away from counting, immediately reminding us to stay rooted in the physical world while exploring our Awareness. And now, he's blocking us from knowing what he doesn't want us to know. Except that isn't what he's doing. I accept it with a loud sigh that makes Kudos roll his eyes at me. Will's protecting us, I can feel it. He's amused at how he knows we'll respond when we discover what he's hiding, but underneath that, he's looking out for us all, easing us through this incredible experience so that we come out of it balanced enough, strong enough, to be able to help our people. He cares about us all, even Prime.

I nod slowly. *Thanks, Will.*

He nods back. *Count, Victor, while you finish your food. Then sleep.*

I sigh again. I seem to be doing that a lot. *Fifty-one. Fifty-two.*

And, Victor?

I'm doing it. I get it. Fifty-three. Fifty-four.

I'm proud of you. So will your parents be, when you see them again.

I stop counting and gulp. As always, Will is telling the truth. He can't do otherwise.

My mind turns to my parents as I finish my meal, don extra clothes for the night, and lie back against my rucksack. They're tired. Not quite as tired as I am, but enough that when they retire for the night, they will sleep instead of staying awake, worrying about me. I'm glad of that. And I'm glad that I'll be able to help them; if Will tells me I'll be able to, then I trust I will, every bit as much as I trust the bay colt.

Trust. A word that is never spoken in Supreme City, a word that has no meaning there except between a few rare parents and their children. A word that, I realise as I drift off to sleep and see the world through my Awareness, barely has meaning in the world of horses, either – for it is a given; when any alternative to trust is unthinkable, then trust itself has no need to exist.

When I wake, the sun is warm on my face. I smile to myself as its light filters gently through my eyelids, making me want to open them and experience a new day. I keep them shut for a few moments longer, savouring the smell of the air that yet holds on to the cool of the night, while slowly becoming laden with the scents and sounds of the day.

I sit up just as Maverick hurls himself at me. I laugh as he licks my face until I'm covered in slimy saliva. When he finally leaves me in peace to move on to a newly-awakened Adept, I wipe my face on my sleeves.

'That's revolting. He's revolting,' Prime tells me. 'I saw him licking his anus just before he licked your face, and you don't even care, do you? You're filthy, you're undisciplined and you don't care about any of things your parents taught you, any of the values our people live by. You're a traitor to Supreme City and you should be disgusted with yourself. Your parents would be if they could see you.'

'Because you know yours would be if they could see you?' I blurt out without thinking. I've never hurt him more. All the times I've fought him, all the times I've hit him with my staff and my fists, every time I've stabbed and shot at him in his training vest, all the times I've really tried to injure him in order to prevent him injuring me, I couldn't have known that voicing the truth he fears the most would cause him the greatest pain. I feel it as if it were mine and despite my dislike of him, I'm overcome with guilt and shame; I feel every bit as bad as I would have had I kicked Maverick or hurt one of the horses. 'Your parents would be wrong, Prime,' I say quietly. He glares at me, his eyes full of the pain and fear that radiates from him... which hasn't turned to anger. Not yet.

Keep going, Victor, Will advises. *The truth opens many doors.*

The truth. 'Your parents told you they were teaching you how to be strong, how to fight for your and their advancement, but they were lying,' I tell Prime. 'Like most people in Supreme City, they hate themselves, and they took it out on you. Maverick feels your pain, that's why he stays close. You never chase him off, because you feel better when he's with you – you don't know why, but you do. I know why; it's because he loves you. You don't trust how that feels yet, but you know you want more of it, and there's so much more of it here. It's everywhere.'

Confusion joins the fear and pain that radiate from within Prime as he sits glaring at me. He still hasn't attacked me, and I don't feel as though he's going to. Maverick whines and slinks to Prime's side, wagging his tail slowly, and repeatedly turning his head away, licking his mouth and squinting. Prime sees him as submissive, weak and no threat, just as Maverick intends, and allows the dog to approach. I feel Maverick's desperation to reach Prime inside as well as outside, to fill him with love so that his hurt is pushed out and away from him. I'm in awe of the dog, as are my friends. Ace can't take her eyes off him. Hero's mouth opens and closes as he watches him. Adept has tears running down her face, a behaviour we have always been taught is a shameful display of weakness.

Will just sits, grinning as usual. I sense how he feels about Maverick, and immediately, I am Aware of the circumstances of their meeting, and much of what came immediately after. My mouth drops open and my eyes widen, and I can do nothing to reverse either; Will was a mess, and Maverick got through to him and turned his life around, paving the way for... his teachers. Amarilla and Infinity.

My heart thumps almost painfully in my chest as I see them in my mind – a slim woman with brown hair and blue eyes, and a black and white horse, also with blue eyes, although a shade lighter than Amarilla's. But that is how they were. I feel who they are now and I gasp. They're like Adam and Peace, only where Adam and Peace are inseparable in All That Is, Amarilla and Infinity are inseparable here, as in, sharing the same body, as if it belongs to them both – yet they're not really "both", because there's just one of them.

Needs must, they inform me cheerfully. *Hi, Victor, glad you had such a good sleep, you have a busy day ahead.*

There… there are two of you, and yet there's only one of you. How is that possible? I think back to them.

It will serve you to merely accept the situation for now. There is much with which your mind would be better occupied, they reply – only where before their thought felt more as if it was coming from Amarilla, now it feels more as if it is coming from Infinity. What the hell?

Will slaps his knee and laughs out loud. 'Of all the reactions to them I've ever seen, that's the funniest. Close your mouth, Victor, before the biters start flying in. Hero, blink, or your eyes will get sore.'

I look around at the others, my mouth still open. Prime is in his own world, looking down at Maverick gazing back up at him, and stroking the dog's head. Ace, Adept and Hero are all looking between one another, me and Will, hoping, like me, that understanding will come. Kudos watches us all in frustration at not knowing, again, what is going on.

'I mean, what do we call them? Amarilla or Infinity? What do you call them?' Hero manages to say.

Everyone looks at Will, who says, 'Believe me, I've called them many things in the past – and don't go looking for that information, because I've buried it as only Amarilla and I know how to – but either Amarilla or Infinity, whichever strikes you first, will do. They answer to both, with them being both, while also being the same. It seems like a paradox, but it isn't really, and as Infinity just wisely advised, there is far more important information waiting to occupy your minds now you've had a rest.' He continues, *It will be a shock when you learn who the rest of my teachers were, but the horses and I will help you past it. Try not to react too violently, or you'll worry Kudos and Prime. I need you to come to terms with what you will find in your Awareness by the time we reach Rockwood, so that you can be of help with the other two.*

The moment I search my Awareness for the identity of the rest of the teachers who were blocked from me last night, they burst into view. Adept finds them too, and collapses in a dead faint beside me. Ace, Hero and I all freeze in position. I think I've stopped breathing.

How could we have been so stupid as to not realise that if humans survived the blasts that wiped out the cities, the abominations they created might have too? We've all seen video footage of the Enforcers in action from when our ancestors lived above ground. We were all threatened with their return if the Elite saw any need to reintroduce them, and we all had nightmares as a result, for they were undefeatable and took no mercy. Little did we know that when we came above ground, when we trusted Will, Maverick and the horses, they would lead us straight into the arms of those who have haunted our dreams since we were children.

Look more closely, Will advises us.

I feel as if I'm going to pass out with terror alongside Adept, but Will's thought is calm and encouraging. I force my mind back to the Enforcers, almost glancing it past them, like using my peripheral vision in the physical world, to spare myself as many of the horrifying details as possible.

They're taller than in the videos that caused me to run and hide from the wallscreen in our apartment; where they were hunched, they now appear able to stand up straight. Their wiry fur, fangs, talons and terrifyingly muscular limbs look the same, so why are they standing up straight? And they appear to be smiling, though their fangs don't let them do it exactly as we do. There are people laughing and joking with them, and there are horses wandering amongst them as they still won't do with the remaining two of our group.

I look directly at the Enforcers in my mind's eye. One of them has his hands on his hips, and his head is thrown back as he laughs so hard, his belly moves up and down. His name is Levitsson, and he's been a good friend to Will as well as his teacher. A friend? A teacher? How can that be? I look at him and into him even more closely.

His yellowy-brown pelt has flecks of grey in it. His eyes are green with the same slitted pupils the Enforcers had, but where their eyes were always tight and glaring, Levitsson's express laughter every bit as much as the rest of his body. He is no Enforcer, he's never hurt anyone in his life. He's brash and speaks without thinking… but that is seen to be one of his many gifts to the people of Rockwood; to the Rockwood Centre where he has worked for more than twenty-five years, helping people – including Will – through whatever blocks they have in their minds to ever greater Awareness, then helping them to balance that Awareness with their personality so that they function as grounded, well-rounded individuals. Like Levitsson himself. He is Aware and he is centred. Always.

I put my hand on the ground behind me as my world spins. Levitsson is an Enforcer, bred to be a killing machine, to obliterate in the most brutal way anyone who disobeys those who control him… yet I can feel that he isn't controlled. There is no computer chip wired into his brain; he's free. And he feels no animosity towards humans. None at all. How can that be? How can he not feel the desire to wipe out those whose ancestors bred his own, treated them so brutally, and forced them to be so brutal towards others?

Because I forgave them. I forgave everything that happened in the past. That is why I stand tall. I recommend the process.

Levitsson withdraws from my mind, leaving me – leaving us all – with the knowledge of how he and the rest of his kind left their past behind.

Adept sits up and I show her everything I've discovered before she has time to think. Her eyes widen and then flick to where Kudos is watching her. 'Um, well, that was w…weird,' she says, 'I don't know what came over me.'

'Your mind is still a bit overloaded, I think, I, um, I felt a bit faint when I woke up, too. Still do, actually,' Ace tells her.

Hero nods and says, 'Me too. I guess it's, err, it's something we're all going to have to get used to?' He looks at Will.

Will grins at the four of us. 'Nothing to worry about, you're all doing great.' *Really great. Well done. You see the challenge in front of us now.*

Prime and Kudos are going to freak out, Hero observes. *We all freaked out and we had our Awareness to help us past it. I sense several hundred Enforcers… no, that isn't who they are. I sense several hundred Kindred living in Rockwood. Prime and Kudos will panic and go straight into fight mode.*

They will, Adept agrees. *The Kindred are big and strong, but they have no aggression now. They won't fight back and neither will your people. A lot of them are going to get hurt unless we all band together to stop Kudos and Prime.*

You've forgotten something, Will tells us. *We will have horses with us.*

FOURTEEN

Will

*a*ll six of them are now staring at me. Prime has finally noticed that something is going on with the others, and follows the gazes of the four who are Aware, as I use mindspeak to explain to them how we will need to proceed once we reach Rockwood. Kudos watches me sullenly.

'Right then, now we're all fully awake, shall we eat and then get going?' I say. 'It isn't a long trek through the forest, but it will be the most challenging terrain you've experienced yet, so I'm not expecting to move at any great speed. Nevertheless, it would be great to reach the village by lunchtime.'

Kudos looks into the trees and then out through the low mist of rapidly evaporating dew, to where the horses are either lying down, snoozing, grazing or grooming one another. 'What about the horses? It doesn't look as if the forest will be very easy going for them, either.'

'They'll take a longer path than ours, but one that's clear of undergrowth, so they'll be able to move at far greater speed. They'll reach Rockwood at around the same time as us.' I look around at the six teenagers. 'You're going to have to prepare yourselves for the fact that you won't be the biggest cause of excitement when we arrive at the village; it's been a good few years since any horses set hoof to cobble there.'

'I'm sure we'll cope with the disappointment,' Prime says.

I grin at him, glad of the sarcasm that has replaced his usual snarls and sneers. Victor did a great job earlier, and of course Maverick has capitalised on the crack that Victor made in Prime's defences, making it bigger.

'Can I have your food again?' Kudos asks me.

'Sure.' I hand him a parcel filled with dried fruit, nuts and grains. 'It isn't the best I've had to offer, but it'll give you more of a taste of what's to come.'

'How do we know your people won't just poison us?' Kudos says. 'It's what my people would do, either that, or they'd put your villagers, as you call them, in the weapons halls to be used as target practice.'

'I guess you don't know, not really,' I reply. 'You could always ask them to eat the food they prepare for you before you do, but I wouldn't recommend that course of action to anyone staying with my grandmother. You may be fit and strong, but believe me, her tongue will flay the skin off your back and her shrieks will pierce your ear drums.'

The Aware teenagers all pick up a sense of my grandmother, Mailen, and chuckle. 'He's not kidding,' Victor tells Kudos. 'She's kind, though, isn't she?' he says to me. 'And she's fiercely protective of you. She's angry you're here with us, and that the rest of your family wouldn't let her come and get you.' He laughs. 'I'm scared of her already.'

'You're pathetic,' Prime says. 'If she's Will's grandmother, then she's old. Too old to be a threat, but old enough to be a burden. She shouldn't even be alive.'

'And yet she is, and very much so,' I tell him, grinning as I picture her in full flow during one of her rants. 'Unlike your elderly, ours are given all the support they need to live their lives to their natural conclusions. Not that they need an awful lot – they eat well, exercise well, and heal themselves of everything that can be healed. They carry experience that the rest of us can learn from, and we miss them when it's their time to pass on, even though they never really leave us. I'm sorry that you never knew your grandparents, Prime. They weren't as afraid as your parents, so they weren't as harsh. You might have liked them.'

Prime's eyes narrow. 'You don't know anything. My grandparents were weak, that's why my parents are still Disposables. That's why I,' he stabs his chest with his thumb, 'am considered Disposable.'

I swallow a mouthful of white gloop. 'Not by me, and not by any of the people of The New. They'll welcome you like the lost son you are, and make you one of their own if you'll let them.'

'Why would I, why would any of us,' Prime swings his open hand around at the other five, 'want to be welcomed by our inferiors? Why would we want to be one of their own when we can rule them?'

'You'll find out soon enough that ruling over them isn't possible,' I tell him.

'They aren't our inferiors, Prime,' Adept says quietly. 'I know you still need to believe they are, but deep down, you know it isn't true. Will doesn't value anything that we've been taught is important, and he's happier for it. He's stronger than we are. He doesn't look it, but he is, you know he is. Let Maverick and the horses help you. They're teaching us all how to be different. How to be better.'

'Neither riding horses nor talking to one another in your heads make you better than me,' Prime says, his voice wavering slightly.

'No, just a better person than I was,' Adept says.

Kudos looks at her thoughtfully, then stares at the horses. I feel the pull they continue to exert on his soul to move out from behind his upbringing and be everything he can be, and increasingly so does he, but still he stops himself, afraid that he might be wrong. He slowly chews each and every piece of fruit, nut and grain individually. He knows it is more than just the different tastes and textures that he's enjoying, but he can't decide exactly what it is about the food that makes him want more of it.

The four who are Aware now glance between one another and the two who aren't, in between eating and wondering how the day will play out. Their musing prevents them from getting lost in their Awareness, and therefore from needing to count what they can see in their physical surroundings, but it is unnecessary and not altogether helpful. What will be, will be.

You've all had a sense of Amarilla and Infinity, I observe. *You know that they are entwined souls, one who took the form of a horse in this lifetime, one who still takes the form of a human. In time, you will learn everything they achieved together and why they exist as they do, but for now, trust me that when they say or do something, it's worth taking notice. One thing they have said over and over, and that you will learn is true, is "everything happens as it should". Feel those words. Apply them to everything that has happened in your lives so far. Then, when you feel their truth, let them settle. They will help you greatly, just as they have always helped me. All the while you're doing that, I won't make you count anything.*

They all grin, and Victor replies, *Marvellous.*

'Right, you've all finished eating, so we'll get going, shall we?' I say.

Everyone gets to their feet, Prime with the most care so as to not step on Maverick, who gets to his feet, his tail wagging as he gazes up into Prime's eyes, waiting for him to move so that he can stay by his side.

I lose my heart to my dog as I've done a thousand times before. He spent the night snuggled up beside me, his desire to comfort Prime tempered by his instinct to protect me from the one he so wants to help, yet knows would still try to kill me if he thought he could do it without coming under attack himself. I can easily withstand an assault from Prime and thousands more besides, but to my dog, I am his pack and he will protect me with his life, whether I need him to or not. The honour is all mine and I will never refuse it.

'Follow me, I'll find the easiest path and do my best to trample the undergrowth as much as I can for the rest of you,' I call over my shoulder as I pass between the first two trees.

'You needn't worry about us, inferior, we're bigger, stronger and heavier than you,' Prime says from just behind me.

'Seriously, Prime?' Kudos says from behind him. 'He healed you when he could have let you die, and you're calling him inferior now?'

'It's no matter, call me whatever you like,' I say, stamping down some brambles. 'I can't guarantee I'll always answer, what with being used to the name my parents gave me and all, but I'll give it my best shot.'

You don't have to give in to him, Hero tells me.

I would only be giving in to him if I were trying to win, I reply.

Ace is thoughtful. *And you're not? I mean, you won the four of us over.*

Hmmm, I wouldn't say I did, not really.

The horses did, Adept confirms.

The horses helped you to balance, and they never fail, I tell them all. *It's not about winning and losing because neither exist when you're only playing against yourself.*

And Prime is part of you. He's part of all of us, because we're all part of All That Is, Victor confirms. I feel a shift in the way he and the others view Prime and Kudos, and their budding determination to help them.

I hone my thought so that the teenagers can't sense it. *They're ready.*

We never doubted they would be, Amarilla responds. I sense her and Infinity's total confidence in me. Where once, Infinity would have used her discarnate energy to fuel events, to power them along so that the best outcome was guaranteed, now she is content to observe the person she helped me to be.

We're ready too, my mother tells me. *The children and any adults not strong in their centres are shielded so the energy of The Old can't knock them off balance. Some of them aren't happy about not having access to their Awareness, but they understand.*

How could they not, after Marvel and Justin gave them a demonstration of how funny people look when they're trying to punch one another. There's no way the teenagers want to be drawn into behaving like that.

Welcome to the conversation, Rowena, I tell her, spitting a twig out of my mouth that has refused to bend away with the rest of its branch. *So, it was Marvel and Justin who did the demo? Aren't you the expert on punching?*

I may have been, once. I'm not proud of it, however I'm still well capable should the need arise, a fact that you'd do well to remember.

That's my Ro, do as she says, not as she does, because whatever she does is right, and whatever you do is wrong, Marvel chips in.

It'll be good to see you both, I tell them. *How long has it been, two years?*

Rowena hurls her thoughts at me. *Don't pretend you don't*

know exactly how long it's been, at the same time as knowing instantly what we've been doing during that time, the thoughts of all of the six following your inexpertly made trail, and the immediate future of all of us in Rockwood, so that you're always one step ahead of the two still holding out on you. I also count it more than likely that you know what we're all wearing.

Curse the clouds, Ro, it's a good job the kids are shielded, you nearly blew my eyebrows off, Marvel tells her.

I chuckle. *I've missed you both.*

Anyway, my mother interrupts, *as I was saying, the children are shielded and in their homes, and your welcoming party is standing by and will be assembled between the woods and the village. Oh, why am I telling you when you already know?*

You're just a little edgy, love, my father tells her.

I'm Aware that he is smiling at her as he always does when she strays off-centre. The two of them have run the Rockwood Centre all this time and, like Levitsson, are both experts at helping people to increase both their Awareness and their ability to balance their sixth sense with their other five – yet my mother can still be knocked off-centre herself when it comes to me or my six sisters, and my father loves her for it. I feel him reach out to her with his mind and steady her until she is grounded once more.

See you all in a few hours, I tell them, and feel them turn their attention away from me and towards one another.

See you soon, Will. Tania is at your gran's, so Breeze and I'll be waiting with the others. Lia's thought arrows its way directly to me. Where most need to put power behind their thoughts in order to bypass everyone else's, hers is soft. She's as confident in her ability to reach me as she is in mine to hear her when I'm Aware of so much else. I've missed her.

Let the fun begin, I reply.

By the time we reach the path for which I have been aiming, I have two very angry teenagers behind me.

'What's wrong with your people?' Prime snaps as he pulls away from the last bramble to snag his trousers before stepping onto the path behind me. 'Why don't they burn all of this to the ground? It serves no purpose other than to slow us down, rip our clothes and cut our skin. And why don't you have anything to kill these... biters, as you call them?'

'We do have repellent against them, but those who've been feasting on us this morning are nothing. It's when they start swarming that the repellent comes out. And we don't burn a forest down just because some of it is in our way. The natural world is in balance, and we're a part of that. We accept it and enjoy it, even when it's inconvenient.'

'You enjoy being scratched and bitten?' Kudos says, slapping at a tiny biter on his hand as he steps onto the path.

'Accept it and you'll barely notice it.'

Maverick has found a stick and races delightedly up to Prime, dumping it at his feet and looking expectantly up at him.

'Not sticks, Mav, here, have a pine cone,' I say and lob one into the undergrowth on the other side of the path. He launches himself after it, barking, and there is rustling and snapping as he searches for it. When he jumps back onto the path of decaying leaves, he has a bramble stuck in his fur and trailing after him. His eyes are bright as he throws the cone at my feet, ready to go again. 'When you're as happy as Maverick always is,' I say to Prime and Kudos, 'nothing else matters.' I throw the cone down the path and step on the bramble so it comes away from Maverick as he tears after his new toy.

'He's a dumb animal,' Prime grumbles.

'There's nothing dumb about being eternally happy,' I say and raise a hand to the others as they come into view from between the trees. They step out onto the path, one by one, with wonder on their faces and completely oblivious that their clothes and skin are in far worse shape than Prime's or Kudos's.

Kudos looks all around us. 'I don't see the horses.'

Adept puts a hand on his arm. 'They're finding their own way, like Will said. They know where we are, and they're coming. Don't worry.'

'I bet it's a better way than the inferior just led us,' Prime says.

'If we'd gone with them, it would have been nightfall before we reached Rockwood,' Hero tells him.

'Listen to you being smug because you think you know everything,' Prime says.

Hero's grey skin darkens. 'I'm not being smug, I'm just saying,' he says quietly.

'They're back that way,' Adept says to Kudos, pointing in the opposite direction to that in which I've begun to walk. I throw Maverick's cone ahead of me and he races off in delight.

Prime sniggers. 'Well I could have told him that. There are no hoofprints beneath us, so they haven't already come this way. That means they're behind us.'

'Don't you ever shut up, Prime?' Kudos says.

I stop and turn around just as Prime punches Kudos in the face, then as Kudos steps back in surprise, kicks him hard in the stomach. Kudos lands heavily on the ground and then leaps to his feet with incredible speed... but Victor is faster. He holds a hand to both Prime's and Kudos's chests and says to Kudos, 'Don't. I beat you before, and that was before I could read your mind. Just... don't.' He looks at Prime and says, 'That's the last time you'll ever do anything like that.'

Prime doesn't need to be Aware to recognise that Victor isn't threatening him, but merely stating a fact. He scowls as he considers his options.

Maverick arrives back with his cone and places it very carefully on one of Prime's boots, then gazes up at him hopefully.

Victor looks at Kudos. 'Okay?'

Kudos takes a step back and nods.

Victor turns back to Prime. 'Okay?'

Prime lifts his right nostril and the corner of his mouth into a snarl. Maverick barks. When Prime looks down at him, he nudges the cone on Prime's foot and then looks crestfallen when it rolls off. Prime's snarl disappears and his eyes soften. He looks back up at Victor. He says nothing, but we can all see that the rage has gone out of his eyes. Victor steps away.

'Now we've got all that sorted, we'll go on to the village, shall we?' I pick up Maverick's cone and hurl it behind us all. He barks and races off after it as the rest of us head for Rockwood.

Within a few minutes, the trees begin to thin out and the path becomes lighter. Maverick tears on ahead, his pine cone grasped firmly in his mouth so that his barks of excitement at being nearly home come out as muffled yelps. I grin as I sense who is coming to meet us. A dot in the distance soon becomes a grey dog tearing along the path. When Maverick reaches his brother, he sniffs him all over, his tail wagging as furiously as Breeze's. Then they both race back towards us.

Prime hesitates, then strides to catch back up with me. 'Two of them?' he says.

'Everyone, meet Maverick's brother, Breeze,' I reply as Lia's dog hurls himself at me. I catch him in my arms and laugh as he licks my face. When I put him on the ground, he sniffs Prime's leg briefly before licking his hand, then moves on to greet everyone else in the same way.

'Great,' Prime says. 'Now there are two anus-licking animals among us, and that isn't even counting Victor and Hero.'

'You're just scared you won't be able to resist two of them,'

Ace says acidly. I make a mental note to keep her away from Rowena… but then decide that listening to the two of them exchange verbal punches will be very entertaining.

The two dogs race on ahead and disappear into the distance. I feel Maverick's delight when they reach those waiting for us, and the joy he spreads as he throws himself at each and every one of them before tearing back towards us. Despite himself, I catch a glimpse of the beginnings of a smile on Prime's face as Maverick reappears on the path in front of us.

'Who did you present the pine cone to, Mav?' I ask him when he reaches us. He jumps up and down in front of me, wanting me to throw him another. 'It was Lia, wasn't it? And she was delighted.' I laugh and rub his head. He licks my hand and then trots between Prime and me as if all the excitement of the last few minutes never happened.

We're nearly at Rockwood, I tell Victor, Ace, Hero and Adept. *Some of my family and friends, including two of the Kindred, are waiting for us. For once, I want you to focus most of your attention on your Awareness, otherwise you won't be able to help feeling afraid of the Kindred and your training will take over. The horses know what to do and as long as you stay in your Awareness, you'll know what they need you to do. Okay?*

I sense their anxiety, but also their determination to do as I have requested. *Good on you,* I tell them. *Reach out to the horses in your Awareness now, and stay with them, especially those who helped each of you to balance.*

They need no further encouragement. Their minds stream out into All That Is, to the horses they trust above everyone and everything else.

I step out of the woods and wave to everyone standing there. The sun is behind them, so the teenagers have to squint. They all lift their hands to shield their eyes.

'Welcome to Rockwood,' my mother calls out. 'I'm Katonia, and I would like to introduce you to Jack, Lia, Amarilla, Justin, Rowena, Marvel, Holly, Vickery, Levitsson and Fitt.'

It is a few moments before our eyes have adjusted well enough for us all to make out those to whom my mother has pointed. When Prime and Kudos notice the two Kindred standing smiling at them, the terror that consumes them almost blasts the other four off their feet. I'm proud that the Aware teenagers manage to hang on to their sense of the horses even as their compatriots' fear batters at them, enticing them to let it take them with the two who have dropped into their fighting crouches and are now rapidly advancing on Fitt and Levitsson. They have no weapons but they also have no choice; their training has taken them over and they will fight to the death rather than die without even trying to stay alive.

I weave an energy net around Maverick and feel Lia do the same for Breeze as the two dogs race to trot either side of the fighting duo, staying just out of the teenagers' reach.

There is a thudding noise behind us and then around us, as the horses burst out of the forest.

FIFTEEN

Victor

I can barely stand; my knees are trembling and the world is spinning around me... but then the horses arrive. Where the bay colt was in my mind, he now fills my vision as I watch him and the rest of the herd canter slowly, calmly, to circle the two who are rushing to attack the two Kindred, blocking them, Maverick and Breeze from sight. I feel the terror that still consumes Prime and Kudos, but it isn't so overwhelming, so all-consuming, now that they can't see the object of it. They move to crouch back to back as they weigh up the new threat that now surrounds them.

None of us are immune to the energy created by the horses' synchronised movement. It's as if by moving in a circle all together as they are – their feet all touching the earth in the same order at the same time, their outward breaths leaving their bodies as the last foreleg in the slow, three-time sequence hits the ground, their inward breaths taken as their muscular hind legs begin the next stride – they draw us into their very being... for there is only one of them and one of us.

It seems ridiculous to be standing apart from them and I have no idea why I still am. I take a step towards them with my left foot in the same instant that Will, Ace, Adept and Hero do the same. All of us except Will jump, and Adept giggles... but the horses' movement draws us onward. Just as they move in unison, the five of us walk easily, comfortably towards them, step for step.

Will is slightly ahead of the rest of us, and reaches the horses first. Ember appears from within the herd, slows his canter almost to a halt until Will is astride him, then retakes his place in the synchronised dance of the herd.

I sense Ace hesitate and wonder if she can do what Will just did – but then her reservation is swept away as quickly as it arrived, by the horses passing in front of us. Her brown colt is the first of our horses to appear. Like Ember, he slows his canter down by shortening his strides, the rhythm of his movement never deviating from that of his herd. I sense Will in Ace's Awareness with her, reminding her body what to do... and she is on the colt's back and away. Hero's grey mare arrives next, and a few moments later also rejoins the others with her rider. Next is Adept's chestnut filly. By the time she carries Adept away with the others, I notice that some of Will's family and friends are also now astride some of the horses. I can't remember which is which, but the man with white hair who grins Will's grin at me whilst cantering past astride a chestnut colt, has to be his father.

I sense the bay colt moving to the outside of the horses' circle before I see him, and then I am Aware of nothing else. I take a step forward as he slows in front of me, then rest a hand on the base of his neck and vault up onto his back as if I've done it a thousand times before... which I realise I have. Will is with me in my Awareness, but he didn't need to help me to vault on like he did the others, he didn't ride with me until my body remembered what to do, because he knows I have remembered for myself. The realisation almost knocks me off the colt's back, but like everything else that isn't balance, my shock is carried away by the horses.

Memories that aren't mine flash through my mind – and yet they are mine. I have lived before, many times, and my last incarnation was as one of the Horse-Bonded. I remember knowing the truth of reality then, too, and I remember how it was a Kindred who helped that truth to become part of me. As soon as I felt my oneness with him, we both knew what we needed to do. He killed me and I left my body so that I could incarnate again, soon, when I would be needed. I felt for those who grieved my loss, but maybe they will let me make it up to them when they realise who I am. I glance down at the bay neck in front of me. He has the same black mane as Spider, but his coat is a lighter brown. I smile as memories of the horse who was Bond-Partner to me when I was Shann, come flooding back. He is the horses, all of them, just like they all are. Just like we all are. Just like those who stand in the middle of our circle, crouched down, their backs to one another, are. And soon, they will know it.

Maverick and Breeze lie calmly on either side of Prime and Kudos, waiting as the horses continue to demonstrate what it means to be truly powerful. Muscles ripple as they move with the same calm, beautiful elegance whether they carry riders or not, none of them appearing weaker than any other as the herd energy shifts, as always, to give the youngest and oldest members the strength they need to move with the rest.

As one, the horses lengthen their strides so that their speed increases. Kudos gasps as his fear of the Kindred – of everything – is sucked out and away from him by the vortex of energy swirling above us. He stands up straight and walks towards the circling horses, his trembling hand outstretched to them, desperate to touch those who have welcomed him as part of them. Ember and a bright white filly slow in front of him. I sense Will's unspoken invitation to Kudos to allow him to help, and Kudos nods without hesitation. Within seconds, he is cantering around with the rest of us, Will riding the filly through him, showing him the way as he did for the rest of us.

Where the four of us who went before him struggled to release everything that held us back from being able to balance perfectly, Kudos does it almost immediately, such is the strength of the horses' dance. We all laugh out loud with delight for him as the fear his body has carried for so long is sucked into the vortex, where it cannot help but become all that the horses are, before dissipating into the ether.

I notice that all of Will's family and friends are now astride except for his mother, his wife and the male Kindred. I gaze around until I find the other Kindred, Fitt, a dark brown female with bright green eyes, sitting astride the largest mare in the herd – a grey mare with a black mane and tail – as if she is part of the horse, just like the rest of us. She is the rest of us, I remind myself, and can't help grinning from ear to ear at the beauty of it all.

Prime stares at each of the humans riding, then at Fitt. He frowns and shakes his head at the sight of inclusion that we represent; three races descended from the humans of The Old, who should be enemies currently engaged in battle, but who are instead part of the same massive, powerful, mesmerising beast that encircles him, Maverick and Breeze. His shoulders shake as he drops to his knees and hides his face in his hands, sobbing in terror and confusion. Maverick and Breeze sidle up to him and sit down, leaning into him on either side, letting him know that he isn't as alone as he feels. I feel the hearts of every person present go out to Prime as we feel the fear that was repeatedly beaten into him, lashing around within him. We and the horses pull at it, calling for it to leave him be, but it hangs on to every bone, every muscle, every nerve, every cell within his body, refusing to allow him to trust that which surrounds him, refusing to let him believe that there is any way to feel other than terrified.

Bright white light appears around each of those who were Horse-Bonded, and shoots towards Prime from many directions at once. I smile, knowing what they do and knowing I can do it too. I feel love for my parents, for the horse beneath me, for all of those around me, and push it outside of myself where it becomes light every bit as bright as that which already surrounds Prime. I direct my own flow of light towards him, as do my friends. When Will adds his light to the rest of ours, Prime's fear stands no chance. It is blasted away from every part of his body to which it has held on for so long, and swept away by the horses, all of whom deny its existence so that by the time it rejoins All That Is, it is love.

As the horses slow to a trot and then to walk, Prime lifts an arm and puts it around Maverick, drawing him closer, then lifts the other and encloses Breeze. Both dogs squeeze themselves as close to him as they can, filling his delicate, tentative Awareness with love and reassurance.

The rest of us slide from our horses' backs and follow them to where there is a long line of stone water troughs. We wash them down and when they have drunk their fill, they wander off to graze with the others, surrounding Prime as he still kneels with Maverick and Breeze.

The rest of us look around at one another, none of us able to find anything to say. Even those who were Horse-Bonded are deeply moved by that in which we have just been included by the horses, in their quest to bring balance where it is needed.

I find that I now recognise Rowena, Jack, Vickery, Marvel,

Holly, Justin and Amarilla as the friends they were to me... then my heart lurches as I remember that Justin was my best friend, and Rowena more than a friend. I skim my attention over them so as not to alert them to who I am; I feel the need to reconcile everything I now know for myself, before addressing it with them.

Will's thought is the tiniest sliver as it reaches my mind. *This is how to bury something when necessary.* He takes my memories of being Shann and pulls them behind my experiences in this life so far, which are so much more prominent in my mind. *If anyone is determined to go looking, you'll need to bury them deeper, but that should do for now. I understand why you want some time to sort it all out in your mind, but as you come to know your old friends in your Awareness, you'll learn that they aren't who they were when you knew them before. They don't need protecting.*

Thanks, Will.

I feel eyes on me and meet the gaze of Amarilla... and Infinity, for I know as soon as I see them that it is Infinity's pale blue eyes that look out at me from behind Amarilla's darker blue ones. They know; Infinity is a horse and the horses know everything in every instant.

Your secret is safe with me – it takes only a split second for me to come to terms with the fact that their use of the word "me" when referring to themselves has the same meaning as, and is interchangeable with, "us" – *however Will's counsel is sound.*

I grin delightedly at their complete lack of convention and normality.

That grin is Shann's, however, they continue. *Now that you have remembered yourself in your entirety, he is as much a part of you as we are of one another. Even if you want to, you will not be able to hide who you were for long.*

Why has this...

Happened to you? Amarilla interrupts as she wanders over to me, smiling, her hand held out for me to shake. *Shann was as open as it was possible for one of his time to be. He sensed the truth of reality from the moment he was born, and as a result, never took life too seriously. His openness, his confidence, his quickness to accept whatever presented itself to him, his ability to lift everyone around him, are much more prominent in you now that you remember your life as him. You will advance even more rapidly than his being part of you has ensured so far, and you will take your friends with you. Your people need you, Victor, all six of you.*

I shake her hand as gently as I can, for it is tiny, her fingers barely extending past my palm. *Yes, I guess they do.*

'Okay, well, lovely as this has all been, I think we need to get you lot bathed, fed, and dressed in clothes that aren't hanging off you in shreds,' Rowena says, both hands in the air for attention. 'What were you thinking, Will? Dragging them through the middle of the forest?' She holds a hand up to him as he opens his mouth to reply. 'Never mind.' She looks around at the five of us newcomers still standing, her eyes, every bit as dark as I remember, lingering on me in a glare as I chuckle at her all-too-familiar bossiness, before moving on to Adept and then Ace. 'Hmmm, you'll have to let me know if your new clothes need any alterations, but I think I've got most of you right.'

'Um, new clothes?' Adept says.

'Yes, I've made a selection for you all,' Rowena replies. 'As soon as you decide where you'll be staying, I'll have them sent to your lodgings.'

'Just so we're clear, I take it by "having them sent", you mean you'll order me to deliver them?' Marvel says. I can sense that he adores Rowena as much as she adores him and I'm glad.

'Does that mean I get my kitchen table back?' Justin says.

Rowena glares at both of them, who look at one another and grin.

'Ro, you can take up as much of the table, in fact of our house as you want, and you know it, don't waste a glare on Justin,' Amarilla says with a fond look at the man who was my best friend, and who has been her partner for the almost thirty years it has been since I was last with them both in person. I chuckle to myself. I can't wait to remind him that I told him all he had to do to have the relationship with her that he wanted, was be patient.

'So... we get to decide where we'll be staying?' I say. 'Ah, I see, we decide using our Awareness. Okay, I'll go with Will and Lia then, if that's okay.' I know Prime will want to stay with Maverick and Breeze, and I think he might also need me. Shann. Whoever.

Will grins at me and nods. *You'll both be very welcome.*

Lia smiles and comes to stand in front of me, taking both of my hands in hers. Like Amarilla's, her hands are so small that she barely grasps the edge and little fingers of my own. 'You'll be very welcome in our home. I'm afraid our daughter is noisy though, it might not be a very restful stay.'

I grin. 'I can't wait to meet her. Thank you, I'm looking forward to my time here in Rockwood.'

'Whoever chooses Amarilla and Justin, just be mindful that you'll also be choosing to share with me and the fountain of all knowledge that is Rowena,' Marvel calls out.

'They're all Aware now, Marvel, they're struggling to be anything other than mindful,' Rowena retorts.

Marvel lifts both hands and points them to Rowena. 'I rest my case.'

Ace flicks a glance at me, but is Aware of the reason I've chosen to stay with Will and Lia. She looks at Rowena, Marvel,

Amarilla and Justin in turn. 'I'd like to stay with you all, please.'
She receives four warm smiles by way of reply.

Hero looks at Holly. 'I'll come and stay with you, if that's
okay?' Holly puts an arm around his waist and guides him
enthusiastically towards the cottage she explains that she shares
with Vickery. Vickery follows them both, grinning at her partner's
enthusiasm.

Adept chooses to stay with Katonia and Jack, and is ushered
off towards the grey stone buildings we can see in the distance,
with Katonia telling her that she will be staying in Will's old
room.

Kudos surprises me by asking to stay with Levitsson,
especially since he is Aware that Fitt is already staying with him;
less than half an hour after he was intent on killing the two
Kindred, his fear of them has been so quickly replaced by
curiosity and a desire for friendship, I can't quite reconcile it in
my mind.

I look over to where the horses are grazing peacefully. They
reached me the first time I looked closely at them, but even so, I
had absolutely no idea of the extent of their influence, their
capability and their power. My people won't know what has hit
them.

Will speaks quietly to me as the others pass us by on their way
to Rockwood, all chatting animatedly. 'Don't forget that with each
increase in status from Disposable to Regular to Elite, your people
are exponentially more fearful and paranoid. You saw what it took
to reach Prime, the most fearful of the six of you. The Elite won't
give up everything they hold dear without the fight they'll be sure
is necessary. We'll help those we can help more easily, first.'

'My parents,' I say as we stand watching two of the horses
wander up to Prime. They sniff him all over as his canine
guardians press against him. The dogs hold him together

physically while the horses surround his mind, ensuring it doesn't fragment as he tries to make sense of who he is now that the part of him which has always been so dominant, has gone.

'It won't be easy, but you'll get them out, Victor, as long as you can remain centred. If you can't, you'll be swept away by everything that will fill your Awareness once you're back in the city.'

'I understand. I'll make it my priority alongside dodging Rowena and Justin.'

Will grins. 'It's true, they'll be the next to recognise you, but like I said, it won't be a problem; just a distraction you don't need at the moment.'

Lia says, 'I'll go back and fetch Tania from your gran's, Will, then I'll pick up Victor's and Prime's new clothes from Amarilla's cottage, to save Marvel a job. See you back at home soon?'

Will glances at Prime. 'I'm not sure about soon, but yes, we'll see you back there.'

Will and I sit down where we are, so as to give Prime space while the horses and dogs help him. I ask Will about his friendship with Jonus, and he transfers so much information about the friend who is in the past, still helping others to adjust to being Horse-Bonded, that I almost lose myself... almost. I count the threads of fabric hanging from my shirt. I count the scratches on my legs. I count the blades of grass amongst which we sit – anything to keep myself centred. Where before I believed my parents' survival depended on me returning to Supreme City with a coherent and helpful report, I now know it depends not on my physical abilities, but on those of my mind.

I'm fascinated by Jonus's people. Where my ancestors hid

underground, creating what they believed to be a safe haven in which they and their descendants could survive for as long as necessary, Jonus and the other ancestors of The New – the Ancients, as they are called by Will's people – struck out into the wilderness, risking death from starvation, animal attacks, disease, poisoning from unfamiliar food sources, and exposure to the elements. My ancestors believed their survival to be dependent on their physical circumstances, and bred a people even less mentally stable than they were. Jonus and the Ancients felt that their survival depended less on being physically safe and more on their freedom to live as members of the natural world; as such, they founded a way of living that has resulted in a level of mental stability that my people are incapable of even recognising, let alone comprehending.

When I witness the Ancients learning how to perform the Skills, I stop counting, only continuing when Will gives me a friendly nudge.

'That's how you healed me and Prime,' I say. 'But the Ancients sang out loud. You didn't sing, we were standing right next to you, we'd have heard you.'

Will chuckles. 'The Skills have moved on since Jonus's time, thanks to my aunt and her Bond-Partner.'

I sense him focus his attention on a blade of grass by my boot. He extends a tendril of himself out to it and resonates with it until he becomes it. Then he draws everything it needs from the soil, the air and the sun, and fuels its growth with his intention. I watch, fascinated, as it grows up and around my foot.

'Tree-singing, without the singing,' he says. Amarilla learnt how to do the singing Skills silently when Fitt's Bond-Partner, Flame, needed healing and Amarilla was too far away to be able to reach the horse with her voice.'

'She learnt how to do that? What, just spontaneously?'

'Adam helped her. Remember him?'

I search both my memory and my Awareness. 'Adam, who was bonded to Peace. They helped the ghosts who terrified my people for centuries, to move on.' I see them in my mind, an old man and a huge brown and white horse. 'I knew them both when I was Shann and they were alive. I had no idea what they were doing when they weren't at The Gathering.'

'You didn't know much of what they were doing when they were,' Will says with a chuckle. 'Adam recognised Amarilla and Infinity as the catalysts for change they were, just like you did, but unlike you, he paid close attention to everything they said and did. When Infinity announced that the Skills could be performed by everyone, he took it on board and within days was quietly experimenting with all of the Skills – and advancing them. He had passed on by the time Amarilla needed to do as he had done, but he was there to give her the information she needed.'

'He's always been there for her. He's always been there for all of you,' I murmur as I absorb everything Will knows about Adam – which, Will being Will, is everything. 'For all of us.'

Will nudges me. 'There's movement over there.'

The horses are walking away from Prime, and both dogs are getting to their feet. Maverick and Breeze both shake themselves from head to tail, then watch Prime as slowly, shakily, he stands up. Maverick jumps up and gently rests his front paws on Prime's stomach, and Prime strokes him... and smiles.

'Your eyebrows have nearly disappeared into your hairline,' whispers Will.

'He's never smiled before. Never,' I whisper back. 'It feels strange to him. Why do I find myself wanting to give him a hug? We've hated each other since we were little. And why are we whispering?'

Because... you think... I can't hear you. Prime's thought is as shaky as his legs, which wobble even more when I grin in response. *You... can... hear... me?*

Will and I jog to his side and each take one of his arms.

'Not helpful at the moment, Mav,' Will tells his dog as he leaps up and down in delight, trying to lick Will's face. Maverick barks and races around and around us in a circle, his eyes bright, ears pricked and tail held gaily aloft. Breeze bounces over to him and they wrestle, then tear off together, barking as they race for home.

Yes, we can hear you, Prime. I'd ask how you're feeling, but I can sense you feel like you've been tumbled around in a washing machine and squeezed out to dry. It does get better, I tell him.

Your... thoughts... hurt... my head.

'Sorry. Is this better?'

He nods. 'How could our people have got it so wrong?' he says, his voice hoarse.

'There's no such thing as right and wrong, not really,' Will replies. 'When you're ready to talk about that further, let me know. I wouldn't risk discussing it with Amarilla; if she and Infinity get started, you'll wish they hadn't. Your people are just playing out what they need to in order to learn from it, that's all. We've all been there at some point in our souls' lives.'

Prime nods. 'I can feel that's true, but how can it be?' His knees buckle.

'Let's worry about that another day,' I say. 'The others have all chosen who they want to stay with. What about you? What do you want to do?'

He smiles again, and it's every bit as unsettling as it was the last time. 'Don't pretend you don't already know. I'm like you now, remember? I know what you're thinking. We'll get back to Will's shall we?'

I grin at him. 'Sure.'

'But first...' I feel his uncertainty and the echo of the pain that sustained him for so long; that influenced his posture, the way his body functioned, the way he thought and felt. Now that it has fled, he is left like the toddler he was when it was first inflicted on him. He reaches for the horses to gain the strength he needs to say, 'You, er, you mentioned a hug?'

I can't bear the look in his eyes, so I don't hesitate. I pull him into a hug my father would be proud of, slapping his back firmly in brotherly solidarity, then more softly as I feel the desperation with which he hugs me back. I worry that he's broken, but then I sense the horses' energy still filtering around his mind and body, sustaining him where before he was held together by fear. I should have known. He just needs rest.

'Come on, can you walk if Will and I hold you up?'

Prime lets go of me and glances at Will. 'This little stick of a man, hold me up? What are you, nuts?' he says, and grins uncertainly.

Will and I laugh, and Will says, 'I'm stronger than I look.'

'You're not even kidding,' Prime says as he allows Will and me to place his arms over our shoulders and begins to stagger towards the village. 'Oh, you're not serious.' He and I both watch in amazement as the stone water troughs – ten of them – float through the air next to us. 'You're doing that, I can feel it, I just can't... make... sense... of... how.'

'Don't try,' I advise him. 'He's rock-singing without the singing. Trust me, your mind is going to need a whole lot of rest before it's ready to get itself around the Skills.'

Prime snorts. 'He can heal, he can move stuff, he can disable weapons, all without saying anything or even moving, and I'm sensing we'll be able to do all those things too? Our people won't know what's hit them.' His knees buckle again as he begins to laugh, and I stumble as I try to keep him upright. Will, however, walks on beside him as if he isn't taking any extra weight at all. Because he isn't, I realise. He's not only moving the troughs with his mind, he's using it to support Prime.

Prime picks up on my realisation. 'Of course he is,' he says. 'The rest of the world is the opposite of what we thought, why should that be any different?' He laughs even harder when Will and I laugh with him.

SIXTEEN

Will

_I_t's good to hear the lads laughing, and to feel the effect it has on them; Prime's arms rest easily on my and Victor's shoulders as if he hasn't been terrified of human contact his whole life, and the two chat as the friends they should always have been.

When we reach the cobbles of Rockwood, Maverick and Breeze hurl themselves at us in welcome, full of joy at having just done the same to Lia and Tania. Prime feels no shame at swaying on his feet as he relinquishes my and Victor's support and crouches in order to hug and stroke both dogs. Victor moves to stand behind Prime, ready to lean into him if he overbalances backward, but he isn't needed; Maverick's and Breeze's attentions impart a boost of energy to Prime that gives him the strength he needs.

When he stands upright again, he looks over his shoulder at the pasture closest to the village, where the horses are now settling down to graze. I lower the water troughs at intervals around the edge of the meadow, knowing my sisters, mother and grandfather are more than strong enough Rock-Singers to be able to move them to the cottages for easy filling when necessary.

We all jump as shrieks of excitement emanate from the nearest cottages. A front door is flung open and three children tear out, followed by their mother, who calls after them, 'Slowly, you know the horses won't appreciate you running at them, screaming.' She glances at me. 'Will, I'm sorry, Katonia just let us know it was okay to lift the shields around the children. As soon as we did, obviously they were Aware that the horses are here.' She notices Prime and Victor and smiles. 'Welcome, you two, we've all been looking forward to having you and your friends staying here with us.'

The lads just stand and stare at Sertha while her children run past them as if they don't exist.

Smile back and say hi, I tell them.

'Er, hi,' Prime manages to say.

Victor rallies. 'Hi, Sertha, and thanks. It probably doesn't look like it, but we're glad to be here, it's just that everything's so different from what we're used to, so unexpected and so strange, we don't really know what to do with ourselves. Please excuse us.'

Prime looks at Victor as though he's never seen him before as he both senses Shann's influence, and sees it in the lopsided grin Victor now wears.

Victor nods towards Prime. 'Case in point,' he tells Sertha, and winks. I find it hard not to laugh.

Sertha smiles. 'I completely understand. Once you've had a chance to settle, everything will seem easier.' She looks at her rapidly retreating children and says, 'I'm sorry to rush off, but I'd better go and supervise them, I'll see you around.' She hurries off, shouting, 'Kall, Cynthia, Ty, calmly, now...'

More shrieking drowns out her cries as more children and their parents hurry out of their homes, many of them accompanied by dogs, and race towards the horses, calling out greetings as they pass us. Prime and Victor watch them all with fascination and astonishment.

I chuckle. 'I did warn you that you wouldn't be the biggest cause of excitement when we got here.'

'I can feel their happiness,' Prime says faintly, 'actually feel it, as if it's mine, which is beyond weird because I've never even felt it for myself before.'

'I'd tell you to start counting them like I am, but I don't think you have the wherewithal,' Victor says with a grin. 'You need to sleep.'

Prime looks back to where the villagers are now wandering amongst the horses. He senses their Awareness of how they need to be in order for the horses to find them acceptable company, and watches them walking slowly and calmly, even the children who only moments before were so full of excitement. If any of them are approached by a horse, they stand still and allow themselves to be sniffed, then continue walking when the horse moves away. Some of them sit down, unwilling to relinquish the feeling of being part of the herd – of just being.

'Why are the horses here with us?' Prime says. 'They've helped us all to be Aware, to know who we really are, so why are they still here? Why don't they go back to where all the other horses are, above the city?'

'They're here because we're here,' Victor says. 'We're no longer part of the problem, we're part of the solution.'

Prime stares at him as he once again puts his arms around his friend's and my shoulders. 'What's happened to you? We're all different, I know that, but you even look different, and it's like you're sure of yourself in this strange world in a way you have no right to be. Not this quickly.'

'I just remembered a lot of stuff when we rode the horses just now.'

'When you all rode them, you mean,' Prime says and trips on a raised cobblestone.

'They gave you a day's grace, Prime, don't count on them giving you any more than that,' I say, steadying him with a combination of tissue-singing to influence his muscles, and by transferring some of my energy to him in the way of the herd.

They want me to ride, like you guys did? He reaches out to the horses, searching for any hint that it is true.

They drew you to Awareness, but you will need to achieve perfect balance for that Awareness to be complete, I tell him. *You will only find your way to absolute balance by riding a horse, for only they can show you where your blocks are, and allow you to sense when you have bypassed them all. When you have nothing blocking you from perfect balance, there'll be nothing blocking you from any part of your Awareness. It's a long time since horses have been willing to help us in this way, and the fact they're doing it now reflects the severity of the situation.*

'We need to be completely Aware and balanced, because our people are the complete opposite,' Victor breathes. 'We're their counterbalance.' *But aren't you and your people already that? Why do you need us?*

Because you're part of the collective consciousness of Supreme City, within the collective consciousness of humans as a whole. Many of your people have felt the pull from the rest of us to step aside from their fear and know of their connection to everything, but more have not. That will begin to change now that some of their own have joined the pull, and when they see what you are capable of, it will change even more. The horses have made you into their secret weapons in the fight for balance. Ironic, isn't it? 'Here we are, oh look, Tania's coming to welcome you.'

Maverick and Breeze jump the waist-high gate that separates the cobbled front path to our home from the street, and run to where Lia has put my daughter down just beyond the front door. Tania puts a hand against Breeze's and Maverick's sides to support herself, and waddles down the path to meet the three of us, chattering away to the dogs in her language of squeaks and gurgles. She puts her hands up to me and I lean over the gate and pick her up.

'Hey, little one, did you miss me and Maverick? Huh?' I say and kiss her on the cheek as I turn her to the lads. 'Say hi to Victor and Prime.'

Without knowing she's doing it, she senses which of the two is the more comfortable in his skin and reaches a pudgy hand to Victor, who smiles and offers her his little finger. She grasps it in both of her tiny hands, and gurgles.

'Look at you, with your pink skin where your dad's is brown and your mum's even darker. You're all different colours, here, aren't you?' Victor says as if he's complimenting her on the dress Lia has put on her. He lifts his finger up and down and she giggles as her hands go up and down with it. She lets go and reaches for him. His eyes widen as he looks to me for guidance.

'Here you go, you'll learn soon enough that what Tania wants, Tania gets, if we want any peace around here,' I say, handing my daughter to Victor. She wraps her arms around his neck and cuddles into him like she does with the dogs when she senses they won't mind.

'She's completely unafraid, isn't she? I can feel it,' Victor says. 'I look so different from you, from everyone here, but she's not even the tiniest bit afraid.'

'We're all different colours, sizes and shapes, but that's not the only reason she isn't afraid of you.'

'She's Aware we're friendly,' Prime confirms, bending over

and holding on to the gate in order to stay on his feet. 'At her age? How old is she?'

'Nearly eleven months. She knows your intentions better than you do. She doesn't know she knows, and she doesn't know how to be any different.'

'That's a lot of knowing,' Lia says, holding a hand out for Prime to take so that she can open the gate, 'and meanwhile, this poor lad is exhausted beyond his ability to stand. Welcome, Prime, Victor, to our home. Come on, Prime, I'll show you to the bathroom where there's a bath waiting for you, then you can get some sleep.'

Prime hesitates to take my wife's hand. 'Lia's also stronger than she looks,' I tell him, 'but more importantly, she's her daughter's mother. It's a lot easier to just do as she says.'

Lia smiles up at Prime. 'He's not wrong. Take my hand.'

Prime does as he is told and his mouth drops open as he finds he barely needs to lean on Lia at all as she holds him up with her mind and energy in the same way I did. I wave Victor through the gate in front of me and follow him and my daughter up the path, sticking my tongue out at Tania as she watches me over Victor's shoulder.

It is more than an hour before Victor comes downstairs to where Lia and I are just sitting down for lunch.

'So, no machines anywhere, huh?' he says.

'No machines,' Lia confirms. 'It feels weird to you, us living like this.'

Victor grins his new lopsided grin, his purple eyes sparkling mischievously. 'Conversations go so much quicker when we don't need to tell each other how we feel, don't they? Yes, it feels weird.

Your way of life seems so primitive compared with how I've grown up, but I know it's far from it, and it's so... peaceful.'

Lia smiles and points to a chair. 'Sit yourself down, I've put you opposite Tania so you're as protected as you can be from the food she likes to fling about, but it's no guarantee I'm afraid. How do your new clothes feel?'

Victor sits down and rubs his hands down the front of his pale blue shirt, then down onto his beige trousers. 'Amazing. In the city, we're all given the same clothes in the same synthetic fabric, from when we're born to when we die, so we never think about it – just like with the food, I guess. But this fabric is so soft, I can hardly feel it, and so cool. It feels weird to not be wearing brown or green.'

Lia nods. 'That was intentional. Rowena was determined you would feel like the people of The New that you are now, and not, well, you know.'

Victor grins Shann's grin again. 'I know, so we wouldn't feel like the arrogant, aggressive, paranoid people we used to be. Don't worry, no offence taken.'

Lia looks at me and nods towards Victor. 'Our guest thinks I'm worried about causing offence.'

I shake my head and sigh. 'Victor, this is the time to use your Awareness to full effect. You may have Shann's experiences to draw on, but our people have moved on a lot since he passed.'

He laughs. 'My mistake. So, it isn't just you who takes everything anyone says as if it isn't personal. Got it. Ah, and now I understand why you think Rowena and Justin will accept who I am without too much grief.' He stops laughing. 'Rowena made all of the new clothes on my bed – all of our new clothes – herself? By hand? You don't do everything using the power of the mind, then?'

I chuckle. 'Rowena certainly designed and cut your new

clothes, but she'll have enlisted everyone capable of holding a needle, in order to get them ready in time. I don't envy any of them, she's bossy and a perfectionist. I doubt Prime is the only one sleeping off his exhaustion.'

'So, you don't make clothes using your mind, and okay, I see now, you make things from wood with your hands too. And you enjoy it.'

Lia passes him a plate. 'We prepare food by hand too. There are those of us more drawn to create with our minds and those happier working with our hands. Some are equally happy doing both, and both ways of working are valid and necessary. When we create something with love and positive intention, it makes a difference, as I know you've already found out. I'm hoping you're going to enjoy your meal; Will let me know that you enjoyed his grandmother's vegetable pie, so I made one similar, only also containing cheese, and those are chips, which are fried strips of potato.'

Victor's stomach rumbles loudly and Tania laughs at the noise. His grey skin darkens. 'Sorry, I'm not used to looking forward to eating. This smells amazing. I'm sorry for Prime that he's missing it, but he was snoring loudly enough to make the walls shake when I was dressing after my bath, so I guess he's where he needs to be.' He puts a forkful of pie in his mouth and then manages to say while chewing it, 'Seriously, I think all we need to do is take a load of this and leave it by the lift to bring my people around. As soon as the smell of it wafts down, they'll be pouring above ground and begging you to let them join you.'

Lia smiles. 'It would be lovely if it were that easy, wouldn't it?' She looks directly at Victor. 'I'm sorry about what has happened to your parents. They're good people.'

Victor stops chewing for a moment. 'Yes, they are.' He looks at us both, his eyes bright with optimism. 'And they're going to love it here once I've got them out.' He smiles and cuts himself a huge forkful of pie, then occupies himself with trying to get it into his mouth.

Lia glances at me, her thought precisely and expertly targeted so it only reaches me. *He's everything you said he would be.*

He is. The others are strong enough too, they just need the time to get themselves centred before everything they are now is put to the test. We have just seven days before they're expected back at the city.

Her nod is barely perceptible. *You're here, the horses are here and the Horse-Bonded are here. Seven days is plenty.*

The days fly past. By the end of their first full day in Rockwood, Prime has ridden his way to perfect balance, and by the end of the second, all six of the teenagers, with nothing to occupy them other than the exercises given to them by their mentors, are doing well at finding their centres and remaining within them for short periods of time.

Lia and I mentor Victor and Prime between us with Tania's help; our young daughter's effortless and unconscious ability to constantly be herself whilst reacting to everything in her Awareness is both a reminder to the two of them, and an unintentional challenge that drives them both to ever more vigilance over themselves.

Lia balances out my tendency to push the lads to the maximum of their ability, with her softer tool of distraction. When she senses that Victor is caught up in his Awareness of Ace and how she is faring with Rowena as her mentor, my wife asks him to tell her all about Supreme City's custom of having spouses chosen for one another by those of the status above. Then she gets him to explain how he feels about now having the choice for himself, and about the fact that the partner he has chosen is so like her mentor. I am in awe of my wife's skill as Victor settles into a balance of that of which he is Aware and that about which he knows, without even realising it.

When Lia senses Prime trying – and failing – to relate the behaviour of those they meet as they wander the streets of Rockwood, to his previous experience of people, she gets him to reach out in his Awareness to everyone whose behaviour confuses him. His smiles come quicker and his frowns less frequent as he learns to use both his Awareness and his five senses when people smile, wave or stop to speak to him, so that instantly, he understands both their words and the intentions behind them.

It is always heartwarming when the teenagers meet each other when out and about in the village or when they are with the horses. They run to one another and hug, smiling and laughing as they recount verbally or in their Awareness – usually both – to one another everything they're learning. Often, they compare their abilities with the Skills, and there is always excitement as they egg each other on to even greater heights.

Adept has found a love for tree-singing and weather-singing. She is often out in the fields, assisting the farmers with crop growth and encouraging favourable conditions. My mother or father are always close by, reminding her to identify all of the crops with which she's interacting, and recite their uses, so that she remains centred.

Hero is becoming an avid Herbalist and enjoys Vickery's teaching. He regales the others at every opportunity with all the herbs he can recognise, and their uses, until they beg him to stop.

Ace puts most of her energy into glass-singing, and is soon at work creating ornaments of horses that the villagers of Rockwood display enthusiastically in their front windows for all to see as they pass.

Kudos absorbs more and more of Levitsson's humour and enthusiasm for life as the days go by, and is loud and passionate about his favoured Skill of rock-singing.

Like their friends, Prime and Victor develop ability in all of the Skills, but both lads prefer to focus on bone-singing and tissue-singing. Where Prime is fascinated at his ability to heal, Victor is several steps ahead. Having sensed Lia and me supporting Prime when he could barely walk, he already sees how to use the ability to help his parents. I feel his intensity whenever he asks me to demonstrate again exactly what we did. As soon as he can tune a tendril of his energy in with the muscles of my legs, he practices using his intention to affect the way they operate whilst explaining to me exactly what he's doing, so that he remains centred. When he can both heal injuries I create, and support my muscles beyond their natural endurance, I turn his attention to perfecting the other Skills he will need on his return to Supreme City.

It is when our charges are with the horses that I and the other mentors can take a break from our vigilance over them, and relax. The teenagers all know that it is never they who decide when they will ride. When the horses sense that any of them, in their efforts to remain centred, are either doing the opposite or straining themselves, they call the teenagers to them and within minutes, the riders are smiling, the lines of concentration gone from their foreheads, the tension in their stomachs released, their shoulders relaxed and comfortable.

During the evening of the fifth day of their stay, all six are called by the horses at once. The sun is low in the cloudless sky, the heat with which it has pounded us all day finally lessening as the trees in the distance finally shelter us from its glare.

Lia and I sit in the grass, taking it in turns to tickle Tania behind her ears with wild flowers, while Prime and Victor stand stroking the horses who have drawn them here – Victor as always by the bay colt, Prime by the elderly brown mare who helped him to reach perfect balance. Tania shrieks delightedly and tries to grab the flowers, which we let her do, only to have another one ready with which to tickle her.

'At least she had a good sleep earlier when it was really hot,' Lia says, 'otherwise she'd be screaming by now.'

'She'd be wanting to scream by now, you mean,' I reply. 'You'd have her in an energy net before either of us could blink, and she'd be fast asleep, despite the racket those two are making.' Tania jumps at a particularly high-pitched bark by Breeze, as he and Maverick take it in turns to chase one another. She giggles and then shrieks as I tickle her again.

'Nothing like two dogs and a toddler to break the peace of an otherwise tranquil summer evening, is there?' Rowena calls out with a wave as she, Amarilla, Marvel and Justin part from Ace, and make their way over to us.

'Or the shouting of a middle-aged woman,' Marvel tells her, catching Maverick in his arms and laughing as my dog licks his nose.

'As soon as the brown colt called to Ace, we sensed you were here, hope you don't mind,' Amarilla says, knowing full well we don't. She nods to where all three teenagers are now mounted. 'Aren't they great?'

I nod. 'They are. Not that it's a surprise; I pay far more attention than I should to what goes on in your house, largely due to the Rowena and Ace situation.'

'Solely due to the Rowena and Ace situation, as we're all very well Aware,' Justin says with a grin.

Rowena plops herself down beside me and holds her arms out

to Tania, who falls into them, gurgling. 'I'm glad to be of such an amusement to you all, but I'll remind you, it was Ace who chose to come and live with us.'

'And you who chose to mentor her as soon as she did,' Justin says. 'I'm not going to pretend my home is a harmonious place to be at the moment, but I have to admit, it's highly amusing witnessing Rowena mentoring a teenage version of herself.'

Rowena scrapes a hand through her long, thick hair, more grey than black now. Her eyes, dark as ever, flash with feigned anger. 'She's nowhere near as feisty as I was, you take that back, Jus.'

'I see we're not a moment too late in witnessing the pretend arguments you lot still insist on having,' Levitsson says. We all turn and grin at him, Fitt, Holly and Vickery as they sit down behind us while Kudos and Hero join the other three.

We watch in silence as the five exhausted teenagers ride towards the rejuvenation of their bodies and minds.

'It's hard not to be reminded of ourselves, isn't it,' Marvel says softly. He reaches out to Broad, his Bond-Partner who is always with him in mind and spirit as he no longer is in body, and remembers what it was to ride the horse he loved so much. 'They're luckier than they know.'

'Luck does not exist,' Infinity reminds him. 'Everything is as it should be.'

We all nod. It isn't new counsel from Amarilla's Bond-Partner, but it is as relevant as it ever was.

'As such,' Levitsson says cheerfully, 'here are the last few who should be here.'

I raise a hand to welcome my parents, who, by the time they make it past Maverick and Breeze, find Tania standing unsteadily before them. My mother sweeps her up in her arms and holds her up in the air, then swings her around as she knows my daughter loves.

'This is quite the meeting,' my father says. 'I don't know where to look – at the six of them down there,' he nods to where Adept has just vaulted on to the chestnut filly's back, 'at Ember,' he nods to where the most recent incarnation of his Bond-Partner stands watching the members of his herd being ridden, 'or at you lot.'

'If you want to join those of us missing our Bond-Partners, I'd go for Ember,' Marvel says. 'If not, then I'd say you can't go wrong with us lot, we're far more attractive than those youngsters, for all their incredible eyes and stomach-churning muscles.'

Jack chuckles. 'The youngsters it is. Their horses haven't all called their riders here at the same time by chance. What's coming, Will?'

'The horses are helping them to remember everything they've grown to be in the last few days, because they've now been away from Supreme City for eight days. They're expected back first thing the day after tomorrow, so whoever is going will need to leave tomorrow. It's time for them to decide the roles they'll play in the days to come.'

Fitt's raspy voice carries from behind me. 'Which you already know, but keep hidden from us. I understand. We all have our lives to live.'

Holly giggles. 'Nicely done, Fitt; Rowena meltdown averted.'

'Why is it always me who's got at?' Rowena retorts. 'You all want to know what's going to happen as much as I do. Except you, Am, I know you'll already know too.'

'We're just better at accepting it isn't going to happen,' Marvel says.

'No, we just don't waste energy pretending it's an issue,' Levitsson says.

'I forgot you were here,' Rowena says and laughs. 'Always around to keep us all honest, aren't you, Levitsson?'

'Can you come and live with Ro and me when we go home, Levitsson?' Marvel says. 'I know you'll be missed around here, but seriously, you'd make my life so much easier.'

'I would take away your whole reason for conversing,' Levitsson replies and we all laugh.

'They're dismounting,' Katonia says, and Tania gurgles in agreement from her lap. 'How do you want to do this, Will?'

I shift back a little and turn so I can see everyone sitting in two rows to the side of me. 'Your charges will need your approval and your support, so give it, whatever they choose to do. It'll be important to them.'

Everyone nods and watches as the teenagers make their way over to us.

SEVENTEEN

Victor

I have been having the time of my life. I've felt guilty at times, and have reached out for my parents in my Awareness, always wishing they could hear me while I tell them about my day – everything I've learnt, everyone I've met, how the six of us who left Supreme City what feels like years ago are all such good friends, and how Ace and I have become so much more than that. I never expected to even like my future spouse, let alone love her. I know my parents will be so happy for me when I tell them that my life partner and I have chosen one another ourselves, and that we'll never live the lives into which we were born. Never. It's not even a half-life compared to the one we've been offered by the horses and the people of Rockwood.

My friends and I are all so different from the people we were. I glance around at the others as we ride the horses who, for the first time since we arrived here, have called all of us to ride together. Where once we would all have been stealing sly glances at one another whilst learning to fight – trying to assess who was the biggest threat, who was learning new moves that could defeat us and who were easy targets – now we openly watch one another with smiles on our faces, encouraging and congratulating each other whilst riding as one. Some of us are more centred than others, some favour Skills that manipulate the elements while others favour Skills that heal the body; we're all different, but we all work together, each a vital part of the team that will heal our people. And all because of the wondrous, heart-stoppingly beautiful horses who carry us willingly and effortlessly as they empower us, encourage us and remind us yet again of who we are within ourselves and to one another.

When the horses finally come to a halt, I grin as Kudos lands beside Hero and instantly reaches a hand up to ruffle his friend's hair, teasing him about the fact that Hero's eyes searched for Adept as soon as his feet touched the ground. Adept smiles, not looking at Hero, but Aware of his admiration as she silently sings the breeze that cools the horses and all of us. I wave my thanks to her and then turn to grin at Ace who smiles back at me while drinking in all of the details of my bay colt, ready to sing his likeness out of glass for me in the morning. Prime smiles to himself, his hand resting against the neck of the brown mare whom he loves as he's never loved anyone or anything before.

We all follow our horses to the troughs and wash them down. When they wander off to graze, Adept says, 'How did we ever get this lucky?'

'Luck doesn't exist. Everything happens as it should. Infinity tells me that repeatedly,' Ace says.

I wink at her and Kudos pretends to vomit.

'We're wanted up there,' Prime points to the mound on which our mentors all sit, watching us. They're eerily still and we all sense their anticipation.

'I can't pick up from them what it's about. Can any of you?' Ace says.

We all shake our heads. 'They're hiding it, but I think we can all guess,' Kudos says.

'We'd best get up there then, hadn't we?' I say and with a last, longing look at the bay colt, I lead the way to where Will, Lia and the others are sitting.

Maverick and Breeze come belting across the pasture to meet us, greeting each of us in turn before settling to trot at Prime's side. We all sense the reason, and we all love them for supporting our friend; he is as Aware of his connection to everything as the rest of us, but he has the most trouble finding and staying in his centre. He suspects, as we all do, that our mentors want to talk to us about our return to Supreme City. The peace and oneness he has just experienced with the brown mare, with all of us, has deserted him and he is angry; angry at those who tortured him, angry at the regime that allows and encourages that behaviour, angry at himself for being angry. The dogs soothe him back to Awareness.

As soon as he is back with us in our minds, we all stand around his mind with our own. None of us think anything, because advice isn't what he needs. He feels our support, our affection for him as our friend, and he smiles. He reaches out to the brown mare and reassures himself that everything is as it was before his anger took him. Maverick barks and bounds around in front of us all – if we're all happy, then it has to be time to play. He play-bows in front of me and I jump forward, landing in what I hope appears to him like a return play-bow. He spins, barks excitedly, and races off. I run after him, laughing, and am soon overtaken by Breeze.

By the time I arrive at Will's feet, his legs out in front of him as he sits in the grass, I'm dripping with sweat. I bend over, my hands on my knees, panting. Maverick and Breeze have already circled back to try to entice the next of my friends into their game.

'I guess... I could have just... pretended I was going... to chase him... and it would have... had the... same effect,' I manage to say.

'You think?' Rowena says, rolling her eyes.

I stand upright and grin, and her eyes go wide. She stares at me, then at Justin, whose brow, usually so low and so serious, lifts in surprise. I see the recognition in his dark brown eyes at the same time that I feel it.

He gets to his feet and puts a hand over his heart. 'Shann.' I feel everything he wants me to feel. He smiles as he strides towards me. He pulls me into a hug and whispers, 'It's so good to see you, I've missed you so much, mate. You were right. About Amarilla, about everything. And now you're here, it all makes sense.' He releases me and moves to the side so that Rowena can take his place in front of me. She glares up at me with her almost black eyes, and my heart surprises me by hurting.

I remember everything I just felt when I rode the bay colt, and grin again. 'Don't pretend you're angry, because I can feel you aren't. At least you are, but only at yourself, because you want to be angry at me and you can't find it within yourself to be.'

She slaps my arm. 'Oh, you're as impossible as you always were. Come here.' She throws her arms around me and hugs me, then steps back. 'Only you would come back here with purple eyes.'

I look around at where my friends are almost upon us. 'Er, well not only me, I mean here are five others who have done the same, and there are thousands back at the city. I admit, mine have the richest colour, and have you noticed the dark purple line around the outside of my irises? Not everyone else has...'

My words are drowned out by laughter as Marvel, Holly and Vickery all come and hug their welcome now that they too recognise me as who I am.

'You hid it from us,' Rowena says, and her eyes flick to Will. 'One of these days, Will, when your daughter is everything you are and every bit as capable of your mind tricks, you'll know what it's like to feel like an idiot.' She looks at Amarilla. 'I'm glad you're not pretending you didn't know about this too.'

Two pairs of blue eyes look up at Rowena, the darker blue ones smiling, the paler blue ones steady. Then they gaze at me. I see again one of them at my feet, mortally injured, the other by my side, screaming as I lock eyes with the Kindred who injured Infinity. I felt my connection to him then and knew my place in the dream. Just as I know it now.

Amarilla nods, as do all of the others in front of me.

'You knew them before,' Kudos says as he reaches my side.

'Not all of them. You died before you could meet some of them,' Adept says.

Ace stands beside me and takes my hand possessively. 'You were very close to Justin. And Rowena.'

'Ace, feel your way back to your horse,' Rowena advises her. 'You've just ridden him, your energies are still entwined. He's right there, feel for him.'

'Why should I do anything you tell me?' Ace retorts, jealousy flooding through her as she focuses on who Rowena and I were to one another.

'Because this isn't something you'll get your mind around by yourself. Shann…' Rowena shakes her head in frustration. 'Sorry, Victor, is here because he's needed. Please, don't distract him from what he needs to do. If you love him, reach out to your horse and let him help you.'

Ace looks at me with pain in her eyes. I squeeze her hand. *Come on, we'll do it together.* I reach out to her horse and find, as Rowena said, that a part of Ace is still with him, just as he is always with her. Intent as Ace is on searching my Awareness for everything she can about my previous lifetime, her attention is pulled along with mine, to her horse. She sighs as everything about our individuality, our personalities, is rendered meaningless.

It doesn't matter. Ace's thought is faint, peaceful. *None of it matters. Not really.*

Rowena takes Ace's hands, telling her, 'I'm more proud of you than I can say.' She looks around at us all. 'What you've all achieved in less than ten days, took me, took us – she waves a hand to her friends – years to accomplish. We all have a difficult time ahead of us, but you're ready, each and every one of you. Just remember, whenever things get difficult, trust the horses. Remember your connection to them, and know that it makes everything and anything possible.'

We all reach for the horses as we nod.

Marvel claps. 'Jus and I were only saying yesterday that we were overdue for one of your motivational speeches, Ro, and I think everyone will agree,' he looks around at everyone, nodding, 'that was one of your best.'

Our mentors all laugh. We pick up the history behind his teasing, and are soon laughing too. Rowena shakes her head and smiles. Marvel puts an arm around her and hugs her.

'Which brings us to why you want to talk to us,' I say. 'Any survivors among us are expected back in Supreme City the day after tomorrow.' I can't prevent myself from shuddering.

Will nods. 'It's time for you all to decide who, if any of you, will go back. None of you have to, you're all welcome to carry on living here as you have been, you know that. I can go back and extend our invitation to them all.'

'But Victor will still need to be there to activate the lift,' Adept says. 'And if you arrive down there, they'll know that either Victor has conspired with you, or that you've killed him and used his thumbprint to get in. They'll kill you on sight.'

Will grins. 'I don't need Victor to open the lift, and I can both defend and heal myself, as you all know.'

'Metal-singing without the actual singing,' Kudos says, nodding to him. 'You can affect the door mechanism of the lift, and their weapons. You can't stop them killing you with their bare hands, though.'

I grin. 'I wouldn't bet on that. It's hardly the point though, is it? I need to go back. They won't see me as a threat. I'll make them believe it's safe to come above ground, and I'll get my parents out, one way or another.'

'If you're going, I'm going,' Ace says.

I turn to look at her, then look past her to our friends. 'We've all just ridden. We're at our most balanced, and that won't have come about just before we have this conversation, by chance. Stay connected to your horses while I say what I'm going to say, because I'm going to be completely honest.' Ace squeezes my hand, but I feel her and the others all do as I ask. 'We can't keep anything from one another. I know that none of you want to go back. In any case, only Hero and I are strong enough in our centres to be able to hold to them once we're back amidst everything we know Supreme City to be, and the Elite will never believe that Hero survived when the rest of you perished.' I glance at Hero. 'Sorry, mate, but you know it's true. You're the strongest of us inside, but that isn't what they – what we used to – see as strength.' Hero nods, and I continue, 'I'm going back alone.'

'I feel like a coward,' Prime says miserably, 'but I know you're right. I don't trust myself to not be the person I was if I go back there. All my life, I thought I was strong, but I'm not. I know that now.'

'My Bond-Partner's name was Oak,' Rowena says quietly. 'He taught me what strength really is, and in line with that, I would say that you're one of the strongest of all of us here, Prime.'

Immediately, we are all Aware of her horse's teachings and nod
our agreement.

'I guess I could disrupt the life support systems as I was doing
when I was there in person,' Adept says. 'And the rest of you
could help. Once we find in our Awareness the bits I've already
tampered with, it'll be easy to disrupt them further, and much less
dangerous than doing it in person. Will that help you, Victor, if we
time it so it takes some of the attention away from you?'

I grin. 'It will, thanks, and it'll make them more desperate to
believe what I'll tell them…'

'Which will be the truth,' Will interrupts. 'It's important that
everything you tell them is the truth. They aren't used to hearing it
any more than you were when you first met me, which will make
it all the more powerful.'

'He can't do that,' Ace says. 'The truth is dangerous in
Supreme City. Victor, look what happened to your parents. You
have to say what they want to hear, or they'll beat you, they'll kill
you, and then they'll kill your parents.'

Will looks directly into my eyes. 'If you tell them what they
want to hear, you'll be fuelling their belief system, their paranoia,
and you'll find yourself being sucked right back into it alongside
them. There is only one way to deal with fear and aggression, and
that is to refuse to be influenced by it, refuse even to recognise it.
You must stay centred and stick to your truth, however hard it is
and whatever the consequences.'

I nod. 'I get it, it's like what you did to us; you disarmed us
with your words and how you are as well as by trashing our
weapons.'

Kudos steps in front of me. 'Will had the horses and Maverick
to help him get through to the six of us. You'll be down there on
your own against thousands of them. It's suicide, Victor. I'm a
good fighter, I'm coming with you.'

'You know as well as I do that two of us – even six of us – against them all is no better than one of us,' I reply. 'It won't come down to fighting. And I'll have the horses and Maverick with me too, I can reach for them any time I need them. Will's right, I can feel it. I have to stick with what I know is true and let that guide me. I did it before and it brought me to this lifetime, along with all of you. I can do it again.'

Ace pushes in front of Kudos, takes hold of my arms and shakes me. 'You died last time! Never mind what's true, tell them whatever they need to hear in order to make it back to the surface, where Will and the horses can protect you.'

I lift my arms until she lets go, then put my hands on her shoulders. 'I don't need protecting, Ace. None of us do, and you know it. Feel that? The bay colt is with me every step of the way, not because he's trying to be, but because he can't not be. I'm part of their herd, part of the oneness, just as you are.'

'You don't think you're coming back,' Ace whispers and a tear rolls down her cheek. 'You came into this role in this lifetime because letting go of life is something you're already good at.'

'I came into this role in this lifetime because the experiences of the man I was, combined with those of the man I am now, will ensure I can do what's needed without worrying about the consequences, that's all. I'm coming back, Ace.' Movement catches my eye as our mentors nod and smile at me.

Will slaps me on the shoulder. 'I'll return to the city with you and wait above ground as emissary for The New.' He looks around at my friends. 'You're all in agreement? You're staying here?' All except Ace nod uncertainly. 'Ace?'

I squeeze her shoulders and put my sense of the herd into my thought. *Let the horses in, Ace.*

Finally, she does. She sighs deeply and all her fear for me, for us, wafts away into the ether. She nods. 'Okay, yes, I agree.'

Rowena says, 'Marvellous, that's settled, then. Those of you staying here will still have a role to play, because Adept's idea is a good one. You can all keep track of Victor's mission and if you sense things getting difficult for him, you can cause a distraction by affecting the life support systems. Nothing too drastic, mind, you won't want to risk causing a panic, or disrupting the systems to the point that everyone down there is in actual danger. You'll be doing that at the same time as continuing your studies with us, so that when Will and Victor get back here with your people, we're ready for them.'

'You know they'll come here with every intention of subjugating you all and taking Rockwood for themselves, don't you?' Hero says.

'We know,' Amarilla replies, looking up at as all. Infinity's gaze bores into us. 'They will insist on a battle. We will ensure they win.'

EIGHTEEN

Will

*L*ia scoops Tania out of the grass and puts her on my shoulders, where my daughter grabs hold of my hair. I'm just at the point of grimacing when she lets go and settles for wrapping her arms around my forehead instead.

Lia smiles up at her and breathes to me, 'That went well. I was concerned for Prime, but he seems to have accepted his decision well enough.'

I nod as we begin to walk behind all of the others. Fitt walks with Prime while tripping over Maverick and Breeze as they trot circles around him. I sense both Fitt's Bond-Partner, Flame, and Prime's brown mare with them as Fitt counsels the lad about forgiveness. He listens intently and I sense him sharing Fitt's memories of how she forgave the humans of The Old for everything they inflicted on her ancestors. The lad will be fine.

Jack and Katonia each have an arm around Adept as the three of them discuss what lies ahead. Kudos laughs with Marvel and Levitsson as the three of them walk together, enjoying what is clearly a great joke. Hero walks between Amarilla and Vickery, his relief at staying in Rockwood carried on his voice as he asks their advice on his latest herbal discovery. I grin. Amarilla will be no more forthcoming with him than Adam was with her when she was his Apprentice, no matter how much Hero pesters her – and he'll be as good a Healer as she is because of it.

Ace and Victor walk hand in hand just ahead of us, with Rowena and Justin either side of them. All four are keenly Aware of the danger into which Victor has volunteered to plunge himself, and those who love him are determined to make the most of the time they have with him before he and I will need to leave.

'It'll be hard for them to let him go again, however much they'll try to hide it,' Lia says quietly, nodding at Rowena and Justin.

'They'll get through it like they have done everything else,' I reply.

'You know, I think with you being Aware of so much all at once, you forget that none of us except for her ladyship up there,' she smiles up at Tania, 'have your level of perspective. We're Aware and we're good at balancing ourselves, but that doesn't mean we don't still hurt sometimes.'

I put my arm around her shoulders and pull her to me. 'Fair enough.'

She sighs and leans her head on my shoulder. 'It's scary, but kind of exhilarating, all of this, isn't it?'

'Life?'

'Yes. Life.'

Lia and I decide to leave Victor to his own devices on his last morning here. He is strong both in his centre and in the Skills he will need for what lies ahead, so he is best left to relax and spend some time with Ace. When we tell him so, he grins delightedly, bolts his porridge down and shoots for the door.

'Young love,' Lia says with a smile as the door bangs shut behind him.

Prime looks as miserable as I know he feels. 'Fancy a walk?' I say to him.

He sighs. 'I guess.'

Warm porridge hits my cheek, and Tania shrieks in delight. I scoop a little porridge on my spoon and flick it back at her. It hits her in the middle of her forehead and she shrieks again. When Maverick and Breeze jump up on either side of her high chair and lick the porridge off her, she laughs. The corners of Prime's mouth twitch.

Lia chuckles and says, 'Any minute now, we'll have vomit joining the scene in front of us. Excuse us, Prime, we're not exactly model parents.'

He is serious again. 'I wouldn't know.'

Both dogs leave Tania and slowly, carefully, place their paws either side of Prime on the chair, stand up tall and push into him. He puts an arm around them both and smiles. Porridge splats against his chin and Tania's laughter turns into a full belly laugh. Breeze is quicker than Maverick, and quickly licks it off. Prime chuckles, then scoops up the last little bit of porridge from his own bowl with his finger and flicks it so that it lands on the tip of Tania's nose. Maverick barks in delight at the new game and, being the closer of the two dogs, leaps to lick it off her.

'Right, off with the lot of you, before this kitchen is covered in porridge,' Lia says.

'But I haven't finished my...'

'Take it with you,' Lia interrupts me. 'Prime can carry Tania.

Go on, go. I've got a busy day in front of me at the Rockwood Centre; we've a lot of parents wanting advice on how to shield their children from negative energy of the strength that will accompany the people of Supreme City when they come. I would guess we have less than a week to make sure they all feel happy and supported, and with you not going to be here to help or look after Tania, I need to make a head start now.'

'Say no more, we're going. Come here, little one,' I say, lifting Tania out of her high chair and handing her to Prime. 'She'll love it on your shoulders, you're so much taller than any of us.' My daughter warbles happily as Prime lifts her over his head and holds her hands until she wraps her chubby arms around his forehead.

'There you go, now you know how it feels to wear a child,' Lia says. 'See you all later.'

Holding two pieces of toast and my porridge bowl, I follow Prime as he stoops through the front doorway so as to give Tania's head plenty of clearance. Maverick runs past us all and down to the end of the path, where he jumps the gate and then puts his paws atop it, watching us come down the path as if he's been waiting for ages.

'Breeze will stay with Lia,' Prime notes as he holds the gate open for me. 'I love the way the dogs like being with you both so much. The horses are amazing to be around – I mean there's just nothing like it when they include us in who they are – but with Maverick, Breeze and all the other dogs here, it's amazing in a different way. There's nothing keeping them with any of you, no reason for them to want to be with you all the time – they can feed themselves if need be and they've got all the other dogs for company – but they want to be with you. And when they're not around, it's as if something is missing. Something we don't need, necessarily, with us being Aware, but that makes everything seem easier.'

I nod. 'I know it only too well.'

'You do? You don't ever seem as if you need anyone. Not really.'

'I'm every bit as human as you are. I'm not better than you, Prime, I just have a different role to play in all of this.' We wander along the street in the morning sunshine, smiling and waving to those we pass. 'You know, whether Victor had wanted anyone with him or not, you would still have been needed here.' I sense Prime's mind searching mine for the lie he can't hear yet believes has to be there.

'I don't see how I can be needed anywhere,' he says finally. 'It's all very well trying to balance my personality with my Awareness, but I don't have a personality now. When the mare showed me how to balance and I released everything that had been keeping me from it, barely anything was left. All I know is how to look for weaknesses in people, and how to use those weaknesses against them. Now, I'm surrounded by happy, loving people, and I don't know how to be like that.'

'Yet you're carrying a young child on your shoulders, one who knows all of us better than we know ourselves, and is equally as happy up there as she would be if Lia or I were carrying her. And my dog trots along at your side, looking up at you the same way he looks at me. You have a personality, Prime, you're just having trouble recognising it because you let go of so much of the person you were forced to be. Rowena was right yesterday; you're stronger than most of us. Here we are, this is my grandparents' cottage. We'll stop off here, shall we? I'd rather not carry my breakfast bowl for the whole walk.'

I have only just lowered my hand to the catch of the front gate when the door is flung open and my grandmother flies down the path in a whirl of long, curly white hair, brightly-coloured skirts and outwardly-flung arms. 'Will!' she screeches. 'At last. And Tania! Oh, stop it, Maverick, just because you get away with jumping all over everyone else, doesn't mean you get to do it to me.' She pushes him away with a look of disgust, and his tongue, deprived of its target, flicks saliva all over her hands. She grimaces and rubs her hands down her skirt, then holds them up to Tania as Maverick bolts past her into the house.

'Prime, this is Mailen,' I say as my grandmother reaches up and pulls Tania down from the lad's shoulders, and cuddles her against her substantial bosom.

My grandmother squints up at him. 'So, you're one of those who has kept my grandson from us for weeks on end, are you? And then there'll be more of you coming, causing trouble where there's peace…'

'Gran, behave,' I tell her.

She looks at me and scowls, then her eyes twinkle. 'Oh, very well.' She holds a hand out to Prime. As he shakes it, her eyes widen. 'Oh my, you poor, poor love, what your parents did to you was unforgiveable. My grandson will tell you to let it go, but there are some things that should never be glossed over, and treating family members badly, even the small things like not coming to see them for weeks on end,' she glares at me, 'is one of those things. Come in, now, come in, you need feeding, and it just so happens that I have a cake in the oven.' She ushers a bemused Prime up the path in front of herself and Tania while my daughter occupies herself by examining a fistful of her great-grandmother's curls.

My grandfather stands on the front step. He allows Prime past him with a smile and a nod, then squeezes against the doorframe to allow Gran through with Tania. He opens his arms to me. 'Behave,' he says as he hugs me. 'That's all you have to say to your grandmother, and she gives in. I've tried lots of words in every tone I can produce, but she takes no notice. What's the secret, Will? I detected no use of that all-encompassing Awareness of yours.'

I grin. 'It's in the eyes, Grandpa. You have to have the look.'

He throws his hands in the air and lets them drop against his sides. 'The eyes! Why didn't I think of that? Go on in, from the sound of it, Maverick's already causing chaos.'

'Shoo! Shoo, I tell you,' my grandmother scolds from inside the cottage. 'I won't have you setting a bad example to the little ones. That's it, Arvella, take him outside. No, not that way, this way. THIS WAY.' The large brown and white dog who is hurtling down the hallway with Maverick in pursuit, slides to a halt, turns and shoots back towards the kitchen. Maverick barks and races off after her. 'That's it, out of the back door, both of you.'

I enter my grandparents' large, airy, stone-walled kitchen to see Gran waving a tea-towel behind the dogs as Maverick's tail disappears through the far doorway. Prime is standing motionless, looking at seven puppies in a large pen in the corner of the room. One of the puppies is standing on her hind legs, her front paws resting against the mesh sides of the pen, her little tail wagging so hard, it's a blur.

I feel Prime's heart thudding in his chest as if it will burst right out, as the little black puppy with a white stripe running up the middle of her nose begins climbing up the mesh. Her brothers and sisters, all brown and white like their mother, bounce around below her, but none of them try to follow her.

'Oh, you naughty little girl,' screeches my grandmother, rushing over to the pen. 'I knew you'd be trouble when you were born the image of your sire, and I was right.' She scowls at me as if it's my fault that Arvella and Maverick achieved an unobserved tryst.

'Gran, stop,' I say, and nod towards Prime.

My grandmother stops in her tracks as she too becomes Aware of the thread linking Prime and the puppy. It flares to life when Prime reaches the pen just in time to catch the puppy in his huge, grey hand as she flops over the top of the mesh. She licks his hand and when he lifts her to his chest, reaches up and bites his chin. He laughs – not the unsure, self-conscious laugh I've heard from him before, but a laugh of pure joy from deep within himself. 'You're a feisty one, aren't you?' he tells the puppy. 'Yes you are, Mailen's right, you're trouble.'

Gran gently puts a hand to Prime's elbow. 'And she's chosen you,' she says to him. 'What are you going to call her?'

We all know as soon as he decides, but he says it out loud anyway. 'Hope.'

'Good enough,' Gran says, then firms up both her grip on Prime's elbow and the tone of her voice. 'She can't leave here yet though, she's barely six weeks old. Get yourself back to Will's and fetch your stuff, you're moving in here with me and Frank.'

'Thunder and lightning, Will, did you even warn the lad before you brought him here?' Grandpa whispers beside me. I wink at him, and he sighs and shakes his head.

'Err,' Prime says, but is prevented from saying anything else as Hope licks his chin where she bit it, then his mouth.

'That puppy is the canine version of your gran. He doesn't stand a chance with the two of them,' Grandpa whispers.

'Um,' Prime tries again, holding Hope away from his face. She kicks her little legs almost at the speed her tail is wagging, so that the bottom half of her becomes a frenzy of movement. She emits a high-pitched yap and lunges forward with her upper body, trying to lick his face again. 'I mean, is that okay with everyone?'

'It's more than okay,' I say. 'When Hope's ready to leave her mother, you can decide whether you want to come back to ours, stay here, or have us help you to build somewhere of your own.'

'Nonsense, there's nothing to decide,' Gran says. 'The boy is an orphan to all intents and purposes, and I won't have him living on his own.' She turns to Prime. 'I expect the monsters from whose loins you sprang will be coming here fully intending to murder us all in our beds?'

Prime opens his mouth to answer, but doesn't get the chance. He'll learn.

'Just you wait until I get my hands on them,' Gran continues, 'I'll show them how to bring up a child. I had four, did you know that? And one of them was Amarilla!' She sticks her chin out and manages to look down her nose at Prime, despite being two feet shorter.

Grandpa puts a hand to his forehead, but Gran doesn't notice and continues, 'If I can bring up a child as strong-willed as she was without raising a hand to her, your parents have no excuse for what they did to you…'

'Mailen, that's nothing to do with us…' Grandpa attempts to cut her off, but I put a hand on his arm. He smiles as he senses the same thing I do; Gran's maternal instinct is wrapping itself around the thread between Prime and Hope, adding strength to the lad's growing sense that at last, he has a place into which he feels he fits.

He just needs time to find himself, Grandpa observes. *And a lot of love. Well, he'll get that with us. You did well to bring him here, Will.*

We'll need him when his people get here. Gran will want to barricade the front door to keep him safe here, but you can't let her.

Grandpa nods almost imperceptibly. *I learnt a long time ago how to appear to be going along with your Gran's wishes while doing completely the opposite, even if I did have to take lessons from your aunt. Prime will be where he needs to be, have no fear.*

I'll go and get his stuff. They won't even notice I've gone. I nod to where Gran is manhandling Prime into the biggest of the kitchen chairs – Grandpa's chair – so that he can eat the enormous slab of cake she's promising him he'll eat while he's "keeping that naughty puppy out from under everyone's feet".

Do you think she'll notice if I'm gone? Grandpa asks.

His thought barely has time to exist before Gran says, 'Frank, you'll be needing to clean the puppy pen out while Arvella is having a break from her babies.'

I grin. 'Sorry, Grandpa. See you in a bit.'

I close the front door almost silently behind me, yet still manage barely two steps down the cobbled path before Maverick comes tearing around the side of the cottage and skids to a halt at my side. I chuckle and crouch down beside him, scratching his neck. 'I could never lose you, could I, mate? Your little girl has found someone to rescue, just like you rescued me. Do you remember when we first met? Huh? Where would I be without you? Where would we all be?' He lies down and wriggles around on his back. I rub his chest and belly, allowing my sense of him to be all of me as I often do when I need a break from myself. Immediately, I merge with the collective consciousness of all of the dogs who have ever lived, and everything becomes simple; I exist to love and protect my pack.

'Shape-shifting in public, Will? You know it frightens the elderly.'

I stand up and grin at Justin, knowing he sees both the man who is his nephew and friend, and a million different dogs as they look out of my eyes, hunch my back and elongate my face. 'Yet you don't appear to be afraid,' I retort, knowing my human grin will reflect the bright eyes of the dogs as they recognise a member of the pack we love and protect. I focus on my sense of self and feel Justin relax as my physical appearance returns to normal.

'Any particular reason for it this time?' he says, rubbing Maverick's ears as my dog stands on his hind legs at the gate. 'Ah, your grandmother, I see. Well, we all need a break sometimes, don't we? So, Prime has a puppy? Yes, that will work, but it's caused you to take a trip down memory lane, understandable...'

'Aren't conversations with one's own Awareness usually Rowena's domain?' I ask him.

He grins. 'They are. Forgive me. I came to drop these off for your grandparents.' He holds up a basket of herbal preparations. 'Hero put them together under Am's supervision. He's as good as she is, as I'm sure you knew he would be.' He hands the basket to me. 'Stick it on the step, would you? If your gran's in full on mother hen mode, I'd rather stay out here.'

'Sure.'

As I come back down the path, Justin is pacing back and forth in front of the gate. He stops and looks at me, his brow low over his dark eyes. He rubs his chin and I know he's wondering whether to say what he's thinking. Then he remembers it's me and I already know, so he shrugs and comes out with it. 'I know you know how the next weeks, months and years will play out, Will, and I understand as well as everyone else does, why it isn't helpful for us to know what you know; we all need to live our lives without the distraction of the future, even though you and Am both manage to live with what you know of it. Just... well... if you can... oh, I don't know why I'm saying this, when you already know what I want and you also know I know it isn't possible...'

'You want me to do everything I can to bring Shann back alive,' I say. 'You know everything happens as it should, but you're so happy to have him back with you, even in the way he is, you can't help but say it anyway.'

Justin shrugs and opens the gate for me. 'Daft, isn't it? And you don't even need to answer that, I've already had a lecture from Infinity about embracing my humanity rather than trying to deny it.'

I put a hand to his shoulder as we start to walk. 'I've had a similar reminder from my wife.'

Justin reads from my mind the conversation I had with Lia yesterday evening, and chuckles. 'She's good for you. And she's not wrong. Remember that while Victor has come into his own remarkably quickly as a result of the horses' and Shann's influences, he isn't as strong as you, won't you, Will? Look after him, and look after yourself. I'd better get back, Marvel is currently restraining Rowena on his own from going after Ace and Victor, and I'm sensing he needs reinforcements.'

I grin. 'Good luck. They need the morning to themselves. Let me know if you want me to shield her so she can't spy on them. I can, you know.'

Justin stops in the street and stares at me. 'You would actually do that? Your courage astounds me.'

'By the time she's worked out it's me, Victor and I will be long gone.'

'Physically, yes, but have you really forgotten what it's like to have her haranguing you in your head?'

I laugh. 'Good point. Try and get her to understand, though. Victor is Victor more than he is Shann.' I look at him pointedly.

He lifts a hand as he turns away. 'I know, we both know, it's just that we see Shann on his face and we hear him in his voice. I'll be there to wave you off later, Will. Have a restful morning.'

I wave in return and wander back to my cottage, stopping to chat to pretty much the whole village on the way. Many of the humans are frightened at the thought of what lies ahead, but more of them are not, and none of the Kindred have the slightest concern. My parents, Lia, Amarilla, Justin, Holly, Vickery, Fitt and Levitsson have been doing a brilliant job preparing them all and sorting them into those who will need to be shielded both from their Awareness and from the scene the ancestors of The Old will insist on creating, and those who won't. They'll work right up to the moment the energy of The Old meets that of The New, and then it will be down to us all and the horses.

Victor, Ace, Lia, Tania and I eat lunch together, then we all and the dogs make our way to the pasture that has been grazed down low by Ember's herd. The other four teenagers from Supreme City are there to see Victor and me off, along with their mentors and my grandmother. She announces that she's there to wave me off, but we all know she's really there to make sure Prime doesn't go with us at the last minute. He knows it too, and he loves the feeling it gives him.

Victor and I – and Maverick – work our way along the line of them, saying our goodbyes and receiving hugs. When we get to the end, I kiss my wife and daughter and Ace throws her arms around Victor. A soft thudding of hooves causes her to finally let go. She wipes her face on her sleeve and smiles at Victor as the bay colt sidles into place between them.

I vault onto Ember's back alongside the colt and Victor, and both horses spin around and trot back to the herd. The horses are all well rested and eager to run. When the lead mare takes off at a fast canter, all follow eagerly, none of them slowing when they reach the forest.

As always, Ember brings up the rear of his herd. Victor's colt is just in front of us and Maverick as the horses disappear into the gloom of the trees, the sound of their hooves altering from a pounding of the hard, sun-baked ground to a soft thudding as they hit the leaf litter of the forest floor. They stay to the path, so have no need to slow down until we reach the grassland on the far side of the forest, where they stop for water.

Victor and I slide off our horses' backs to let them drink and have a roll. Maverick is panting hard and hurls himself into the stream from which the horses are drinking. He has a belly full of water when the herd is ready to move on, so I'm glad the lead mare settles on a brisk walk. She knows what she's doing.

Victor turns around to me and says, 'Phew, that's a relief, for me as well as Maverick. If we'd carried on at that pace, I wouldn't have been able to walk tomorrow, herbs or no herbs. It was amazing though, wasn't it, all of us moving at that speed together?' He leans forward and throws his arms around the bay colt's neck. 'Thank you, colt. Colt?' He turns back to me. 'I can't keep calling him that. After everything he's done for me, everything he's still doing for me, I can't call him that, it'd be like me calling you "man".'

I shrug. 'It's all the same to him, you can feel that as well as I can.'

'Yet Ember has a name.'

'He does. He doesn't need one, but it's convenient for those of us who talk about him regularly.'

'I'll never stop talking about this horse as long as I live,' Victor says. 'Whenever I need to remind myself of the truth he helped me to see, I'll think of him. Truth. That's his name. It'll help me to stick to it once I'm back in the city, like you said. I'll think of him and I'll remember.'

The mare continues to walk for a while, then begins to trot before settling into a leisurely canter.

Victor cries, 'Yeehaaaaaaaaaah,' and Maverick barks and races onward to run alongside him and Truth. The herd energy shifts towards my dog and the weaker members of the herd, including Victor, whose muscles have begun to strain. Instantly, Victor relaxes back into his balance. 'Wow, wow, wow, that's amazing.' He turns to me. 'Isn't it amazing? You feel it, right?'

I laugh. 'I feel it. Enjoy it, Victor, and remember it.'

When we reach the hills, the horses stop for water again. Sensing that they will graze for a little while, Victor and I wash down Ember and Truth, then step away from the horses to leave them in peace until they are ready to move on. Victor sits down and leans back against a boulder, shielding his eyes from the sun as he watches the horses. I feel him drinking in every detail not only of Truth, but of all of them. He knows he'll be able to reach for them any time he wants to once he's below ground, but he wants to be able to picture them too, when he's faced with all of the things he doesn't want to see.

'You need to let it back in to your mind, Victor.' He looks at me. 'The city. You need to accept it back into your mind and let it combine with everything else that's there now. You're strong enough, the horses have seen to that. If you continue to hold the city away from yourself, you'll continue seeing it as more frightening than it is. Accept it for what it is, and for the part it has played in this dream of ours. It isn't necessary any longer, but it's brought your people to this point in time. It's allowed them to experience fully the parts of themselves they've needed to express, so that we can help them to move past it all.'

Victor breathes deeply and nods. He pictures the apartment in which he grew up, the wallscreen from which he took his lessons and instructions, the weapons halls, the grey corridors, the grey, purple-eyed people in the brown of Disposables, green of Regulars and red of the Elite. Then he pictures his parents. I feel his concern, but also his love for them and his pride. He lets more of the city in and I feel the fear that leeches along its corridors, into its apartments, through its walls. I feel the battle rage he felt when he beat Kudos, and which has raised or held each and every Elite to their positions of what they believe to be power. He accepts it all as the necessity it has been, exactly as I advised him to. If I weren't already Aware of the consequences of a soul with Shann's experience incarnating into a body bred to be as supremely intelligent as Victor's, I would be amazed.

I get to my feet at the same instant that Victor does. Maverick yawns and stands up, then stretches and yawns again. 'Tired already, mate?' I say to him, ruffling his ear, 'I hate to break this to you, but the horses are keen to get back.'

'We're going to get there in a matter of hours, aren't we?' Victor says. 'It took us two days to get to Rockwood on foot, but the horses will get us there in a quarter of the time, even with them stopping to graze.'

'We didn't exactly set them much of a challenge, did we? What with stopping to argue every few minutes, then you lot needing a long night's sleep, a nap the following day, another interminably long sleep the second night, followed by your fight with the forest – and that was when you weren't all tripping over your own feet.'

Victor laughs as Truth wanders over to him. 'I can't argue with you.'

I rub Maverick's chest and say, 'Ready to go again?' He barks. 'Of course you are.'

I rest a hand on Ember's withers as he pauses briefly beside me. As soon as he feels me land lightly on his back, he trots towards the rest of his herd, his ears flicking back as he passes a pair of fillies play-fighting when they should be taking their places with the others. They spin away from him and disappear into the milling horses. Maverick barks and looks up at me, his tongue lolling and his eyes shining. All time is now, I know it, I'm Aware of it – but this is one of those moments when I want now to be all there is.

NINETEEN

Victor

The sun is halfway between its zenith and the horizon when we arrive back at the grasslands above Supreme City. I sigh as I realise that I'll have to put my watch back on to know the time once I'm below ground again.

My ancestors were so proud of themselves for developing machines to do everything for us – to clean our air and water, synthesize our food and clothing, tell us what to do and when, teach us what we are allowed to know according to our status, monitor where we are at every single moment, listen to us and report us for saying anything against the regime – that they completely forgot how wholesome it is to breathe in air containing all kinds of particles for our bodies to interpret; how liberating it is to drink water that isn't crystal clear and trust our bodies and the herbs nature provides to ensure that we take what we need and expel the rest; how nourishing it is to eat food that is grown and prepared with love and good intentions; how comfortable it is to wear clothes made from natural fibres which nurture our bodies on the outside as our food nurtures them from within; how empowering it is to know whatever we want, whenever we want, because we already have all the answers we need; and how necessary it is for our advancement to know the truth, yet to still have our own opinions and desires, and the freedom to make our own choices. In their desperation to feel safe and powerful, they strived to create a synthetic world that they believed would be superior to any that has existed before – yet what they actually created was a one-dimensional existence that has severely limited the potential of all of us who have ever lived there.

I should feel scared at returning to the city, but as the afternoon has worn on, I've found that the more time I have spent being carried by Truth, the further behind I have left the fear and lies of the city.

The lift is just visible in the distance, jutting up in the middle of all the horses grazing around it. Truth slows to a stop near a water hole, and I jump down from his back and cup water in my hands to wash the sweat off him, making sure to sweep it back away from the clean water. Will does the same for Ember a little further around the hole.

'We carry on alone,' Will says.

'We? Don't you want to stay here with Ember's herd?'

'Mav and I will return to them in the morning, once you've gone below. You and I have a few things to sort out before we rest for the night,' Will replies.

I pick up on his intention. 'The gear we left by the lift. You want me to re-enable all of the weapons. Why?'

'You need the practice. By the time you've re-enabled six weapons and then disabled five of them again, you'll be able to do it without thinking. Come on.' Will hitches his rucksack onto his shoulder and walks off towards the lift. I go to follow, but my legs don't want to move. I grin. I don't need herbs, I can sort this myself. I tune into my stiffening muscles and they follow my intention for them to relax. I stagger slightly and the herd energy shifts in my direction, supporting me.

I rub Truth's shoulder. 'Thank you,' I say to him, knowing I'm speaking to them all. 'I know you don't need my thanks, but you have them anyway.' I hurry after Will.

'That's why Amarilla gave you the herbs,' Will says when I catch him up. 'Healing yourself is a great ability to have, but it takes energy and concentration when you might be better using them for other things.'

'Okay, got it.'

We walk at a leisurely pace amongst the hundreds of horses grazing the vast grasslands around the lift, even Maverick, who has managed to get over his excitement at having Will back on the ground with him again. When we reach the lift, Will instructs me to put everything with a metal component to one side. Once we have a pile of weapons, ammunition and the headband, he takes me with him in his mind to the first weapon. I witness which of its various components follow his intention and begin to straighten where he bent them when he disabled the weapon.

You take over, he tells me.

Like every youth of Supreme City, I can take apart my weapon and put it back together in the dark. I know every tiny component, and within a few minutes, I've reshaped and re-aligned the gun to exactly how it should be.

Fire it into the air, Will tells me.

But the bullets will come back down somewhere, they could hurt the horses.

Not if they are no longer bullets. Do as I do.

With no further argument, I fire into the air, keeping my mind with his. It's easy. We resonate with the bullets and their component atoms – which follow our intention to separate from one another. It takes energy, but we are both strong and the horses are with us, supporting us as always with the energy of the herd.

Approval accompanies Will's thought. *Good. Now re-enable the rest of the weapons, then disable all of them and all of the ammunition, except your own. When you're done, you can get to work on the headband. Figure out the best way to disable it without it being obvious you've done so.*

I grin. *Good idea. Okay, I'm on it.*

Will sits down in the grass and leans back against one of the glass walls of the lift. He pours a bowl of water for Maverick and opens a packet of meat, which he puts at his dog's feet. Then he sets about dividing up some of the food he's brought into a meal for the two of us. All the time, he's with me in my mind, monitoring everything I do. I sense his readiness to add his intention to mine if need be, to either add strength to my conviction I'm doing it right, or to suggest a better way of doing it, but he doesn't.

When I have rendered five weapons useless once more, caused all of the ammunition except mine to disintegrate, and disabled the headband in ten different ways, he nods. *Which option will you go for?*

I point to the headband's disabled fingerpad. *That one. It's the quickest solution.*

Agreed. Come and eat.

As I begin to chew my first mouthful of my sandwich of bread, cheese, tomatoes and lettuce – such a simple meal, yet so enjoyable as a result of the energy it gives me and the pleasure of my taste buds exploding – it hits me again how much I will be leaving behind. Maverick, now chewing on a meaty bone Will has given him, picks up his treasure and comes and lies down between the two of us. He licks my trouser leg then carries on chewing. I stroke his back and sigh. 'You're not making this any easier, Mav.'

As always, Will knows how I'm feeling, but he doesn't say anything. There's nothing he can say. I have to accept my situation for myself. I nod. That's why he wanted to arrive now; so that I have the evening with him, Maverick and the horses whilst being directly above the city. I need to fully reconcile who I am with who I was, and try to figure out a way to be both so that I can do what I need to do. I need to get past the fear that threatens to take hold of me... which I do by reaching for Truth and holding on to him.

The sun is setting by the time I have everything balanced in my head.

I'm proud of you, Victor. Ace's thought is soft, encouraging, strong. *Rowena's been working me as hard as you've been working yourself, so that I reach for Solace instead of for you. I'm managing it, so I guess I'm proud of me too.*

I sense that Ace is with the dark brown colt in her Awareness, and look in the direction where I know he grazes in the evening sunshine with the rest of Ember's herd. *Solace is a good name. He'll be back with you soon,* I tell her.

I hope you are too. I won't distract you any further. I just wanted to tell you I love you and I'm proud of you.

I love you too.

She fades away from me. I sense her focusing on Solace, and feel him and the rest of the herd supporting her and the others every bit as they are me, while flicking their tails, shaking their heads, and occasionally stamping their feet, to dislodge biters as they tear at the grass. They appear to be dumb animals intent purely on filling their stomachs, but they are so much more; they are the bringers of balance.

Yet so are the animals moving from flower to flower in the

fading light, I suddenly realise as I follow a large, yellow and black striped insect in my Awareness. In feeding themselves so that they can breed more beings exactly like themselves, they move parts of one flower to the next. I feel the flower respond to the touch of the particle from its neighbouring flower, and marvel as it accepts it into its being, just like we do when we mate. I sense the history of the plant and am mesmerised. When its flowers are no longer needed to attract the insects who fertilise them, their petals fall to the ground and are eaten and digested by more tiny animals, whose egestions nourish the soil so that more plants can grow. The horses eat those plants while directing part of their energy towards keeping us humans in balance... everything provides something for something else, everything co-operates and balances – except my people.

Determination sweeps over me. I can do this.

Sleep now, Victor, Will tells me.

I wake with the dawn. I've quickly become used to the bliss of the first gentle rays of light brushing my eyelids, easing me out of sleep until my eyes are ready to open, and instantly feel sad to be leaving the process behind. Then I remember how I felt before I went to sleep, and determination courses through me. I sit up, hug Maverick as he licks my face, then stand up and stretch.

Will hands me a sandwich and some fruit. 'Morning.'

I inspect the sandwich and sigh. 'A few bites of deliciousness, then it's back to white mush for me. Honestly, that alone is enough to motivate me to do what I need to do quickly and get back up here.'

Will chuckles but makes no comment.

Once I've eaten, I change into a fresh set of the green clothes that identify me as a Regular, and strap my watch onto my wrist. The time shows as a few minutes after six. I came above ground just after seven. I'll go back down shortly, so that I'm standing to attention outside the doors to The Forum well before seven. That, along with the fact that I am sane and happy to be reporting back, should hopefully impress the Elite enough to listen to everything I have to say.

Which will be the truth, I remind myself. *Whatever happens, I stick with Truth and the truth.*

'And don't forget,' Will tells me through the last mouthful of his sandwich, 'I'll be with you every step of the way. I'll stay small and silent in your mind so as not to distract you, but I'll be with you.' He waves a hand around at the horses who surround us, most of whom are grazing while the others snooze standing up or sleep lying down. 'We all will be.'

I nod. 'I know.'

I wash in the remainder of my water, comb my hair down flat and part it into the city's regulation hairstyle, albeit a longer version of it; that can't be helped, I've supposedly been living rough for ten days. I repack my rucksack, including everything I left behind. 'You'll sort everyone else's weapons and stuff?' I say to Will.

He nods. 'There'll be no sign of it by the time your people get up here.' He looks me up and down and hands me my weapon and helmet. 'You're ready. You have it clear in your head what to say about why you're returning alone?'

'Yes. The truth. I've got this, Will.'

He grins. 'I know you have.' He draws me into a hug, then holds me back from himself. 'See you, Victor.'

I grin back. 'See you, Will.' I bend down to stroke Maverick, then put my thumb to the pad by the lift door and push the button to open it. I step inside the lift, turn to face the man and dog standing watching me, and press the button to descend. Will and Maverick disappear from sight. It hurts even more than I thought it would. I take in a deep breath, breathe back out slowly, and slap my cheeks. I reach for Truth and find him biting the back of a filly while she bites his back in return. They know exactly where I am and what I'm doing, and neither are even remotely concerned, because there is no need to be. Not in truth. I smile and then immediately straighten my face. There can be no smiling in Supreme City.

The lift door opens and I step out into the dull, grey corridor. I realise for the first time that it isn't just the colour that makes it dull. It is barely light in the world I have just left, yet its air is full of scents that please or tickle the nose, and sounds that lift the soul and make the body feel part of something... alive. Here, the air is clean, sterile and unnoteworthy. All I can hear are the whispers of frightened voices, the harsh overtones of aggressive ones, and a myriad of sounds I've never even noticed before – the whirring, whining, clanking and high-pitched shriek of thousands of machines. Fear lashes the walls, turning in on itself and rebounding in search of anyone within whom it can take hold. It finds me and I stand stock still, holding to Truth as it assaults my body, trying to find somewhere to lodge itself. When it can't, it leaves... only to be replaced by the next wave.

Yet there is something with it, something I recognise and that recognises me. It stays with me when the fear moves on, bolstering my determination to hold to Truth; the love with which Adam and Peace infused the city lingers still, supporting where it can. And it isn't alone in its encouragement of me; the herd energy shifts towards me slightly and I sense not only the horses, but Will, Maverick, Ace, Lia, Amarilla, Infinity, Justin, Prime... each and every one of my friends is with me.

I begin to walk towards the lifts that will take me down to the

Forum. To the Elite. However much fear and paranoia pounds through the corridors at this level is nothing compared with what it will be down there. I know it, but I'm ready for it. We all are.

Some Disposables hurry out of an apartment and almost collide with me. Their terror hits me so hard, I have to stand for a couple of heartbeats to steady myself.

The man and woman look down at the ground as the woman says, 'We're sorry, so very sorry. It won't happen again.'

I want to tell them to relax, that there's no problem at all, but I can't. 'On your way, Disposables,' I say and when they look up at me in shock at the softness in my voice, I almost wink at them. I catch myself, then have to catch myself again before I grin as I try to decide whether the urge to wink was as a result of having spent so much time with Will, or due to Shann's influence. The Disposables hurry away and I make my feet follow them.

It feels strange to be walking on a flat, even floor after the past weeks of walking on ground that is anything but. And it feels strange to be comfortable as I walk; to be without the ache in my lower back that used to result from sticking my chest out, to be free from the injuries and stiff, sore muscles that resulted from weapons training, to be comfortable in my own skin.

All of those I see on the way to the lift are Disposables. All avert their eyes and none of them speak, so I'm spared more instances of potentially giving myself away.

Once the lift starts to descend, I wonder whether to stop off at my apartment to make sure I'm presentable and fully centred before arriving at the Forum. I decide against it. The Elite will know I'm back and they will know if I make a diversion. They won't appreciate being relegated to secondary importance. Straight to it, then.

The lift doors open on level -50 and I step out into the corridor of light tubes with their crystal-lined walls. I remember being impressed by the sight before, but now, compared with the natural light and beauty above ground, it seems little brighter than the corridors of level -1.

I'm unsurprised by the fear that hits me, but where it lashed around the higher levels, unadulterated and uncontained, down here it is entwined with enjoyment of its own existence and cleverness into sharp spikes of foulness that prod at my Awareness, probing for weaknesses to exploit and secrets to expose. Deep within each spike is a terror so intense that it would be completely debilitating were it allowed to surface. I almost grin in gratitude for the warning of what will assault my Awareness with even more strength when I come face to face with the source of the spikes, but I stop myself. The Elite are watching and listening, always.

I stride straight ahead towards the doors of the Forum. When I reach them, I lower my rucksack, gun and helmet to the floor by the wall to my left, then stand beside them, feet apart, hands by my sides, my eyes on the wall opposite. I don't see anything; I'm with Truth with all but the tiniest part of myself that listens for the sound of footsteps down the corridor, or of the door opening. Truth is all there is.

I breathe in and out slowly, time after time, and bring myself back to my physical surroundings until I have them balanced with my Awareness of Truth. I have no idea how long I stand that way.

I sense the Elite gathering on the other side of the door in twos and threes, discussing the fact that I have returned and am waiting to report, and forging the alliances they think might help them take the greatest advantage of everything they speculate I will say.

When they finally seat themselves at the table, they take much time preparing themselves mentally and physically. Each knows they must get control of me before any of the others do, and for that, they must be the first to understand what I will tell them so that they can take charge of the situation, whether by words or action. I feel their exhaustion. They have been awake mere hours, yet they drink stimulants to help their minds work even faster than usual so that they can be confident of outthinking one another, of becoming ever more powerful. I refrain from rolling my eyes.

The doors finally open.

'Enter, Regular, and approach your Elite,' says the same Regular who admitted me on my last visit.

I stride confidently to the table, where I once more stand with my feet apart. As expected by all of those watching me, I lift my right hand and place it over my heart even as I sense the shock of both the Regular and the fifteen seated around the table.

As tuned in as we all are to one another's posture and body language so that we can pick up the slightest details that indicate weakness, they all immediately see the difference in me from when I was last here. They can detect no weakness, even though my behaviour is nothing but respectful and submissive. The change in my posture is huge, yet they can't reconcile what they see with any way of feeling to which they relate. Where I am concerned, they are blind and it terrifies them way over and above the fear that drives their actions day to day.

'Explain your presence here, Regular,' says the woman at the opposite end of the table to where I stand. Where before her voice was soft, calculating, dangerous, now it is husky, spoken as it is through a throat that is tight with fear. I am Aware that her name is Eminent, and that the fingers of her right hand are clasping a handgun in the pocket of her robe.

I'm almost dumbstruck with fascination at the reactions of those who sit before me, writhing within their skins at the sight of me standing so comfortably within my own. I swallow, re-centre myself and gaze downward. 'I have spent ten days above ground as ordered, and stand before you now to report my findings.' I find it desperately hard to keep my eyes down; I'm not scared of them anymore. But I must succeed at my mission. I breathe and focus on the toes of my boots.

'So, report,' says a man. He tries to keep his voice steady, but his voice breaks on his second word. The other fourteen all shift in their seats, wondering whether to move against him now or later… but they can't think straight because of me and all that I represent. They all turn their attention back to me and I breathe through the spikes of their terror that poke at me, desperately trying to find any sign that I am the same person they sent above ground.

Truth. I sense his calm acceptance of All That Is as he grazes in the warm, early morning sunshine. I am him and he is me as I remember that truth has a power of its own. I speak clearly and calmly. 'The five who went above ground with me no longer exist as people of Supreme City.'

'You killed them.' There is an avid tone to the woman's voice.

'I did not. They succumbed to a power greater than anything I possess.'

They don't believe me. They are incapable of believing I didn't kill those who would steal for themselves some of the glory of returning to report to the Elite, because it's what each and every one of them would have done. They are even more frightened of me, but they need to know what I know.

'Continue,' Eminent says.

'The ghosts have gone, the air is breathable and the water is drinkable.' I sense relief all around. 'I met a man who took me to his village. He and his people welcomed me as one of their own. They showed me how they produce their food and clothing, and how they build their homes. I stayed with the man, his wife and daughter, and the family's two dogs. The man came back with me and as I report, waits above ground. On behalf of the villagers of

Rockwood, all seven hundred and seventy-eight of them, he extends the same invitation to everyone of Supreme City, that he did to me. We are all welcome to live alongside them as people of The New. They will show us how to survive above ground; how to build homes, make clothes from natural fibres, grow and prepare food, and how to heal ourselves.'

The Elite's relief turns to outrage.

'They will show us how to do these things?' Eminent hisses, 'They will do no such thing; they will do them for us, they will serve us, that is what they will do. You dare to stand there and suggest that we accept an invitation from them? Why did you not kill the inferior for uttering such disrespect to you? You may be a mere Regular, but you are a citizen of Supreme City. He should have knelt at your feet as soon as he saw you.'

It is all I can do not to laugh at the thought of Will kneeling at my feet in supplication. 'He has the same appearance as our ancestors, but he's different. He's powerful. All of the people up there are. You would be wise to accept their invitation, for you cannot defeat them.'

Everyone gasps and their spikes of terror poke at me with more force. 'You lie,' hisses a woman sitting to my left. 'Regular, the headband.'

A headband is lowered around my brow. By the time the Regular has put his thumb to the fingerpad in readiness for his next instruction, I have deactivated it.

'Tell us the truth,' the woman says.

I look up at her just as she nods to the Regular behind me. He presses the button that should result in blinding pain behind my eyes. I look straight into the woman's eyes and feel her shock turn to outrage. I hold to Truth. 'I have been completely honest, Peerless.'

She leaps to her feet, points a gun at me and fires. I blink as the trigger clicks. No bullet comes my way. I continue, 'The man I met goes by the name of Will.'

Eminent stands. 'You dare to LOOK AT US, REGULAR?' She flinches at her loss of control over herself and glances around at the others to see if any will try to take advantage. They are all too stunned at my behaviour. 'You dare to mention the name of AN INFERIOR in our presence, as if he is equal to us? As if he has power over us?' She looks at the Regular behind me and says, 'Maximum pain.'

The Regular presses another button on my headband.

I stare straight at Eminent and say, 'Will is accompanied by his dog, Maverick, and hundreds of horses. It was the horses to whom the five with me succumbed. They're powerful in ways you can't imagine. Far more powerful than we are.'

Eminent draws her gun and fires it at me, but like Peerless's, it merely clicks, as will any of the other weapons I disabled before I set foot in the room. If they take them apart to fix them, they will find dust where each bullet should be.

'Will and his people can help you to stop being afraid,' I say, looking at the Elite in turn. 'They can show you a better way to live. They can show you what power truly is. Please, all of you, accept their invitation, for your own sakes and for those of our people. Regardless, the horses will ensure that you do.'

I sense Eminent's fear rising as she realises that she has not only disclosed her fear of the others by revealing that she, like all of them, carries a handgun to protect herself, but that she has left herself appearing even weaker due to the fact it didn't fire. The others are wondering whether to take her power from her physically, or by retaining their focus on getting control of me. Their brains operate at the immense speed necessary for them to survive as members of the Elite while they consider all of the possible moves they could make against her and one another, and all of the possible consequences.

A man whose name I am Aware is Sovereign, sitting halfway along the table to my right, is the first to arrive at his decision. He leaps to his feet and onto the table with heart-stopping speed, and in a few strides is flying through the air at me. This is it. I close my eyes and am wholly with Truth as Sovereign takes me down. I stay with the bay colt through each and every blow the man delivers to my head and body. I am punched, stamped on and kicked, Sovereign's battle rage driving him on far beyond the point where he has my silence. When my arm breaks, I sense Will drawing the bone back together. When two of my ribs crack, he pulls the splinters back into place and heals the fractures. When my pelvis shatters, he's there in an instant, his intention stronger than I had any idea was possible as he insists that it becomes whole again.

I endure it all through Truth. I'm with him in my Awareness, riding him again for the first time, releasing the fear I held that stopped me being in perfect balance with him and everything around me. I release all of the traces of fear that try to take hold of me now, so that my body doesn't resist Will's intention as he continues to heal the damage being inflicted on my body.

A loud bang reverberates through the Forum. I trace it back to its source and sense my friends sitting in a circle, holding hands in the pasture their horses grazed before leaving with Will and me. Adept has led the others to the parts of the life support systems that she weakened when she was here in person, and the five of them are causing them to disintegrate further. There is another loud bang and I sense the terror not just of the Elite in the room with me, but of all of them. They already believe the life support systems are failing, and now they fear that the failure of the city is far more imminent.

My friends move on to the next weakness and just as I'm fading out of consciousness, I hear a crash. I suspect it is even louder than it seems to me with my blood pulsing through my ears in the way it is. The beating stops. There is another crash, followed by a hissing sound.

'Regular, take this specimen and dump him with his parents,' Sovereign says. 'Tell the Disposables on prison duty to ready the three of them for execution.' No one argues. His calculation has proven correct; by taking control of me, he has taken Eminent's position of power.

As I'm dragged out of the room, I hear Sovereign calling more Regulars into the Forum and barking orders at them. Some are told to clear up the mess my beating has caused, others to find out what is causing all the noise and report back immediately. The Regular dumps me on the ground as he waits for the lift. I never hear it arrive.

TWENTY

Will

$\mathcal{K}$nowing what would happen to Victor doesn't make it any easier to witness first hand, but the lad is every bit as impressive as I foresaw. Shann's experiential knowledge that what happens to the body need not affect the soul, combined with Victor's determination to hold on to the horse named for that which he knows to be important above everything else, has resulted in an individual capable of withstanding anything.

I've done all I can for him. I've healed all of his fractures and the wounds to his organs and tissues, and eased his muscles out of the protective tension they adopted – but both the beating and the healing have taken a lot out of him. The horses are with him, allowing their energy to ease itself through his being, supporting his body as it recovers and soothing his mind so that when he wakes, he will instantly remember his role in the dream and what he must do next. He will be tired and bruised, but capable.

His friends are doing a great job. Adept's knowledge of the inner workings of the city is now all of theirs, and they have used it to great effect to disrupt parts and sensors in many different areas of the life support systems throughout the city; they have made it appear as if the systems are on course for catastrophic failure, when in fact the damage is minimal and the people are perfectly safe.

Nevertheless, Supreme City is in turmoil, and Victor's execution is forgotten for now. The Elite have had no choice but to order all hands to help fix what they can, while they take an army to secure the new home for them all above ground that Victor has reported is waiting.

The Elite are gathering at the lift now, their mistrust of Victor far less than their fear of losing their lives when the city fails. The Elite of the Forum, now with Sovereign in charge, fill the first lift, along with their favoured Regulars as guards.

As I sense the lift beginning to rise, I weave a net of calming energy around Maverick. He sits down and nestles close to my leg. The horses also sense who is approaching. Those closest to the lift snort, then stretch their necks out towards it, their nostrils flaring. As one, they turn and gallop away. By the time the top of the lift comes into sight, all of the hundreds of horses who have gathered here are standing in a massive, distant circle around it, just close enough to be visible while being far enough away to satisfy their survival instincts.

The lift comes into sight, a mass of green-clothed Regulars – whose violet eyes all fix on me, then Maverick, and then the horses in the distance – visible, standing, rigid with fear and clutching their weapons, around the red-robed Elite.

The lift door opens. I know that it is Sovereign who barks, 'The first five out of the lift, surround the inferior and his beast. The rest of you, form a circle around the lift and your Elite. Face outwards and shoot anything that moves.'

Two of the five Regulars who move to surround me begin to

sneeze as a result of the grass pollen they have just breathed in, as do four of the Elite.

Sovereign curls his nose and the corner of his mouth up into a snarl. 'Weaklings,' he sneers, glaring around at the six who are affected. He struts to where Maverick and I are waiting, with two others just behind each of his shoulders. The Regular blocking me from his view hastens to one side. The five Elite stare coldly at me. Sovereign says, 'You will look at the ground when I address you, Disposable.'

Peerless steps forward to stand at his right shoulder and adds, 'You will look down when any of your superiors address you.'

The Regulars who surround me join the Elite in glowering at me as I gaze around at them all and say, 'I know Victor has told you that my name is Will. I'm very pleased to meet you.'

I strengthen the energy net around Maverick as one of the Regulars hits me in the face with his gun and snarls, 'Eyes down.'

My broken jaw and flesh wound are already healing by the time he is resting his weapon back against his shoulder. Maverick whines but stays in place by my leg. I open my mouth and flex my jaw, then continue, 'I would like to welcome you all above ground, and to repeat the invitation I know Victor has already extended to you from me and my people; we would love it if you would allow us to help you settle up here.'

I feel the blood drain from the faces of those around me and race to their frantically beating hearts, leaving their skin almost white as they all stare at me in disbelief.

Sovereign rallies first. 'Shoot the…' He sneezes. 'Shoot the do…' He sneezes again.

I raise my voice. 'You'll find yourselves unable to shoot Maverick, but should you try, I'll feel much less inclined to offer any of you the remedy I have here for your allergy to the grasses growing all around us. Sneezing is only the beginning. Soon, your eyes will start watering, then your airways will swell, affecting your breathing, and you may well have nosebleeds which can be heavy and extremely annoying.'

The speed at which all of the Elite process the information and come to a decision, despite the terror that grips them at the sight of my intact face and as more of them start sneezing, is impressive.

'Take his rucksack and search it,' Sovereign says, before Challenger, one of the other Elite, can say it.

I hand my back-sack to the nearest Regular, who scowls as I meet his eyes, but says nothing. He upends it so that my and Maverick's food, my dog's water bowl, my flask, and the huge pile of packets of herbal preparations given to me by Amarilla, Vickery and Hero, all fall to the ground. All of the packets of herbs are labelled with initials or symbols rather than words.

Sovereign sneezes again and nods to the packets. 'The cure for this… allergy. I will have it now.'

A hard-faced Elite whom I know to be Eminent steps up beside him. Her voice is soft as she says, 'It is poison. He would poison us.'

'You,' Sovereign nods to one of the Regulars who has just sneezed violently, 'will take it first.' He looks at me. 'Give it to him.'

'I must first insist on your assurance that you won't try to harm Maverick,' I say. 'You won't believe it now, but in time, you'll come to love him.'

Sovereign leans forward until his nose is almost touching mine. 'You don't get to bargain with me, Disposable. You're only alive because I haven't taken everything I want from you yet. Give the remedy to the Regular beside you, or I shoot the dog, then make you wish you'd never been born.' When I don't flinch, he nods to where the horses stand watching in the distance. 'I understand they have some superstitious importance to your people. They have no use to us. I'll make sure you're still alive when we start shooting them.'

'That would be a mistake. As I'm sure Victor has told you, without the horses, you won't survive.' I allow the shard of panic that flares in everyone within ear shot to sweep straight through me as Sovereign takes an involuntary step back. 'Your records of history won't show it, but the ancestors of the people of The New were escaping the cities of your ancestors for years before the cities were destroyed. They would never have survived had it not been for the horses teaching them how. That's why they're here now, to help you, because you need them every bit as much as you need me, my people and the dogs, including Maverick.'

All of them stare at the horses standing calmly, silently, in the distance, and I feel their uncertainty and its resulting fear that only adds to the layer upon layer with which they already somehow manage to function.

'Horses?' Challenger sneers. 'Your ancestors needed horses to teach them to survive? That's preposterous. Horses are beasts. We have nothing to learn from them, we are humans, and Elite humans at that.' He sticks his chest out as he turns to Sovereign. 'Stop hesitating. Shoot the dog and the horses, and have done with it, they'll just get in the way.' He points at me. 'We can use him and his people. They'll serve us until we can't stand looking at them any longer, then we'll get rid of them too.'

A loud crash makes its way up to us via the lift shaft. I manage not to smile in appreciation at Adept's timing.

'As I've already told you, if you try to harm my dog, I'll be less inclined to help you,' I say, looking around at all of those standing around me. I nod towards the lift shaft. 'That didn't sound good at all, I don't suppose you'll be wanting to go back down there. How much food have you brought with you? Enough for a few weeks, maybe? What then? You won't be able to shoot the horses, should you try. I guess you could eat Mav and me, but there isn't a huge amount of us both to go around. My village is a few days' walk from here. The next nearest community is a few weeks' trek if you know where you're going, which you don't, and neither do you have a means of sourcing water. You need me to get you and your people to my village so that my people can show yours how to provide for themselves, and you need my dog to ensure my co-operation. And I'll say this one more time, just so I can satisfy myself that I've prepared you as best I can – you do have a lot to learn from the horses.'

The lift whines as it begins its journey to the surface with the next load of people – the less powerful Elite and their Regular guards. The brains of those already above ground whir into frenetic activity as they consider all of their options and all of the possible consequences. This time, it is Eminent who reaches a decision first.

'I will allow you and that... dog,' she looks at Maverick and shudders, 'and the horses, to live for now. Since I will not take counsel from an inferior, I hereby raise you to the status of Elite. Congratulations, you will go down in history as the fastest to rise so high from so pathetically low.'

I meet her eyes, and smile. She is the cleverest of them all. She recognises my posture and body language as that which she saw in Victor before Sovereign beat it out of him. She has replayed over and over in her mind the image of my face being bloodied and distorted by the Regular's weapon, only to right itself and heal until the last drop of blood was gone, right in front of her. She is desperate to find an explanation for what she saw and her brain searches endlessly for one, but comes up with nothing... other than yet more fear.

She can't beat me as Sovereign beat Victor, because then I am no use to her, and the crash from below has convinced her that she needs me. She can't be seen to defer to an inferior, so she has raised me to her level so as to not lose face in front of those who would challenge her for her position. By being the one to give me Elite status, she has stepped past Sovereign; his control over Victor is secondary to the control everyone, including her, now thinks she, as my sponsor, has over me, so she is once again in charge. Her mouth curls up in response to my smile, but I see and feel the dread in her eyes as she fights not to shudder with it. I'd give her a hug if I could, but it won't help.

She processes my response whilst also reordering her peers in her mind in terms of their relative power now that she is back in control. Sovereign is at the bottom unless he fights her right in this instant, which she judges he can't; his eyes are, as I warned, now streaming, and he is beginning to panic as his steadily increasing nasal congestion affects his breathing.

I pick up the large packet containing Hero's hay fever preparation and tear it open across the top. I lick my fingertip and dip it into the finely ground herbs, then lick the powder that sticks to my finger. I offer the packet to the Regular who is still waiting at my side and now sneezing almost continuously. 'See, it isn't poison. Do as I did, and you'll feel better very soon.' He hesitates. 'I'm Elite, apparently, so you can go ahead,' I say. 'And you don't need to look at the ground, I'm all for eye contact.'

Eminent steps in front of the Regular and holds her hand out to me for the packet. 'The Elite will have the remedy before any Regulars do,' she says.

I move the packet well out of her reach and pass her another. 'With the compliments of one of our Herbalists,' I say, then step to the side of her and nod to the Regular to take the packet I now hold under his nose. 'Help yourself, then pass it around to anyone else who needs it.'

Eminent leans towards me and whispers, 'I made you Elite for my own purposes. Never forget that I can squash you in an instant.'

I grin and wink at her. 'I highly doubt that.' I look around and call out, 'Just lick your finger and then dip it in, that's right, that'll be plenty to ease your discomfort for now, and ensure there's enough for all of the fifty-six of you who'll have hay fever symptoms.'

Eminent steps away from me and narrows her eyes as she stares at me, moving me up in her estimation as the biggest foe yet to step into her path. She's terrified of me, yet in the way of her people, she twists her fear around her intelligence and believes it makes her even more powerful. Her dread turns to fascination. 'You can't possibly know how many will show this weakness.' She nods to Sovereign and the other four Elite also suffering and turns up the corner of her nose. I feel her glee. She has just put all five of them down at the bottom of the order of power within the Elite.

I wink again. 'Fifty-six.'

The lift door opens and more Regulars file out, followed by the red-robed Elite for whom they have been given guard duty.

'Let's all move away from the lift, shall we?' I call out, scooping my possessions into my back-sack and hoisting it onto my shoulder. 'Give your friends room to breathe and take in their new surroundings? By the way, you need to make sure your skin is fully covered, or you'll burn in the sun. When we get to Rockwood, you'll all be given a supply of sunscreen, but I couldn't carry enough to protect you all, it's the glass jars you see, they're heavy. My apologies.'

'Burn?' Eminent says, narrowing her eyes. 'I have read no reports in our history of anyone burning in the sun.'

'Your ancestors who lived above ground weren't allowed outside for long enough at a time to be affected. Once they were living below ground, those who returned from scouting missions weren't coherent enough to report the cause of the blisters on their skin, even had they been sane enough to know. You can believe me or not, it's up to you. It would have been helpful for you to have brought Victor with you, he could have given you the benefit of his experience from the past ten days.'

'Do not dare to say his name in my presence,' Sovereign snarls, then sniffs as his nose begins to clear.

'Feeling a bit easier?' I say. 'Great news, let's move away then, come on, that lift's going to be working hard today, isn't it?' I bend down and stroke Maverick's head. 'Come on, Mav.' I walk between the Regulars put in place to guard me, and once clear, call over my shoulder, 'I'm going to spend some time with the horses. I'll be back later when all five hundred of you are above ground, then we can make plans to get going.'

I sense the brains of the Elite whirring as they try to work out how I could possibly know how many they have ordered to come with them. Eminent is the first to put it to one side in her keenness to keep apparent control of me. 'You will stay where I can see you,' she orders.

I turn around and grin. 'Oh, you'll be able to see me.' I lift a hand and wave to her, then turn and begin to jog towards where Ember is waiting. Maverick barks in delight and bounces up and down beside me. 'Want to run?' I say to him. 'Shall we run?' He barks again.

I feel fifty-two pairs of eyes on us both as we run away; fifty-two brains taking in what they see and fifty-two minds ordering the information, storing some of it away for later, while using the rest of it now to assess the new situation, what it all means and how they can use it to their advantage. They have become so like the computers they idolise, they are missing the beauty that surrounds them. They don't allow it to touch them, to awaken their souls. It's time to start work on that.

I turn more of my attention to Victor as Maverick and I run. His parents have cleaned all of the blood off him and are now mystified as to where it all came from; he has surface cuts and bruises, but apart from that, he appears to be uninjured. They hold his hands while they plead with him to wake up. He'll be out for a little while yet, but he's doing fine – the horses have got him.

Ember whickers as I draw near. My heart lightens as it always does whenever he, Maverick and I are together; I am capable of much as a result of my heritage and upbringing, but without the two of them, I would still be an angry man, unable to connect my personality with my soul. We are three who have much to do together, and we are having a blast doing it.

I rub Ember's forehead between his intense, orange eyes, and grin as I remember the cheeky foal he used to be. His muscles ripple beneath me as I vault onto his back. He strides forward, his black coat gleaming in the sun, his fluted ears pricked, his weight and mine balanced on his powerful hind legs so that his front feet barely touch the ground. I sense his herd releasing him. They know he must do this without them.

'It's fun time, Mav,' I say as my dog looks up at me, his acorn-brown eyes bright, his tail wagging happily. He barks once and then falls in beside Ember as we canter towards the people of The Old.

I'm Aware of them readying the weapons I have already disabled. When we sense they are close to firing, Ember turns away and canters across in front of them. Though the sun is behind them, they squint at us as they try to make the three of us out from one another. One moment they see us as man, dog and horse, then they see something they can't believe they are seeing. That is all we need. In the moments when they question themselves, they see the truth. They don't know that's what they are seeing, but their souls do – and they are beginning to stir.

Ember veers away and canters back to his herd; he is the expert at bringing balance and he knows we've done enough for now.

I jump down to the ground once my horse has retaken his place among the others, and Maverick, frothing and panting, play-bows to me. I chuckle. 'You're too hot to play now, crazy boy.' I pull my flask strap over my head and shoulder, and cup some water in my hand for him to drink. Ember has no intention of moving from his place in the circle, so I pour the remainder of my water over him to wash his sweat off, then scrape the excess fluid away with the edge of my hand.

I head for the water hole, holding my flask. 'Come on, Mav, let's refill this, shall we?' He barks and tears off ahead. I feel far more eyes on me and Maverick now as the lift continues to do its job, and on the horses as those who watched Ember's display try to pick him out from among the rest. I smile. The very act of focusing on the horses will take them further along the path that Ember has opened up for them.

Their fear, so much a part of them that they can't help sending it to the horses along with their focus, usually comes hurtling back to them, having been multiplied by whatever they see. But the horses draw it within themselves and since it can find no place to reside within them, it wafts away into the ether having been changed by the horses to something else, leaving the observers feeling a fraction calmer. The more they watch, the more of their fear is taken from them, and the more they want to carry on watching the huge, incomprehensible beings in the distance who stand so still, so calmly, observing them in return.

I wander among the horses so that their watchers have a reason to keep doing so.

The sun is at its zenith by the time Maverick and I get back to the lift. There are people milling around everywhere, including now, some in the brown of Disposables. A man in the green of a Regular pushes between some Disposables and approaches me, his eyes cast down.

'Eyes up, Boss,' I tell him.

He stops in his tracks and glances up before lowering his eyes again. 'Eminent requires your presence. I'm to take you to her.' He whispers, 'You're not supposed to call me by my name, I'm below you in status.'

'Look at me, Boss. Properly, I mean. Pretend it's okay.'

He manages to look me in the eye, then lowers his own eyes to my chest before setting his shoulders and meeting mine again.

'You aren't below me in status, the whole idea is ridiculous,' I murmur. 'I know you don't believe me, but I'm going to repeat myself until you all do. You can just point out to me where Eminent is, if you're busy?'

He frowns in disbelief. 'Er, no, I've been ordered to take you to her. This way.' He turns and leads me back the way he came. I weave an energy net around Maverick again to keep him calm and protect him from the energy that his instincts will drive him to want to either comfort or protect me against, and follow Boss. 'How did you know my name, anyway?' he murmurs over his shoulder. 'No one apart from my wife uses it, and even she doesn't if she can help it.'

'The same way I know her name is Duress. It must be exhausting, constantly having to avoid using names. Mine is Will, although I'll answer to pretty much anything. Inferior has been used before with some success.'

Boss swallows loudly. 'Here she is.' He hurries away before I can hurt his ears any further with my insurrection.

Eminent is seated upon a red chair encrusted with stones that sparkle brightly in the sunshine. Four of the other Elite are also seated, albeit on slightly less ornate chairs, and all five are being fanned by Disposables flapping what appear to be shirts and blouses. The remaining ten of the Forum are standing, shifting from foot to foot as they watch the lift and glare at Eminent in equal measures. It takes me back to the playground at school, where the loudest children would choose who was included in their games and who wasn't.

The lift opens and five more chairs are carried out by Disposables. Regulars direct them over to us, and Eminent nods to me and then four of the Elite. The Disposables place the chairs as directed in front of me and the four others, in a semi-circle in front of Eminent. The next four Elite to have their places in the line of power confirmed by the possession of a chair, sit down.

I stay where I am, behind them all. 'You only have three more lifts' worth of people to bring up, but it's lunchtime, so we'll eat before journeying to Rockwood,' I call out. All who are seated, apart from Eminent, turn in their chairs and look up at me.

Eminent waves me to the empty chair. A wave of fury hits me from the Elite still standing as Eminent attempts to put me above them in standing. In the way of the horses, I don't give their emotion anywhere to lodge within me, but feel it change to something far less toxic as it passes through me. By the time it is released, it cannot harm any of those standing nearby.

I grin. 'Thanks, but that looks really uncomfortable. Maverick and I are going to sit and eat over there,' I wave to an area clear of people, 'where I can see the horses. Then we'll get going. My people are so looking forward to welcoming you all to our village.'

I see as well as feel their contempt for me that, despite the status Eminent has awarded me, they don't bother to hide. They have believed in their superiority for so long, they refuse even to consider that their army can possibly be withstood by humans so apparently inferior to them, let alone welcomed by them.

Despite their brainpower and despite the fact that I am one unarmed man among hundreds of them who has, in the space of a few hours, been accepted into their midst and given a place of what they deem to be power, their fear urges them to believe that I am naïve and stupid; it cannot allow them to do otherwise. The injury to my face is invisible, despite it having been inflicted in front of them, yet they have also managed to put that and Ember's demonstration of his oneness with Maverick and me, to one side, unable to allow themselves to believe they saw that which they can't understand. Such is the effect of fear, yet the inroads I have already made are as a result of that which they don't recognise having its own effect; they can't fight what they refuse to acknowledge, which makes it even more powerful.

The second that Maverick and I sit down in the grass, I sense the horses moving out of their standing circle and dropping their heads to graze. A murmur passes through the crowd and I am Aware of nearly five hundred pairs of eyes flicking between the horses and me. I open a pack of meat for Maverick, then set about my sandwich.

TWENTY-ONE

Victor

I am with Truth. I don't have a body and neither does he, but I know we're together because we can't be apart. Everything is grey – or is that because I don't have eyes, and my mind has filled in the gaps with the colour it knows best? I shake off my question as soon as it occurs to me. It doesn't matter. Nothing does. There are no battles, no threats, nothing of which to be frightened. Frightened? What is that? I know I've been frightened for nearly all of my life, so why can't I remember? Truth draws me onwards through the greyness and understanding dawns; fear doesn't exist here.

If I had a mouth, I would be grinning the lopsided grin that entices people to smile back at me. I'm Victor and I'm Shann and I'm a thousand other personalities – I remember them all. My soul runs through each and every one of them, allowing them to change me with their experiences until I am back where I started – part of the whole but now consciously so, as I could never have been without having experienced myself as the opposite.

Nothing can keep me from the truth now that it runs so

strongly through me, any more than I can hold myself apart from Truth – for even as he now follows the army of those yet to hear their souls, with the rest of his herd, he can't be anywhere other than with me. None of them can. I feel all of the horses around me, holding me together, holding me to a life I haven't finished living; Victor's life.

I hear someone calling me, which is strange, because sound doesn't exist here. The horses close in around me, pressing at me and focusing my thoughts. It is my mother who is calling... but she and my father aren't here, they are incarnate in the bodies that gave life to Victor. To me.

'VICTOR, PLEASE WAKE UP, VICTOR!' my mother shouts.

'Please, son, please come back to us,' my father pleads.

I open my eyes. 'There's no need to shout, Mum, I can hear you.' I sit up and grin at their stunned faces, then hug them back as they throw their arms around me and hold me so tightly, I can barely breathe. 'I've missed you both,' I tell them when they finally let go. 'I was angry at you for getting yourselves arrested, but I've still missed you. I'm going to get you out of here.'

'Shhhhhh,' my mother whispers, 'you know they can hear you.'

I chuckle. 'Not any more. I disabled the cameras and microphones while you were squeezing the air out of me, and my friends will keep them far too busy to come and check on us or fix the damage.'

My parents sit back on their heels, only just visible in the almost dark; clearly, the prison warrants even less light than the apartments and corridors of Disposables.

'Your friends?' my father whispers. 'What friends? And what do you mean, you disabled the cameras and microphones? That's not possible. Victor, what's happening, what trouble have you got yourself into? When they dumped you in here, unconscious and covered in blood, we thought it was to punish us further, but none of it makes sense. The blood wasn't even yours, so whose was it?'

I squint around myself in all directions, and manage to make out other people sitting on the hard, cold floor of our barred cell, as far from my parents and me as possible. I'm Aware that, as with those in the cells surrounding ours, none of them want any involvement with anyone or anything that might keep them in here any longer than their current sentences.

'It was mine,' I say. 'But don't worry about that. I'm here to get all of you out.'

'Keep your voice down,' my father hisses.

I shuffle forward onto my knees, put an arm around each of their shoulders, drawing them close, and whisper, 'All my life, you've taught me what you were expected to teach me, but you laced it with hints that there's more to life than being scared – and I know why. You feel it. You feel that living as part of this twisted regime is living less than a half life, and you're right. I was sent above ground to lead a scouting party of five others my age, and we met horses, people and dogs who between them, changed us all. The others stayed with those who helped us, but I came back to report to the Elite that it's safe above ground, and to get you out. I know this will seem like craziness, but please, both of you, trust me.'

I sit back on my heels and look from one of my parents to the other as they stare at me, then one another, then at me again, their mouths opening and closing. Even in the dim light, I can see that they are both dirty and their silver hair, previously always regulation length and style, tumbles down past their shoulders. Both have the tell-tale scars of headband torture running across their foreheads. One of my father's eyes is swollen shut and he's missing several teeth, and my mother is deaf in one ear and without several of her fingernails.

'I can't do anything about your missing teeth and nails, but I can heal everything else, if you'll let me?' I say into the silence, already tuning into the tissue of my mother's forehead that has healed in such a fashion as to cause her pain whenever she changes her facial expression. 'I'm going to take the shocked silence as a yes,' I add with a wink.

My mother puts her hands to her forehead as she feels her scar tissue follow my intention to soften and disperse. As fresh, healthy tissue forms in its place, she gasps. She watches my father's forehead heal, then holds her head as I heal the broken bones in her ear, pull them back into place, and persuade the surrounding tissue to knit back together.

'I can hear properly,' she whispers and looks at my father. 'Winner, I can hear.' She almost stops breathing as the swelling around his eye dissipates. He opens it and they both look at me in fear and disbelief. Truth. It's the only way.

'Don't be afraid, be glad,' I say. 'That feeling you've always had, that there's more to life than we've been told? Trust it, because it's your soul talking to you. That urge you've had to reach out past the fear they put into us all? Trust that too, because it's the souls of all of the other humans alive calling to yours to join them.'

My mother reaches forward and takes my face in both of her hands. 'I don't understand what's happened to you, or what's happening now, but the urge to be something other than afraid that you describe, I do have it, and it's even stronger now you're here. I trust you, son. What do you want me to do?'

My father puts a hand on my shoulder and squeezes it. 'You healed us. You really disabled the cameras and the microphones? Of course you did,' he continues without waiting for my reply. He looks around at the others and says at the top of his voice, 'Listen up, everyone, Victor's here to get us out.'

I get to my feet and speak loudly enough that all of the forty-one prisoners in our cell and those that surround it, can hear me. I tell them of my experience above ground, my recent experience in the Forum, and of the five hundred Elite, Regulars and Disposables who have been persuaded by my friend's sabotage and Will's personality, to follow my friend to Rockwood. They don't believe me any more than my parents did at first, until one by one, I heal them of their wounds. Then they listen avidly to my plan.

No one is allowed any possessions whilst in prison and there are no clocks, so nobody knows the time – but I do. I reach out to the Disposables moving around in their apartments and when their wallscreens instruct them to retire to bed for the night, I turn wearily to those in my cell.

'Okay, it's twenty-one hundred hours. Everyone except those still working on the damage to the life support systems is in bed. They're all exhausted, my friends did a great job keeping them busy.' I tune into the metal parts of the lock that holds our cell door shut. When the lock clicks, I pull the door open and beckon everyone out in front of me. 'You know what to do. Use the food and clothing stores on this floor only, then get to the lift and take it to the surface. I've just disabled the fingerpads and locks on both the stores and the lift, so they'll open for any of you.'

A woman with long, matted hair stops in the doorway and asks, 'How can you be so sure all those you say went above ground earlier have gone? That there isn't anyone up there waiting for us?'

'The same way he knew they went up in the first place, the same way he knew about all of our injuries without even being able to see most of the others, and the same way he healed us all,' my mother says. 'Go on, Quell, it'll be alright.'

The woman smiles at my mother's use of her name, and at the encouragement. I smile at the fact that by throwing in prison anyone with rebellious tendencies, those in charge have unwittingly gathered together those most open to the truth, making it so much easier for me to get them out. Further, by putting the prison on level -1, closest to the surface and therefore most vulnerable, they have made it as easy as possible for us to escape.

My parents are the last to file past me. 'You're exhausted, son,' my father says. 'I may not understand exactly how you've healed us all, but I've watched it taking more and more out of you. Are you sure your mother and I can't stay here to help you?'

'I'm fine, and I'm sure. You'll be helping me by keeping the others moving, as Mum just did. They need to get supplies and be ready to go up to the surface as soon as possible. I'll release everyone else and be close behind you.'

He sighs and nods, then draws me into a hug. When he releases me, my mother hugs me too, whispering, 'Don't be long, I'll worry about you all the time I can't see you.' Then they both disappear into the gloom.

I move from cell to cell, unlocking the doors and encouraging everyone out, dismissing their thanks for healing and releasing them in my hurry to remind them where to go, what to do, and to be as quiet as possible.

I try to ignore the mounds that remain, unmoving, on the floors of most of the cells. The smell that emanates from those who have died is meant both as extra punishment to those still alive, and a reminder not to resist anything the guards choose to do to them. It sickens and angers me, but I breathe in and out slowly as I sense Truth steadying me. I remember why I named him, and re-centre myself.

Keep going, Victor. Ace's thought wafts softly, unobtrusively into my mind. *I know you're tired, but the horses have got you. We've all got you. Keep going.*

A burst of energy almost knocks me over and I sense Rowena and Holly drawing Ace and the other four away from me and showing them how be more subtle about giving support. I smile, appreciating my friends' intention, if not entirely the result.

When I've released all of the live prisoners, I follow the last of them through the gloom of the prison, and out into the corridor of level -1.

Ace was right; the horses are with me every step of the way as I persuade my feet to keep moving, one after the other, until I reach the clothing store for the floor. I gather a laundry sack and several fresh sets of clothes, then keep myself moving until I get to the food store. I collect enough food tubs for the few days it will take to reach Rockwood, deposit them in the laundry sack with the clothes, then shuffle towards freedom.

When I reach the lift, it is just coming back down from having taken up the first half of the prisoners – my parents clearly not among them as I asked them to be, because I see them hurrying towards me. They close in either side of me and almost carry me to the lift, where they lower me to the floor.

'Everyone's here?' I say.

'Yes, son, everyone's here,' my father says.

I nod. 'Let's go then.'

The lift door clicks shut and I feel the lift floor push into me suddenly as it begins to rise. I smile as I look up at those chattering excitedly around me, and revel in how different an experience this is from the last time the lift took me up to the surface.

I close a hand around each of my parent's legs as they stand either side of me, and when they look down, I grin up at them.

'This is the beginning of the rest of your lives,' I tell them and then pass out.

When I come around, it is getting light and I am being shaken. The ground upon which I am lying has tremors passing through it in a steady rhythm that I recognise.

'Victor, huge animals that match your description of horses, are coming. What do we do?' my mother asks.

I smile without opening my eyes. 'You're already doing it. Watch them. Just watch them.'

I sense the gentle energy of the horses still weaving its way through my being, supporting my recovery from my beating and all of the healing I both received and performed yesterday. I feel them cantering towards us, one herd out of the four waiting above the city to bring balance as soon as the opportunity arises... and it doesn't take long in this instance. The Disposables who were imprisoned with my parents have long felt both Adam and Peace's loving influence wending its way through the fear of the city, and the pull of our human collective consciousness drawing them ever closer to Awareness. Their willingness to move past their fear and rebel in a hundred tiny, yet significant, ways, leaves them ready and willing to succumb to the horses' influence.

I sit up slowly, rubbing my eyes as the horses appear out of the low mist of the dawn and canter around those watching them. A woman laughs with delight as she not only sees them, but becomes Aware of them. She is joined by my father, then my mother, then gradually, by everyone else.

'You're beautiful, thank you,' someone calls out to the horses as they canter away, taking with them the last of the fear and dread of those they have so rapidly helped to Awareness.

They don't go far. When they reach the area they were grazing, they spread out, drop their heads and tear at the grass once more.

There is cheering, and everyone hugs each other. My mother begins to protest when I am pulled to my feet, but then laughs as everyone piles in to hug me. None of us speak out loud; we don't need to.

I sense the danger a split second before Will's mother speaks in my mind. *Victor, please tell them out loud that I and the others are here with them all to help, so that it's less of a shock to them. We need to act quickly to help them to ground themselves, or you and they won't be going anywhere.*

'Listen up, everybody,' I call out. A few turn around and look at me with vacant eyes, but the rest stand where they are, not seeing or feeling anything of their surroundings as they explore everything that enters their Awareness.

'EVERYONE, LOOK AT ME, RIGHT NOW,' I shout as loudly as I can. That does it. 'At some point, someone will bother to check on the prison, hell they might even remember to take us some food, and when they do, they'll know there's only one place we could have gone. We need to be away from here before then, otherwise, trust me, the fear and aggression you'll feel from them will floor you before they've even touched you. You're all Aware now, just like I told you happened to me. You can sense your connection to everything, which is amazing and wonderful, but if you're not careful, you'll get lost in everything you can feel. I know you're all sensing my thoughts as well as hearing my words, so follow what you feel from me… that's it, these are my friends. They'll help you to stay grounded in your physical surroundings, in your lives here, while being Aware. Let them help you.'

Immediately, Katonia allocates a mentor to each of my group, out of herself, my father, Lia, Levitsson, the other staff at the

Rockwood Centre, and the Horse-Bonded currently in residence in the village – all of whom get to work. The eyes of those around me come back into focus as some of them look around and begin counting while others move their mouths in silent conversation with their counsellors.

'Okay, everyone,' I say, 'let's get going, we'll eat as we walk.'

My mother smiles at me in between counting, and my father nods, his mouth forming unspoken words as he converses with Levitsson. When I begin to walk the path of flattened grass already trodden by the hundreds who have gone before us, everyone falls in behind me.

Well done, Victor, I never doubted you, Will tells me cheerfully.

I grin, knowing he's grinning too. *You never doubt anything. Thanks for healing me. I couldn't have done it myself – I couldn't have done any of this without you and Truth. A strong will and a dose of truth go a long way, don't they?*

He is chuckling now, I can feel it. *I guess so. Stay Aware of us, okay? You'll catch us up if you're not careful, this lot have weighed themselves down with so many weapons, they can barely walk and the Elite have insisted on having those hideous red chairs of theirs carried along with us as well.*

We'll stay out of sight. I don't even try to tone down the admiration for him that accompanies my thought. I remember fully how much concentration it took for me to move my Awareness between the Elite when I was before them in the Forum, so that I knew what they were thinking and how best to respond. Will knows the thoughts simultaneously of all five hundred he has with him, and can respond to any or all of them when necessary – as well as being completely Aware of what I and my group are doing and conversing with me. When I was in prison, I healed the others one by one, just as I disable weapons and bullets one at a time – I am Aware that Will disabled all of the weapons of the hundreds with him in an instant, while chatting amiably with those who want him dead. He's awesome.

And he knows it, don't make his head any bigger, the Elite will notice, Rowena interrupts my thoughts.

Much as we all appreciate – and in fact would find it hard to live without – your moral compass, do you think this is the time, Ro? Marvel retorts.

I sense the fondness for Rowena and Marvel of all of those currently focusing their attention on supporting me and my group in our endeavours, and their amusement as the pair cause all of us – including my family and friends – to smile.

It's always the time, I broadcast to them all. *Those of us from the city have lived our whole lives without being allowed to show affection, lighten the mood or support one another in the way you guys do. Bring it on, I say.*

Marvel, Justin and Levitsson all manage to make their thoughts groan. *Victor, you really should have allowed Shann's experience to influence you before letting Rowena loose,* Justin advises me, *especially as she and Ace are fast becoming one and the same. Don't say I didn't warn you.*

I'll consider myself warned. Thanks, all of you, for helping my parents and friends. I suppose I must have looked as vacant as they all do, when I was first Aware.

What makes you think you don't still? Ace asks, her thought laced with relief that I am okay.

See? You only have yourself to blame, Marvel observes.

Everyone fades from the conversation as I tell Ace, *I've missed you too. You know your parents are with the army, don't you? Prime's are too, and Hero's.*

I sense her bristle at the thought of her parents, then she remembers what has made them the way they are. *It'll be alright.*

I'm glad your parents are okay. I've missed you and the horses though. Solace is there whenever I reach for him, but the pasture just seems so empty without them all here.

We're on our way.

I can sense where Will is and I can remember the way between Supreme City and Rockwood that I have travelled twice before, but even if I couldn't do either, I wouldn't be able to miss the path travelled by those currently marching towards Rockwood. Even were the grass not trampled by hundreds of feet and littered appallingly by discarded food tubs, the hoof prints and dung of the hundreds of horses maintaining a moving circle around Will, Maverick, and the Elite, Regulars and Disposables making up the city's army, would have told me I was on the right track.

I and those with me pause to collect each and every piece of litter we can find. We are very mindful that we are, as Will advised, travelling far more lightly and therefore at a far greater speed than those we are following, but more than that, we are keen to clear up both the physical evidence and residual energy of the casual disdain the army has inflicted on the beauty that surrounds us all.

The tubs fit inside one another and are light, but even so, we can't carry them all in our arms. My father stuffs my mother's supplies into his own laundry sack and shoulders it as she opens hers for us all to deposit our finds. I smile to see them both counting the tubs as they go in, as per their mentors' instructions.

By the time we move on, the sun is hot and I advise all with me to drape spare clothes over their heads, and pull their sleeves down over their hands. I sense their fatigue as they follow me onward; they are unused either to this form of exercise, or the heat. I draw on the energy of the herd that yet supports me, and shift some of it to my people at the same time as silently tissue-singing to support the muscles of those who are struggling the most – one of whom is my mother.

Careful, Will warns me, *or you'll pass out again.* I sense him joining his intention with mine, and immediately, all of those who were tripping and stumbling around me find themselves walking more easily. *Focus on keeping yourself going, I've got them,* he tells me.

Thank you. I put all of my gratitude behind my thought, even as I sense that, like the horses, he doesn't need it.

When we stop to eat, sadness sweeps over me as I sense Truth moving further away from me, however slowly. He is with his herd – as he always is and always will be until the time comes for him to leave and form a herd of his own – and his herd is needed with Will so that my friend and Ember can do what they need to do. I understand it, it's all as it should be, but I yearn to be physically close to the magnificent bay colt. Soon.

'It's amazing that he allowed you to ride him, isn't it?' my mother says, sitting down next to me and leaning back against the same boulder. 'The horse, I mean. Well you know that, you knew it before I even started talking. Do we even bother to carry on talking anymore, or do we just talk in our minds from now on?'

I grin and put an arm around her. 'Do whatever comes first when you think of something to tell someone. For now, it's a good idea to talk out loud as much as you can, it'll keep your attention here so you don't get lost in your Awareness. And yes, it's amazing. Since the last bonded horse passed on, only the Horse-Bonded have ever been invited by the horses to ride them. It was necessary for them to invite me and the others, though.'

My mother is silent for a while. Then she murmurs, 'You call him Truth. It's what he showed you about yourself, about...' She falls silent.

'Everything,' I say. 'It's so simple, but so powerful. When you hold on to the truth, no horridness can touch you. It hurt when Sovereign beat me, but it didn't really hurt, if you know what I mean?' I look sideways at my mother and then at my father as he sits down in front of me. I sense them feeling their way around the meaning of my words. They both begin to nod.

'I have Levitsson helping me to be centred, as he calls it,' my father says. 'You've met him?'

I nod.

'So, you know he's a descendent of the Enforcers. He should hate me, but he doesn't, because he knows the truth. It transcends us all, doesn't it? We're all one. That's it.'

I look around at everyone sitting in small groups or by themselves, taking in their surroundings as they continue to follow the instructions of those helping them to centre themselves. They are still dirty and dishevelled, but they all now wear fresh clothes and their faces are free of both fear and the worry lines that have defined them for so long. They smile as they eat the white gloop that soon, they will never have to eat again. We just have a little hurdle to get over first.

A little hurdle? My father's thought is incredulous. *An army is more than a little hurdle.*

I grin at him and my mother. *For us alone, maybe. For the horses, the Kindred, Will, the Horse-Bonded and the people of Rockwood? We'll see.*

We're all shattered by the time the sun is setting, despite Will's help. 'Okay, everyone, we'll stop here for the night,' I call out. 'Choose a spot where you'll have shelter from the breeze that's just getting up. Can you feel it?' Everyone nods. 'It'll chill you if it can reach you while you sleep. In any case, you'll need to put extra clothes on top of those you're wearing to keep you warm now the sun is going down.'

As everyone mills around between the boulders and bushes of the hillside, choosing where they will rest for the night, I reach out to each of them in turn and note that they all took heed of the advice I gave them to cover up, and not one suffers from sunburn. It strikes me that none of them are suffering from hay fever either, or as a result of having drunk the water with which we refilled our flasks – which Will clearly knew would be the case, since he left none of his herbal supplies behind for me.

I reach out to him and immediately know why; those with me are healthy in body and mind. I healed them and the horses have ensured that they accept without reservation their new lives and surroundings. They move through the energies that surround them without resistance or the need to fight – so nothing resists or fights them in return. It occurs to me to wonder whether the same will apply to the wild cats and dogs that Will warned me and my friends about when we slept in the hills. I hope so, as we are without his protection.

'I wouldn't say that.'

I spin around just as Maverick's front feet land against my chest. He bounces up and down on his hind legs, trying to lick my face, and I catch him in my arms, grateful for the energy boost his presence immediately bestows upon me. 'How did you creep up on me like that?' I say to Will, opening my mouth as little as possible to keep Maverick's tongue out of it.

He chuckles. 'You were so deep in thought, a herd of horses

could have crept up on you. Oh wait, look, they did.' Ember and Truth appear from behind the bush around which Will has just stepped, and I sense the rest of their herd grazing nearby.

Truth fills my Awareness. He steps past Will, his front feet barely touching the ground as his hind legs step far underneath him, taking his weight. No one moves; everyone around me is as Aware as I that his presence is a privilege. He sniffs my shoulder and I sense the invitation that doesn't exist except for in my human mind; we both know his intention. I put a hand to his withers and vault up onto his back and Will mounts Ember in the same way.

Neither of us speak as the horses take us back the way we have come, leaving the rest of their herd grazing the hillside. My body follows Truth's easily for the most part, but there are a couple of places where I realise I am a little stiff. I release the energy that originated with Sovereign and lodged where he caused me injury, and immediately, I am one with Truth. By the time he and Ember float to a stop back at camp, I'm the person I was before I went below ground. I slide down to my feet and rest a hand against the bay colt's neck. I know exactly what he's done for me and why.

You and me both, Will tells me, still astride Ember.

I frown up at him. *You don't get knocked off balance, ever.*

The degree is different but the effect is the same. The energy of The Old is insidious; no one who is Aware can be completely immune to it. You and I will both need to be everything we can be when we get to Rockwood. Ember and Truth just ensured it.

I nod as I reach for my flask and pour water over Truth's sweaty back. *How did you get away from them?*

I'm not a prisoner as such, I'm Elite, you know. He grins. *While they need me, at least.*

They don't know what they've done, Rowena groans. *They've created a monster.*

Will and I laugh as I turn to the group. 'Everyone, this is Will.'

He lifts a hand in salutation as my father says, 'We're all Aware of that, son.' There's laughter all around.

Everyone calls out their greetings and Will grins and replies to each of them. Then he says, 'Well, I'd better get back, the Elite are getting twitchy. I just wanted to say hello, and to let you know in person how very welcome you'll be made in Rockwood, although I see Maverick's determined to give you a physical demonstration.'

One of our group is flat on her back with Maverick astride her, covering her face in licks. Her shrieks are those of delight as she feels his motive as well as his physical attentions.

'Mav, come on now, we have to get back to the five hundred people who want us both dead,' Will calls out. He says to me, 'Admittedly, though, less so than they did. Every now and then, Ember, Mav and I give them a little demonstration of how things really are, and it's having a little effect.'

'As are the horses circling you all,' I murmur as he brings the events of his day to the forefront of his Awareness for me to peruse, whilst also checking all five hundred in his group of unknowing students, and having a conversation with Lia. 'The Elite are unchanged as yet, but the Disposables are beginning to feel them, as are some of the Regulars. Well, that will help.'

He grins down at me. 'Yes, it will. There are no wild cats or dogs around at the moment, you know that. If any dogs are attracted to you all, they'll be looking for your companionship with the way you are now, not your flesh, so welcome them. If any wild cats wander close, the horses and Mav will know, and we'll come to help you if need be, so you can rest easy.'

'How will you help, exactly?'

Will glances at those watching Maverick as the dog makes his way back to us, licking each and every one of them on the way, then he looks back at me. My heart catches in my throat as, just for a moment, what appear to be thousands of dogs glare back at me in his place. I can sense them all individually – even Maverick and Breeze are there – yet they take up no more space than Will himself. Then Will reappears, though I sense he never left. He chuckles at my wide eyes and open mouth.

'I did tell you that Maverick and I can be quite scary at times,' he says. 'Sleep well, Victor.'

I nod as he and Maverick follow the horses back to where the herd is already beginning to move on. 'You too.'

TWENTY-TWO

Will

I sense both the relief and the revulsion of many of my travelling companions when they catch sight of me, Maverick, Ember and our herd reappearing around the hill adjacent to the one at whose foot they have set up camp for the night. Then I sense the familiar confusion as my dog and I blend in with our herd, becoming all but invisible, then flicker back into sight as I dismount from Ember, and Maverick and I walk back to the Regular guards set around the camp's periphery.

'Eyes up, look at me, please,' I say to those standing in my path. When they do, reluctantly, I nod and say, 'Boss, Honour, Glory, how are you doing? I hope the heat hasn't affected you too much?'

I know it has, but they will never admit they are sweating, uncomfortable and feeling a little faint as a result of dehydration. Glory has a blister on her heel, which I heal immediately.

Her eyes widen, but she says nothing other than to join in with the chorus of, 'Good, thank you. No, not at all.'

I take the lid off my flask and hand it to Boss. 'Drink as much as you need, then pass it on. I'll get more when it's empty.'

He takes it uncertainly, trying to work out what game I am playing and how to avoid the trap I must surely have set. When I nod and grin, he lifts it to his mouth and drinks. His thirst overtakes his fear and he drains the flask completely before handing it back to me.

'Right, well, I'll be back in a bit with more for you two then,' I say, nodding at Honour and Glory, who stare back at me.

I spend several hours refilling my flask from a pool of water – around which the Elite sit in their red chairs – before heading back to all of those who have not yet been permitted to approach the pool, as a reminder that although they are no longer in Supreme City, they are subject to the whims of the Elite.

The Elite are furious at my behaviour. I sense each and every one of them imagining all of the different ways they will torture me when we reach Rockwood, both to re-establish their authority in the eyes of their own people, and to break the wills of the villagers of Rockwood. But they cannot act yet; the Elite, of which they have made me a part, cannot appear to be anything other than united whilst surrounded by so many who would bring them down at the slightest provocation.

I am Aware that most of the Regulars laugh and sneer behind my back at my ignorance, weakness and willingness to serve. My behaviour gives them respite from the confusion they feel as a result of the constant, observant presence of all of the horses who surround us, and from my, Maverick's and Ember's regular and unsettling displays of oneness.

More than a few of the Disposables smile and whisper their thanks for the water, even as they look at the ground, at one another, at the sky – anywhere but at me – unable to meet my eyes even when I ask them to. I smile back, glad at the extent to which the horses are reaching them.

It has been dark for some time before I'm finally satisfied that everyone is hydrated. I wander back to where Boss, Honour and Glory have sentry duty. Glory and Honour are asleep while Boss takes his shift. He stands looking out into the night, feet apart, weapon by his side but ready to be positioned against his shoulder in an instant at the slightest hint of danger.

I stand next to him, listening to the distant sound of Ember's herd – the closest of the horses – snorting in between snatching mouthfuls of the dry, scrubby grass. I'm Aware of Boss's fear echoing that of all the others still fighting exhaustion in their efforts to stay awake.

They have survived their first day of breathing strange air; drinking dirty, strange-tasting water while sweating so much of it back out; tripping and stumbling over unfamiliar terrain; dealing with the discomfort of the heat, biters, and allergies; enduring the constant reminders of their lack of control presented by the strange smells and sounds of which they have no knowledge, no experience and no idea how to defeat; and being subjected to the strangeness of the horses who frighten them yet seem to call to them, to draw them into their strangeness – and it has all taken its toll on them. Those too exhausted to take any more have welcomed sleep as a welcome release, but to the rest, sleep is as much a danger as everything else.

'You're worn out. Sleep, I'll take your shift,' I say to Boss.

His eyes flicker sideways to me in the moonlight, then return to watching the shadows. 'I don't understand you,' he says. 'You're Elite, you can rule along with the rest if you want, but you persist in trying to throw away the power they gave you. They'll kill you, you know, you've given them no choice.'

'They'll certainly try.'

I sense his incredulity. 'You actually believe you can stop them? Are all of your people as stupid as you?'

'I don't believe in beliefs, I just go on what I know. Rest, Boss, I've got this. Okay?'

He hesitates.

'If it helps, that was an order.'

He throws his hands up in the air in the moonlight. 'You're one crazy idiot. Fine.' He hands me his gun. 'Take this.'

I chuckle. 'Thanks, but no thanks.'

He sighs. 'If you haven't the guts to use it, wake me if need be and I will.'

'That won't be necessary. Rest easy, friend.'

He is still shaking his head as he lies down, but I feel my words settle within him. Within ten breaths, he's asleep.

I lie down beside him and Maverick snuggles alongside me as he always does. He is as Aware as I am that the pack of dogs approaching Victor's camp will only add to the joy of their new lives. The two families of wild cats in the far distance are both moving away, having no desire to come anywhere near two large groups of humans, despite the scent of horse flesh that initially gave them pause to consider it. The horses are hydrated, rested and content. I smile. All is well with the world. Within minutes, Maverick and I are asleep.

I wake every time a member of the Elite considers whether to give in to their urge to murder me in my sleep. Sovereign comes the closest to actually attempting to do it; his fury at my most recent behaviour combines with his desperation to wrestle control of the rest of the Elite back from Eminent, making him forget his need for me to show him the way to the village that he thinks he will then rule. It is a loss of control which, were he back in the city, would have cost him his life.

I sense Ember shifting on his feet as Sovereign hunts for me in the moonlight amongst the now largely sleeping army... then I'm Aware of the black stallion settling back into his standing doze as a Regular on guard calls out for whoever is creeping through the camp to show themselves. Shocked back to his senses, Sovereign scurries back to the other Elite, terrified now of losing further status than he has already, by being caught in the act of trying to kill the only one who can lead them out of the hellhole in which they currently perceive themselves to be.

I wake Honour shortly before dawn so that she won't be caught neglecting her duty. 'I took the shift before you and didn't feel sleepy, so I let you sleep on,' I tell her. 'If anyone wants me, I'll be with the horses.'

'No one wants you, we're just stuck with you and that disgusting animal of yours,' she replies, scowling at Maverick, who has just carefully placed a twig of heather by her foot for her to throw.

'That does seem to be the case for now,' I say. 'Come on, Mav, we'll leave everyone in peace.'

I sense Boss's newly opened eyes on my back as I throw Maverick's twig for him and head for the horses. He suspects I must have kept watch all night so that he and the others could rest, but he can't figure out why, any more than he can make sense of anything else I do. He looks to where he can hear the horses, and I sense him trying to pick them out in the dimness of pre-dawn. He doesn't know exactly why he looks to them as often as he catches himself doing, but he's beginning to realise he feels better when he does. I grin to myself.

The first rays of sunlight burst over the horizon just as I reach Ember. He raises his head, his amber eyes reflecting the orange light and appearing aflame. He looked after me when I was a boy and he was incarnate as my father's Bond-Partner, Candour, and he looks out for me now as a member of his herd.

I sit down cross-legged in the grass near his front legs, and he lowers his head back down to graze. Maverick nudges me with a big stick he has broken off a bush. As soon as I look at him, he drops it and play-bows.

I laugh. 'How many times, Mav? Not sticks. Here you go.' I pull a packet of smoked meat from my back-sack and open it, and the stick is forgotten.

I eat my breakfast in the tranquillity of the herd. Every now and then, orders and reprimands waft over from the army camp, but they seem a hundred miles away.

When I sense that Eminent is wanting to get the day's travelling underway, I get to my feet. Maverick barks, as sure as he always is that we are about to do something fabulous and exciting. He reminds me that we are. I crouch down and hug him, grateful to him for the millionth time.

I nod to Boss as I pass him and the others. Everyone else is careful to look anywhere but at Maverick and me as I pass them on my way to where some Disposables are rushing around, packing the rucksacks of the Elite and readying themselves into teams to carry the red chairs.

'In the short time I've had the extreme displeasure of knowing you,' Eminent says haughtily but quietly to me, 'I've come to realise that you have no pride, no shame, no respect and no ambition.'

I nod. 'All true.'

'Explain yourself.'

'There's nothing to explain, really. I have no attachment to how people see me, so I don't have any use for pride or shame. Respect is insignificant in the face of unconditional acceptance, and as for ambition, well, isn't that just wanting something I don't already have?' She glares at me. 'Okay, well I'll take that as a yes, so then I have no need for that either.'

She narrows her eyes and I sense her fear of me – the first person she has ever met whom she can't understand – that she has so desperately been holding to one side, building back up. She must attack me in the only way she can at present.

'You're no better than the beasts whose company you keep,' she hisses. 'You even wander around like they do; you don't have roads and you don't have vehicles. It is amazing, is it not, that in all the hundreds of years your people have lived up here, with all of the raw materials available to you, none of you have thought to create vehicles to transport yourselves? Are you really all so primitive and so stupid?'

'We're descended from those who couldn't stand being disconnected from the living world around us, and that trait has survived. We're rarely in a hurry, and when we have cause to travel anywhere, we enjoy the walk,' I reply.

'You enjoy being sweaty and dirty? You like being vulnerable to the heat and the cold and,' Eminent shivers, 'to water falling from the sky?' She turns to the rest of the Elite and announces, 'I'd be surprised if the inferiors even try to stop us conquering them, we're doing them a favour by taking them on.' They all snigger and she turns back to me. 'Give us a few years and we'll have transport vehicles in the sky, on roads, underground, wherever we can think of to put them, and your people will enjoy building and maintaining them for us.'

'It never hurts to dream, I suppose,' I say to her with a wink. 'Let's get going, shall we? We have another day's walking ahead of us, and by the sound of it, I'd better enjoy it while I can.'

She stiffens, as does everyone else in the vicinity. I feel again the fury of the Elite, and their desperation to obliterate me warring with their need to get to civilisation. I turn to lead the way and notice a Disposable turning quickly away, the hint of a smile on her face. As Maverick passes her, she drops a hand to trail across the top of his head. He licks it and carries on his way.

A long, hot day follows of walking out of the hills and across the grasslands to the woods between us and Rockwood. I'm well Aware of the misery of most of the army as they slap at biters in between constantly rearranging their clothes so that their heads and hands remain covered.

Many of the fifty-six suffering from hay fever are struggling, since the Elite have kept for themselves the packets of remedy I distributed. I walk from one sneezer to the next, offering herbs from a further packet I keep in my back-sack, and which none dare to take from me. The Elite have also kept the body cleansing herbs which will repel any water parasites, so I dispense more from my supplies to those suffering from stomach cramps. None of them show weakness by complaining, but many nod their thanks for my help.

Once we are well into the open countryside of the grasslands, the horses are far more visible as they continue to maintain their circle around us. I sense more and more of the Disposables and Regulars watching them for longer at a time. Even the Elite forget to hide their glances as they check whether the horses are still there.

'Why are they still following us?' Peerless eventually demands of me.

'They aren't following us, they're surrounding us,' I reply.

'They've remained in a circle around us since we came above ground,' Eminent agrees. 'Why?'

'Circles are fascinating,' I say. 'Did you know that ancient civilisations saw them as representing unity, wholeness and infinity?'

'That is a ridiculous superstition that belongs in the past, just like those who believed in it. Do not insult my intelligence by trying to convince me that the horses believe in it also.'

I hold up my hands. 'I wouldn't dream of insulting any part of you. And no, the horses have no need to attach meaning to anything, their behaviour is purely their response to what they sense. Everything has an energy, and circles are no exception. When it is horses forming the circle, that energy becomes much more powerful. When they move in their circle in the way that these horses are all capable, its power is immeasurable.'

'The Disposable who reported to us on the conditions here dared to suggest that horses have power,' Sovereign scoffs. 'This is what he was talking about? Power comes from a combination of strength, intelligence and a willingness to fight.' He looks around himself. 'I don't see us falling down dead because the horses are circling us, do you?'

'They're not trying to kill you, they're helping you. I know you've noticed everyone watching them, I know you see the effect they're having, even if you don't feel it yourself as yet. But you will.'

'Silence,' Eminent orders. 'The horses are only alive until we no longer need you. Then we'll be rid of them and you once and for all, you can count on it.'

She can hide her unease from those around her, but she can't hide it from me.

By the time we reach the trees, the sun is disappearing behind the hills we left earlier in the day.

'We'll camp here for the night, it'll soon be too dark to fight our way through the forest,' I call out to the Elite.

I know that Ember wants me. I wander to the outskirts of the army, passing the last Regular guard just as Ember appears in front of me. There is a collective gasp from all those nearby as they see him up close for the first time. It pleases me that none of them have even considered attacking him during his approach. They watch in silence as I vault onto his back. As he carries me away, Maverick running excitedly at his side, I am Aware of them suddenly realising that they are still holding their weapons loosely at their sides. They look down at their guns, then briefly at one another, in confusion. They have always been afraid, always on the defensive whilst ready to attack, yet one of those who only yesterday terrified them so much that they would have shot at this range without even thinking, has left them gazing after him, feeling nothing that they recognise.

Ember, Maverick and I canter around the army, most of whom stop what they are doing to watch.

'Everyone, get back to setting up camp, or you'll be shot where you stand,' Sovereign shouts, yet he too can't stop trying to figure out why he can only see one being where he knows there are three.

I sense Eminent's stare as well as the unease that continues to grow within her while increasingly refusing to be pushed to one side. She is trying to decide whether to have me killed now and have done with it, but decides that she still can't risk it. Not quite yet.

Ember brings me back to the same spot from which he picked me up. The Regulars nearby are following their orders while watching the majestic, black stallion out of the corners of their eyes. They are more than impressed. He is far larger than they are, more muscular, and as they have already seen, he is much faster. His orange eyes glint with intelligence. He is everything they value in themselves and more, yet they still can't find it within themselves to see him as a threat. He shows no sign of having even noticed that they exist... and they are beginning to want him to.

Ember canters back to his herd, leaving me to walk amongst the Regulars. Many of them are blinking and either slapping their own faces with both hands or shaking their heads, trying to loosen the effect Ember has had on them. Many of them allow Maverick to lick their hands as we pass, and a few even stroke him surreptitiously. My dog is delighted, but he senses as keenly as I do that they could still turn on him.

I open my heart and send everything within it to my brave, beautiful Maverick. He turns and leaps into my arms, covering my face with licks. When I eventually put him down, those nearby smile at him as he barks and play-bows to me as if he and I are the only ones here. I pick a long stalk of grass and toss it into the air. He catches it and then trots next to me, carrying it proudly as if it's the best toy he's ever had.

By the time I've taken water and herbs to everyone who needs them, the sun has long set and the warm night is still. I wander to the edge of the camp closest to where Ember and his herd are grazing, and look out into the night, far beyond the horses, towards where I sense Victor and his group moving as stealthily as they are able.

You've made good time, I tell him. *They're a good bunch with you, to keep going without complaint.*

They are. Thank goodness for the horses blocking us from the rear sentries' vision, though, otherwise we'd have had to wait for dark before leaving the hills.

You're almost at the path through the forest. You can rest soon. It may be a longer route than the one we'll be taking, but you'll still reach Rockwood before us; getting this lot through all that undergrowth in the morning is going to take time.

And a lot of their energy. You can be a cruel man, Will. I sense an echo of Shann in his humour.

Just pushing them as hard as I pushed you. Complaining?

I know Victor is smiling as he responds. *Not complaining at all. We'll carry on for as long as we can see, then we'll rest. We're flagging, but the dogs are keeping our spirits up.*

I grin as Maverick snuggles in close to me. *They're very good at that. And you can sleep easy now they're with you, no wild cats will dare come close to a pack of dogs. Sleep well, my friend.*

You too, and try not to get murdered, okay? See you in Rockwood.

TWENTY-THREE

Victor

I really thought that my life couldn't get any better; I had my parents with me, I had Truth and the truth. Then, just as I was dropping off to sleep last night, I became Aware that a pack of eleven dogs was approaching, drawn to us by everything we have become.

I shared what I sensed with the others, along with my experiences of all the other dogs I have had the joy of meeting. By the time the dogs came slinking into our camp, all eleven tails wagging, we were waiting to welcome them with food from our supplies. While they took some time sniffing our offerings, they eventually decided it was better than nothing and lapped the tubs clean. Then they settled down amongst us as part of our pack, accepting the sound of our voices as we spoke softly to them, and our hands as we stroked them.

When some of the younger dogs rose to play in the moonlight, wrestling with one another and pretending to bite each other's faces before chasing one another madly between the boulders, we all watched in delight. Tired as we were, their energy and joy for life revived us, and I ended up joining in with the game, as did some of the others. By the time we all settled back down to sleep, it felt as if we had been a pack for weeks rather than hours.

Today, the dogs have lifted us beyond where any of us thought we could be lifted. We're tired, but though we walk on our own feet, we are carried by their energy; they bound around us as if there is nothing they would rather be doing, nowhere they would rather be, and we believe them.

They are larger dogs than Maverick, or any I have seen in Rockwood, and a uniform grey. I am Aware that they are all related; the largest two are a breeding pair, seven are their offspring and the remaining two are the sisters of the lead female. During the day, however, their pack dynamics have become less defined, as if now that they have humans as part of their number, the rules by which they previously organised themselves no longer apply. The lead pair have become every bit as bouncy and daft as the rest and they have all delighted us with their never-ending energy and antics.

They have followed us since we left camp, but now, as we enter the darkness of the woods, it is we who follow them. They bound eagerly along the path we have chosen, never straying far enough in front of us that they disappear into the darkness, and returning frequently to greet us and then turn and trot on again, encouraging us to keep going.

Such is their energy and enthusiasm that we find ourselves walking on through the night, unable to bear disappointing them by coming to a stop. We exit the trees just as the first birds begin to question the dawn. Immediately, the dogs rush to stand in front of us, the fur along their backs sticking upright, their tails erect.

'Stand down, guys, it's all good,' I say, stepping between and then in front of them as I see movement by the nearest cottage of Rockwood's cobbled streets.

By the time Ace and the others are halfway to meeting us, the dogs have decided I am right. They race towards those coming to greet us all, and there are yells of delight when they reach their targets. Ace tears herself away from the melee first and runs straight at me, almost knocking me over when she reaches me.

When she finally lets me go, I keep an arm around her and turn to my parents. 'Um, you remember Ace?' I say to them both.

They don't get a chance to speak; Ace hugs them both, then puts an arm around each of their waists and says, 'You're exhausted. What were you thinking, carrying on through the night like that? Ah, I see the dogs, I understand, but the fact remains, you need food, a bath and then sleep, in that order.' She guides them past me and back towards Rockwood, saying, 'It's a bit of a squeeze at our place at the moment, but you can both have my bed, I mean you're that exhausted, you won't mind sharing, will you?'

'It's unsettling, isn't it?' Marvel grins at me, holding his hand out for me to shake. 'When she's with Rowena, they can't agree on anything, but when the two of them are apart, it's like they're the same person. Well done, mate. Oooooh steady there, I've got you.' He grabs my arms and stabilises me as my legs begin to shake. One of the dogs is by my side in an instant, leaning into me.

'This is Guide,' I manage to say. 'She and her pack have adopted us. They led us all through the night.'

'Okay, well we'll make sure they're all fed and looked after, but for now, we need to get you some food and rest. What were you thinking, giving all your food to the dogs? You know they can hunt for themselves, right?'

'Yes, we know, but they carried us here... you're going to

have to search my Awareness, I don't have the energy to tell you
about it.'

'Just focus on keeping your legs going until we get you to
Will's, since Ace is apparently filling Justin's house with your
parents in addition to her, me and Ro.'

'Is everyone...'

'Everyone else is being looked after,' Marvel assures me. 'You
see, the thing about being Aware is that we're rarely taken
unaware.'

'Well it's rare for Marvel anyway, it's unheard of for the rest
of us,' says Rowena.

I'm too tired to smile. I allow myself to be led back to Will's
cottage, where Lia puts a plate of something in front of me; I don't
even register what it is as I eat it, all I know is that it's hot and it
smells and tastes amazing. When she shuts the bathroom door
behind me, I lower myself into the hot bath awaiting me while Lia
and Tania play loudly outside the door to make sure I don't fall
asleep. I scrub myself all over then wrap myself in a towel. I think
I get the worst of the water off before sinking into a bed of sweet-
smelling sheets. There is barking in the distance, then a pounding
of feet on the stairs. A weight lands on top of me and I'm licked
all over. I smile faintly as the warm, furry weight snuggles up
beside me.

'Thank you, Guide,' I whisper.

I'm being shaken and licked awake at the same time. 'Is it
morning?' I murmur.

'It was morning when you got here and it's been morning for a
long time, in fact it's almost afternoon,' Ace whispers. 'I'm sorry,
Vic, we've left everyone else to sleep, but you have to wake up,

we need you.' The urgency in her voice brings me to full wakefulness.

I sit up and Guide finally ceases licking my face and snuggles up beside me. I reach out to Will in my Awareness and find him almost at the edge of the forest. I look up at Ace, who nods and says, 'It's time.'

TWENTY-FOUR

Will

*T*he army fights the forest as if it is every bit as much an enemy as everything else. I advise the Elite who are closest to me on numerous occasions to look for the path of least resistance, even though I know they can't allow themselves to listen. Not yet.

By the time Maverick and I step onto the path that has been churned up by the hundreds of horses who passed by some hours before, those who step out behind us are even more sweaty and irritable than they were when we set off just after dawn.

No birds sing in the trees, no animals rustle through the undergrowth; all have fled from the five hundred strong army that is forcing its way to Rockwood.

'This will be the first road I order your people to create,' Eminent says, looking up and down the path.

'Maverick, go to Lia,' I say to my dog. He looks up into my eyes and tilts his head on one side. 'Go and find Lia,' I say and he barks, then tears off down the path in delight at the game.

Eminent watches him go. 'Rockwood is that way?' she asks me.

'Yep, just beyond the last of the trees.'

'Put a headband on the Disposable and shoot the dog,' Eminent orders.

A Regular takes aim and fires the weapon I reactivated as soon as the horses were out of sight, after we entered the trees. I turn the bullet to dust before it is halfway to where Maverick's excitement is driving him on to a waiting Lia and Breeze. His part in this is done for now.

My arms are grabbed by two more Regulars as a third lowers a headband around my forehead, tightens it and puts his forefinger to the fingerpad I've just disabled.

I can only turn my head, but I manage to look Eminent in the eye. 'Does it suit me?'

'It'll suit you far more once it has burned into your flesh, causing you to scream and void your bowels and bladder in front of those who would resist us,' she sneers and then laughs. 'Lead us home, Disposable.'

'As you wish. I'll just say it one last time, though; none of this is necessary. You don't need to fight us in order to have food, a home and a place in our community, we're already offering you all of those things.'

One of the Regulars holding on to me punches me in the gut. 'You don't speak until you're spoken to. Eyes down, Disposable, and walk.'

I heal my injury, smile, and walk the path that my dog and my horse have trodden before me. It isn't long before it lightens. I am Aware of the focus of my family and friends as they wait for me to arrive. I step out of the trees and smile at the sight before me as the Regulars tighten their grips on my arms.

Ember is at the centre of a wall of horses who stand watching as I am pushed forward while the army files out of the forest behind me. The horses' muscles ripple as they dislodge the biters that land on them, but apart from that, they are motionless, their eyes gleaming in the sunshine.

'The horses are your defence?' Eminent sneers from just behind me and then says to a Regular with red stripes on his arm, 'Five ranks of a hundred. Prepare to fire.'

The horses remain absolutely still while the army hurries to organise itself as she has ordered.

Eminent says, 'Stand aside, Regular,' to the guard on my left, and stands in his place, looking at the horses and the village beyond. She leans towards me and breathes in my ear, 'That's the extent of hundreds of years of life above ground? A ramshackle collection of tiny, ugly houses, a people too cowardly to come and face us, and a load of filthy animals you've somehow forced to stand in their place?'

I grin. 'I understand completely why you would see it that way. Have no fear though, very soon, everything will become clear.' I look behind me and add, 'We'll just give them a few more minutes to get into position, shall we?'

Eminent takes a handful of my hair and pulls it hard as she turns my head to face her. Her eyes widen, her pupils dilate and her breathing rate increases as she anticipates the pleasure of witnessing my pain. She reaches up and presses a button on my headband. I gaze into her eyes. A hint of a frown appears on her face as she tries to understand why I appear unaffected by the torture she is attempting to inflict on me. There is movement amongst the horses and she releases her grip on my hair as she turns to see what is happening. I grin and wave as some of the villagers of Rockwood appear between the horses and stand shoulder to shoulder with them. None of them speak.

Eminent grabs my arm and shoves me in front of her. I sense

her fear as she returns to her attempts at understanding how I am withstanding the crushing pain I should be feeling from the headband. Her brain works at incredible speed but in vain, until she wonders at last whether she should have paid heed to Victor's warning that she cannot defeat me. The thought begins to eat at her but she has no choice other than to proceed as she has already announced she will, otherwise those waiting to take her place will strike.

'I give you one opportunity to surrender,' she calls out to the villagers of Rockwood. 'There will be no negotiation. Kneel to me, or die painfully. Like this.' She presses another button on my headband, hoping upon hope that the flesh of my forehead will now burn as she is so desperate for it to. Nothing happens. She shakes violently now as she grasps me, terrified not only of the peril she has put herself in from those in front of her, but from those behind.

Amarilla steps beyond the line of horses and walks towards us, stopping when she is fifty strides away. Eminent can't stop herself gasping along with everyone else as they all notice the second pair of blue eyes that looks out of Amarilla's at them all. I grin; I know exactly how it feels to be the subject of Infinity's scrutiny.

Amarilla speaks, but it is Infinity who counsels, 'Just as millions of humans have done before you, you believe that the way to feel safe and worthy is to amass power. Further, you believe that the only way to possess that power is to take it from those whom you believe to be separate from you. It is no more the truth than it ever was but the pattern has been played out so often during history that even after all that has been accomplished by those of The New, its echo yet remains in the human collective consciousness. You have our gratitude for your determination to allow the pattern to play out to exhaustion, for now, together, we will finally clear it.'

I feel the shock of those listening, as much because they are finding themselves listening as because of the words that Infinity blasts into us all.

Eminent rallies first. 'Do. You. Surrender?'

'Constantly. I can recommend it,' Amarilla says, continuing to look from one to the next of those standing behind me. 'I know there are many of you who don't want to fight. You sense the horses as well as see them, and you enjoy the connection you feel with them. So, don't fight. Focus on the horses, who they are and what you feel from them, and know that they and we will protect you.'

Peerless steps forward beside Eminent and laughs. 'You know nothing, Disposable. We've tolerated those filthy beasts because…' The words die in her throat as the Kindred villagers step out from behind the horses and humans. The panic of the people of The Old hits us all like a river in flood.

Eminent shoves me forward towards Amarilla and steps back amongst her army, screaming, 'FIRST RANK, FIRE AT ALL OF THEM, LEAVE NO ONE STANDING.'

Less than the full complement of the hundred in the front row fire their bullets at those of us standing before them.

Amarilla and Infinity gaze at me and smile as I meander over to them whilst thousands of bullets disintegrate all around us whilst on the way to their targets. I reach Amarilla's side and turn to watch the army.

Eminent yanks the gun from the grasp of a Regular who has refused to fire, and hits him with it. I heal his cut and fractured skull immediately, and he sits up, rubbing his head and frowning in confusion.

Eminent hoists the man's weapon and screams, 'SECOND RANK, FIRE.'

'Are you going to take that headband off? It does nothing for you,' Amarilla murmurs.

I take it off and look at it. 'I thought it suited me. Eminent disagreed, obviously, but then she disagrees with everything I say.'

Those of the third rank still willing to fight fire their rounds, followed by those of the fourth and then the fifth. As we all – humans, Kindred and horses – continue to stand, unharmed, watching them, the panic of those shooting only escalates. They all begin firing at will, including all of the Elite. Some shoot those amongst them who are refusing to shoot at us, only to find that their bullets disintegrate along with the rest. I heal all of those injured as a result of being manually attacked by their compatriots, so that everyone else can focus on ensuring no bullets arrive at their targets intact.

When the bullets finally run out, there are less than a few hundred still disconnected enough from the rest of us that they continue to see fighting us as their only option. Knives are brandished, small metal stars are thrown, and metal rods are held out at arm's length as they extend to full length staffs. All disintegrate, but those still needing to fight charge on anyway, fuelled by the battle rage they value so highly. They will kill us with their bare hands. They are convinced of it.

A thunder of hooves precedes the arrival of Ember and the lead mare of his herd alongside Amarilla and me. Within seconds, we are on their backs and joining the huge herd now circling the villagers of Rockwood, protecting them from their attackers while creating the whirlpool of energy that will draw everything to balance as it has so often before.

Those intent on killing arrive at a moving wall of horses, all cantering slowly, powerfully, as if there is no emergency, nothing of which to fear. The horses are from different herds and of all ages, builds and colours, but all move their legs in the same rhythm that doesn't change even as they trample those determined to break between them, or when they are charged by those attempting to leap on them either to reach the humans and Kindred beyond, or to attempt to bring down the horses themselves.

We heal those who are trampled even as their injuries – some of which would otherwise be fatal – occur, so that their pain is momentary and the interruption to their attack short-lived. When they get up and charge again, they are trampled again – and we heal them again. Those who try to leap onto the horses' backs are easily repelled by a buck, a side-step or a kick. When they join those being trampled on the ground, we heal them too, and continue to heal them after every subsequent attempt.

Throughout, the horses are immovable from who they are. They glisten with power as they draw out their attackers' fear, draining the strength of their assaults as surely as does their fatigue from being injured and healed so many times.

I glance around and grin as one by one, the rest of the Horse-Bonded accept the invitations of the horses who slow down beside them until they are mounted. The energy that swirls above and around us is palpable as it gains in strength, drawing more and more fear out of those who surround us and flinging it out into the ether as the love it always was. Some of the Regulars still attacking us pause their assaults and blink, trying to make sense of what they are seeing and feeling. Their hesitation is all their souls need to urge them to look harder, to open to everything they feel.

Many of those yet driven on by battle rage slow the frequency of their attacks at the sight of Fitt cantering past – and in many cases over – them on a tall, grey mare, the Kindred's participation in our circle of unity prodding at them deep inside in a way they don't understand.

It is time.

There is a clatter of hooves on the cobblestones and six horses emerge from Rockwood at a gallop, carrying the teenagers previously of The Old, now of The New.

Eminent processes the new development with the same speed that she does everything else, relating it to everything I told her earlier and everything she has witnessed since. She runs towards the six galloping horses, waving her arms at them and screaming to those still attacking, 'DON'T LET THEM JOIN THE CIRCLE.'

She is too late. The teenagers and their horses reach us and merge seamlessly into our display of connection, oneness and inclusion.

We all sense the shock of the remainder of our attackers as they recognise the new riders – and yet can't place them at all. The muscular, grey-skinned, purple-eyed, silver-haired teenagers look just like the attackers themselves, yet they couldn't be more different. There is a softness to them that only serves to make them appear stronger. Their posture should scream of weakness and lack of fight and ambition, yet they sit their horses with an air of having achieved everything they could ever have wished for. They should be trying to kill the Kindred who rides alongside them, and to beat us humans into submission, yet they laugh delightedly with us all as if we are old friends, as if they have nothing to fear from us and no point to prove – and as if none of us are under attack. They are invincible without trying to be, without needing to be; the horses' strength and power is theirs.

Our attackers' legs give way as the vision before them causes their very idea of themselves to fragment. They are unable to move as the horses canter out and around them and all those who have succumbed before them, until all are included within the circle. We all work together to maintain the vision of oneness and inclusion, but it is the horses' energy that holds together the minds of those who are falling apart, while drawing their souls out to join us in Awareness.

Eminent, Peerless and Sovereign are the last to succumb. We cheer as we sense them finally exhaust the pattern of violence and separation that has gripped humans for millennia, releasing it from our collective consciousness so that, like the fear that created and drove it, it is absorbed back into All That Is as that which it always was.

Our job now is to look after all of those who performed the task for us all; those who fought the final battle and won.

TWENTY-FIVE

Victor

$\mathcal{W}$here I was exhausted, I am now exhilarated. My soul sings within me, drowning out my body's requests to rest while it continues to recover the blood it lost and the energy it has expelled over the past few days. I can't possibly go back to bed and sleep after what has just happened.

I watch all of the horses apart from Ember's herd galloping towards the trees and then disappearing among them. They are needed to help those waiting above Supreme City for the people still below ground, who, now that the pressure of the pattern to fight for power has been obliterated from their consciousness by the Elite and Regulars who held to it, feel that which they have always felt, but have never been allowed to recognise.

Even now, the first of them are making their way to the lift, no longer able to bear the energy of their home now that everything keeping them there has gone. They are spurred on by the love with which Adam and Peace infused the city so long ago and which has sustained them all this time, helping them to stay true to everything they felt even when they were forced to conform.

When they reach the surface, it will help them to recognise the love of the horses who are waiting for them. They will be Aware before the day is out.

The horses of Ember's herd wander amongst those sitting, kneeling or lying in the grass, unable to function now that they have been stripped of all they believed. The villagers also wander amongst them, healing their brains of the chemical imbalance responsible for battle rage, now that they no longer need or want it; now that it has no place. Some of those who attacked us are crying, others are moaning, but most just stare blankly around them, uncomprehending of, and overwhelmed by, everything of which they are now Aware. The horses' energy weaves around and through them all, holding fragile minds together where they would otherwise fall apart.

Maverick bounds around Will, overjoyed to be reunited with him, but all of the other dogs of Rockwood, including those who arrived here with me earlier in the day, walk slowly, carefully, to those who need them.

The Disposables are sniffed, licked and snuggled into as if they are old friends. The Regulars are approached with more caution, the dogs sitting or lying in the grass nearby, then gradually shifting closer until they are able to rest chins or paws on knees and shoulders. Then they are still, just there, loving those whose souls volunteered for such a difficult mission. Aware as the people now are, they sense everything the dogs feel for them. When hands reach for those who love them without reservation, the dogs shuffle closer, the warmth of their bodies emphasising the warmth of their hearts.

The Elite are given far more space than the rest. Dogs lie in their vicinity, their tails thumping on the ground, their eyes squinting and bodies wriggling whenever any of the blank-faced

Elite happen to rest their eyes on those who just want to give them the love they have denied themselves for so long.

I see Prime crouch down in front of a brown-clothed woman. His mother lifts her tear-stained face and reaches a finger up to her son's cheek, tracing the line of his jaw as if seeing him for the first time. They are both Aware, but neither knows how to relate to the other now that everything they were to one another has fallen away.

Will's grandmother kneels down awkwardly beside them, her brightly-coloured skirt billowing out over the grass, and hands Prime his puppy. He smiles as Hope licks his nose, and strokes her head. A ghost of a smile forms on his mother's face. Prime holds Hope out to her, and she holds a finger out for the puppy to lick, then takes her gently into her arms. Hope wriggles around to face the woman and smothers her face in kisses. Prime shuffles closer to her, and Mailen puts an arm around both of them, whispering to them as she pulls them even closer together. Eventually, Prime puts an arm around his mother's shoulders.

I look away and see that Will and Maverick are now sitting in the grass near Eminent. Will laughs as Maverick nudges a clod of earth dislodged by the horses, against his knee. My friend picks it up and throws it, and Maverick tears off, barking. Eminent jumps at the sound, her eyes moving slowly to where the slender black dog with his white-striped face has grabbed hold of what is left of the clod, and is shaking it. She watches in silence as he trots back to Will, dumps a mouthful of soil into his lap and then lies down, panting, just in front of her. He keeps looking away as she continues to stare at him. When she finally looks at Will, Maverick shifts a little closer to her and lies with his head on his paws, looking up at her.

Eminent isn't sure she wants to feel that which she does from the dog; it's too overwhelming. Ember appears behind her and lowers his head to just above hers. His energy wends its way through her, reassuring her even as it surrounds her and holds her together so that she can cope with feeling Maverick's limitless, unconditional love. The three of them will stay with her as long as it takes.

I wander to where Sovereign is kneeling in the grass. All of the wounds he sustained whilst he was attacking have been healed, but he landed on a large stone when he dropped to his knees, and one of his knee caps is fractured. He welcomes the pain, convinced that he deserves it now that he is Aware of his connection to all of those he wanted to obliterate.

Will you allow me to heal you? I ask him. *You no longer need your brain to give you battle rage and the pain in your knee is unnecessary.*

He can't look at me. 'Back... at... the city. I... nearly... killed... you,' he whispers, his mouth moving as if by itself as he continues to stare blankly ahead.

I sit down to one side of him and cross my legs in the grass. Guide appears and after snuggling in to me for some fuss, lies down between Sovereign and me, looking from one of us to the other as if she is part of the conversation – which she is.

'You didn't know what you know now,' I say to Sovereign. 'You're Aware of how I feel. You know I bear you no ill will, in fact I'm grateful to you, all of us are, for what you and the others put yourselves through. The pattern that has plagued humanity for so long has finally been released, thanks to you. Please, let me heal you? It's the least I can do.'

He lowers his eyes to the ground and shakes his head.

'Guilt will block you from greater Awareness,' I say quietly.

Movement in the corner of my eye causes me to look up at Fitt grinning down at us both. *Can I help?* she asks, kneeling down beside me and opposite Sovereign. I immediately sense her intention and nod, fascinated.

Sovereign doesn't acknowledge her but she and I both sense him sinking even lower as he remembers hurling himself at her while she was astride the grey mare, determined to bring them both down.

A whicker precedes the arrival of Truth. He lowers his head to just above Sovereign's and we all feel his energy supporting the man as he draws Sovereign's soul out past what is left of his personality so that he can feel its influence.

Come with me, there is something I would like you to see. Fitt eases her thoughts into Sovereign's mind so gently, so delicately, it fascinates me. *Sovereign. Come with me?* She entwines her mind with his, melding seamlessly with Truth as he reassures, soothes, and encourages Sovereign's soul to be more of him.

Sovereign nods almost imperceptibly. Truth continues to hold him together as Fitt takes Sovereign's mind with her own to the greyness of All That Is… to the decision his soul made to live a difficult life so that he could help to free humanity from the echoes of its past. She helps him to see his life through the eyes of his soul until he sees himself kneeling in the grass with her, with me, with Guide and with Truth. He feels his soul's urging and reaches a shaking hand out to Guide, who is by his side in an instant. She leans into him and licks his cheek as he puts his arm around her. Truth lowers his head further and breathes everything he is onto the back of Sovereign's neck.

Fitt withdraws from Sovereign's mind as gently as she insinuated herself, and winks a green, slitted eye at me. I am Aware of the chestnut mare who stands behind her in spirit if not in body, and sense the mare's influence on everything Fitt does, everything she is. Fitt nods knowingly at me and smiles. She gets to her feet and moves on to the next Elite who needs her help.

'Sovereign, will you let me heal you?' I ask again.

He looks up at me, his eyes containing a glimmer now where they were empty, and nods. His eyes widen a fraction as the pain in his knee recedes and then disappears, then he sits back onto his bottom. Guide lies down and rests her head in his lap. I reach a hand up to stroke Truth's nose as he continues to support Sovereign's recovery, and smile at him and Guide. Luck may not exist, but I feel as if it does.

The sun beats down on us all as we wait with those who were Elite and Regular, while they continue to heal. Gradually, the strangest of battlegrounds clears as those who come to terms with their Awareness and with themselves accept invitations to stay with the villagers of Rockwood. Shades are erected near those of us sitting with those still too shocked to move, large enough for the horses still in attendance to remain in place in comfort. Food and water are handed out, and I notice tents being erected in the paddocks behind the cottages in the distance, as indoor beds are given up to guests.

By late afternoon, it is only those who were the highest of the Elite who still remain dotted around the pasture. Each of them has one of us, a dog and a horse in attendance as their minds gradually meld back together – all except Peerless, who is attended by Amarilla alone. I smile to myself. The power of Infinity is more than enough for anyone. They are all a little stronger now, a little more certain of the person they will be as they listen to the voices of their souls, still drawn out to the surface by the horses so that they cannot be silenced by guilt and grief.

I sense a shift in the energy that surrounds us, and immediately join in. White light bursts out of me in imitation of that emitted by

Amarilla and Will, and surrounds Sovereign. I know I have more inside of me, so I put all of myself behind it and extend my light flow to blend with that of Ace and my friends from Supreme City, as well as with that of Amarilla, Justin, Rowena, Marvel, Vickery, Holly, Fitt, Will, his parents and their extended family. Our love settles over all of those who have put themselves through so much. It blends with that of the horses and the dogs so that none of those still struggling can be in any doubt of our united commitment to their recovery.

When the horses give up their vigils and wander away to graze, we know we're getting somewhere. When the dogs get to their feet, shake the dust from their coats, and wander off to drink from the water bowls placed everywhere, we know we're nearly there. When the new people of The New all look around themselves as if seeing one another for the first time, we allow our light flows to dwindle and wink out.

Sovereign looks at me and smiles a smile that, for the first time ever, reaches his eyes. I am Aware of his fascination with the way he feels; his mind feels light where before it was heavy, and it is strange to be comfortable sitting out in the open without constantly assessing risk. He experiences the scents that previously irritated his nose, as sweet and intoxicating. Immediately, he is Aware of where each and every one has originated, and of the breeze that carries them and the insects that ride it... and what business each is about and why...

I grin and say, 'Okay, Sovereign, I'm going to need you to count all of the yellow flowers you can see.'

TWENTY-SIX

Will

_R_ockwood is a busy place; our five hundred newly Aware villagers have to be monitored not only so that they don't lose themselves in everything they can now sense, but so they can be supported while they discover who they will be now that large parts of their personalities have fled.

We all revel in caring for them, despite camping outside so that our guests can have the comfort and privacy of bedrooms whilst they recuperate. My mother, Lia and Levitsson mentor many of the newly Aware themselves, whilst also advising the rest of us where necessary.

It is soon time, however, for those of us privileged enough to be invited to ride the horses, to be somewhere else. We have all sensed the horses above Supreme City performing their magic on the people surfacing from below ground in their hundreds every day. Many of them are now Aware and in need of our help to centre themselves, every bit as much as are those in Rockwood.

On the second morning after "the battle that never was", as the newcomers have taken to calling it, all of us who sense horses waiting for us race to the pasture, having kissed our loved ones goodbye. Yet there is one of us missing, one whose heart now belongs firmly in Rockwood; Prime's parents have moved in with him and my grandparents, and together, they are learning to be a family with the help of the dogs also living there. When Ember and the members of his herd who are prepared to carry me, the Horse-Bonded and the teenagers of Supreme City, come to meet us all, the old, brown mare who carried Prime to balance remains with the herd.

No words are necessary. Prime's friends all reach out to him with their minds, wishing him well and promising to check in with him regularly. The rest of us send our love, and we all sense his gratitude.

As soon as we are astride our horses, Ember's lead mare – carrying Amarilla – turns for the trees. The horses are eager to be where they sense they and we are all needed. Maverick and Guide race each other alongside the horses as they all tear off in front of Ember and me.

We are the perfection that is the herd as we race through the forest, our energy distributed unevenly between us so that we are evenly matched in strength and stamina. We revel in our Awareness of ourself as one, as well as in ourselves as individual parts of the whole.

The horses carry themselves and those who have passed on, for there is no distinction. When I catch a glimpse of Justin and Fitt, the bay colt Justin rides and the grey mare carrying Fitt are also the chestnut stallion and mare who were Gas and Flame. Holly's and Vickery's horses are themselves but also the grey mare who was Serene and the white stallion who was Verve. I see Oak beneath Rowena and Broad beneath Marvel as their horses race one another, neither seeking to win. Victor rides the dark bay who was Spider every bit as much as Shann rides the light bay who is Truth. And when I catch sight of my father, I see beneath him both the horse he rides and the tall, grey stallion who was Candour yet now also resides in Ember. Because we are one. All of us.

I can't see Amarilla with my eyes, for she rides at the head of the herd and I at the back. But I sense Infinity with Ember's lead mare, revelling in the power and strength of the young, healthy body that is as much hers as the mare's, and as much Amarilla's as both of theirs. Adam and Peace are with us too, the echo of Adam grinning from ear to ear as his brown and white Bond-Partner gallops soundlessly above the forest floor alongside Mettle carrying Jonus, the two of them revelling in the culmination of everything they began.

When we reach the grassland above Supreme City hours later, it is as if only minutes have passed. It's hard to tear ourselves away from the horses – both incarnate and discarnate – who have carried us here in so many ways.

We all dismount near a water hole and wash our horses down as they drink. When they go off to roll, we watch them in silence. Beyond them, people are dotted around in the grass, sitting, stunned at everything of which they are now Aware. Horses wander between them, stopping to graze near some, standing with their noses touching the tops of heads of others, supporting in whichever way they are needed. Nearer the lift, several herds of horses are each cantering their circles of power around groups of newly surfaced Disposables, creating the vortices of energy that will draw them to Awareness that they are anything but disposable.

'Horses forever,' Rowena murmurs.

We all know what she means.

Epilogue

*T*ania jumps up and down on my and Lia's bed. 'Daddy, Ember's back, can we go and see him and the other horses? Can we? Please?' She is joined by both Breeze and Maverick.

Lia groans and puts a pillow over her head. 'Will, take your daughter and the dogs, and leave me be, please?'

I chuckle. Fending Maverick off with one arm, I hold a hand out to my four-year-old daughter and pull her to me. I tickle her until she screams with laughter, while Maverick and Breeze bounce around on us both and Lia.

'Will. Go,' Lia orders from beneath her pillow.

'We're going, we're going,' I say, getting out of bed and swinging Tania onto my back. I carry her through to the room which adjoins ours and deposit her by her wardrobe, telling her, 'Get dressed and then we'll go and see him together.'

She and I and both dogs are soon hurrying down the grey, stone-walled corridor that divides what used to be the healing rooms of The Gathering. We step out onto the cobbled square and, as always, I wink at the statue of Jonus and Mettle at its centre. People are hurrying from all directions towards the paddocks now occupied by Ember and his herd.

The door to the accommodation block bursts open and Victor, Ace and Guide burst out with Hero and Adept hot on their heels. Tania shrieks and runs over to Victor, who scoops her up and puts her on his shoulders without missing a step. I haven't a hope of keeping up with them, or any of the others who were of The Old but have now made The Gathering their home.

Most of them are those who were the Elite; they have more killing and torture in their recent pasts than any of those over whom they ruled, and as such, their guilt is far greater and taking longer for them to work out of their systems. They feel their connection to everything, they know it is their salvation and they work hard to make it more of themselves with the help of those of us who brought them here to heal, and of all of the Horse-Bonded unable to leave The Gathering once their Bond-Partners passed on.

Lia, who is as talented as my mother in helping people to move past blocks to greater Awareness whilst ensuring they stay centred, and Fitt, an expert in the energy of forgiveness, oversee us all – Horse-Bonded, Kindred, and "The New New", as Victor, Ace, Hero, and Adept have jokingly taken to calling themselves – as we work to help the ongoing recovery of those who put themselves through so much so that humankind could move ever forward.

They all wanted to move far away from Supreme City, far away from the power they thought they had and which now scares them. So, we brought them here, and for the most part, they are happy. Where they worshipped fear, safety and control, now they have surrendered to love, Awareness and intuition. Where they relied on technology to keep them alive, now they look to the power of their minds and souls. Where they believed in separation, now they value their connection to everything and everyone. And where they led by rules, fear and aggression, now they co-operate with one another and with all of us in the running of The Gathering. A circle has closed and, in the way of circles, has brought a healing power of its own.

Prime and Kudos and their parents are all well settled in Rockwood. The village has expanded with the addition of cottages for those who couldn't face living anywhere but the place they see as their salvation. Prime visits his parents daily in the cottage he helped them to build, but continues to live with my grandparents, about which Gran is delighted, especially since one of my sisters is showing more than a little interest in her ward.

The remainder of those formerly of Supreme City live in several villages created from the rocks of the hills we all traversed when journeying between Rockwood and their former home. Once their new villages were finished, I was with them in my Awareness as they and the villagers of Rockwood who helped them all linked hands to form a massive circle above the underground city. They focused on the energy of Adam and Peace still circulating around the corridors, and added their love to it. Supreme City was bright with the light of the people, as it never was when they lived there.

Then they tuned into its walls, resonated with them... and collapsed them. The lift shattered and sank down its shaft as the ground gave way and fell into the ruined city.

Earth was sung from the distant hills, and lowered into the hole. Rainclouds were sung to the area, and the water that soaked those standing, singing with their minds to achieve that which previously was done with voices, also stimulated the seeds to germinate within the newly-moved earth. Grasses and herbs shot up through the soil, following the intentions of those lovingly resonating their energy with the plants that now cover everything which has been healed, cleared and is no longer needed.

Eminent walks out of the dining hall doorway as I pass it, and crouches down to accept Maverick's and Breeze's greetings. Then she falls into step beside me. 'They're back.'

'They are.'

'I always feel better when they're around.'

'We all do.'

'Even you? You're with them all the time in that ridiculously all-encompassing Awareness of yours, regardless of what else you're doing. What am I even saying? You ARE them.'

'I'm also human, just like the rest of you. I see what you see, I hear what you hear, I touch what you touch. The horses, like the dogs, make the most of their physicality, and their presence affects me every bit as much as the next person.'

'Even Tania.' Eminent nods towards where my daughter is bouncing up and down on Victor's shoulders in the distance. 'I've never liked children, but she's different.'

'She's different from how we all were, but she's just the first of all those who will come after her. You've freed her to be all she can be, you know. You've freed us all.'

'You all keep telling us that, and when I'm calm and centred, I know it, but as soon as the memories of everything I've done come flooding back, I forget everything I know.'

'And that's why the horses are here. Yet another thing we all have to thank you for,' I wink at her and she laughs a high-pitched, tinkling laugh that softens her shoulders and makes her look years younger than she is.

'You're impossible,' she says.

That's what I've told him over and over, Rowena chimes in. Amarilla, Justin, Rowena, Marvel, Holly and Vickery also join us in our Awareness, sharing our joy that the horses – Ember's herd and others – still drop in and visit us from time to time to support the healing and advancement of the human race, as they always have, and always will.

Horses forever.

Books by Lynn Mann

<u>The Horses Know Trilogy</u>
The Horses Know
The Horses Rejoice
The Horses Return

<u>Sequels to The Horses Know Trilogy</u>
Horses Forever
The Forgotten Horses
The Way Of The Horse

<u>Prequels to The Horses Know Trilogy</u>
In Search Of Peace (Adam's story)
The Strength Of Oak (Rowena's story)
A Reason To Be Noble (Quinta's story)

Tales Of The Horse-Bonded (Short Story Collection)
From A Spark Comes A Flame (Novella)

A regularly updated book list can be found at
<u>www.lynnmann.co.uk/booklist</u> (QR code below)

The Forgotten Horses (A Sequel to Horses Forever)

Tania is supremely Aware and exceedingly headstrong. Her parents have kept her shielded from the full extent of her Awareness in order to protect her from herself, but now that she is twenty, the time has come for them to relax their guard.

Tania's abilities begin to emerge, striking awe into those around her, but when she disappears in the middle of the night, all in Rockwood are left shocked and grieving. All, that is, except for Will and Amarilla, who know exactly where she is and why. They also know that they will need to follow her if she is to survive long enough to help the horses whose call for help she has answered – and help the horses she must, for they are the safeguards of humanity...

The Way Of The Horse (A Sequel to The Forgotten Horses)

Nathan has survived the years since his parents' murders by visiting an equine assisted therapy centre every day, where a devoted mare provides him with sanctuary from his demons. When she and the other therapy horses are taken from the centre by the police and herded out of The City Of Glory, Nathan is ready to kill or be killed.

But then the enigmatic Tania takes his hand and he remembers another time. Another life. Then, he was one of the Horse-Bonded, one who failed to fulfil his potential. Now, he is a scientific research assistant barely clinging to sanity. The fate of The City Of Glory's citizens depends on him staying alive but in order to do that, he will need to embrace both his memory of who he really is, and the help of the horse who won't allow death to thwart them both...

Did you enjoy Horses Forever?
I'd be extremely grateful if you could spare a few minutes
to leave a review where you purchased your copy.
Reviews really do help my books to reach a wider audience,
which means that I can keep on writing!
Thank you very much.

I love to hear from you!
Get in touch and receive news of future releases at the following:

www.lynnmann.co.uk

www.facebook.com/lynnmann.author

Acknowledgments

Fact – I don't thank my husband enough. He is always one of the first to read anything I write, even though reading is nowhere near the top of his list of favourite pastimes. He is a constant source of encouragement. He takes up the slack when I'm behind and need to work evenings or weekends. He comes hiking with me when I need a break, even when he would rather be doing something else. I'm truly fortunate to have him behind me and I know it… thank you, Darren Mann.

As always, I am immensely grateful to my editorial team – Fern Sherry, Leonard Palmer and Caroline Macintosh – for constantly making my work better than I can manage on my own, and pushing me to improve my writing. Thanks also to Amanda Horan for again coming up with a cover design that I absolutely love.

Lastly, my love and thanks go out to all of the horses and dogs I have been fortunate to know. Their influence on me is everlasting.

Made in United States
North Haven, CT
25 November 2023

44537162R00174